M000107539

general editor John M. MacKenzie

When the 'Studies in Imperialism' series was founded more
than twenty-five years ago, emphasis was laid upon the
conviction that 'imperialism as a cultural phenomenon
had as significant an effect on the dominant as on the
subordinate societies'. With more than seventy books
published, this remains the prime concern of the series.
Cross-disciplinary work has indeed appeared covering the full
spectrum of cultural phenomena, as well as examining
aspects of gender and sex, frontiers and law, science and the
environment, language and literature, migration and patriotic
societies, and much else. Moreover, the series has always
wished to present comparative work on European and
American imperialism, and particularly welcomes the
submission of books in these areas. The fascination with
imperialism, in all its aspects, shows no sign of abating, and
this series will continue to lead the way in encouraging the
widest possible range of studies in the field. 'Studies in
Imperialism' is fully organic in its development, always
seeking to be at the cutting edge, responding to the latest
interests of scholars and the needs of this ever-expanding
area of scholarship.

Chocolate, women and empire

Manchester University Press

Chocolate, women and empire

A SOCIAL AND CULTURAL HISTORY

Emma Robertson

MANCHESTER
UNIVERSITY PRESS
Manchester and New York
distributed in the United States exclusively by
PALGRAVE MACMILLAN

Published by Manchester University Press
Oxford Road, Manchester M13 9NR, UK
and Room 400, 175 Fifth Avenue, New York, NY 10010, USA
www.manchesteruniversitypress.co.uk

Distributed in the United States exclusively by
Palgrave Macmillan, 175 Fifth Avenue,
New York, NY 10010, USA

Distributed in Canada exclusively by
UBC Press, University of British Columbia, 2029 West Mall,
Vancouver, BC, Canada V6T 1Z2

British Library Cataloguing-in-Publication Data is available

Library of Congress Cataloging-in-Publication Data is available

ISBN 978 0 7190 9005 9 paperback

First published by Manchester University Press in hardback 2009

This paperback edition first published 2013

Printed by Lightning Source

Dedicated to Lily Robertson and Kathleen Harland

CONTENTS

FIGURES

Permission to reproduce images granted by Nestlé UK.

GENERAL EDITOR'S INTRODUCTION

As Emma Robertson so effectively points out in this book, chocolate remains a mythic product, a symbol both of luxury and of a fantasy world of exoticism, yet also (for many) a workaday requirement providing energy and nutrition. Most people in wealthier societies have some kind of relationship with chocolate, such that it conjures up all sorts of romantic and other resonances. It remains a prime medium of gifts in smoothing many forms of relationships and social interactions. As the concept of hand-made chocolates has re-appeared in modern times with the spread of private chocolatiers, many of these characteristics have been re-emphasised. The product has, in some ways, become even more prominent on our high streets, all the more opulent as an aestheticised item (enhanced by such politically correct tags as 'fairtrade' or 'organic' with prices to match). Yet all this masks an essentially imperial relationship with cocoa producers whose living standards are very different from the consumers at the other end of the chain.

Since Robertson stresses the importance of anecdote and personal nostalgia in the collection of oral evidence, perhaps I can indulge myself in a couple of chocolate reminiscences. When I lived and worked in Africa, I (ironically) found chocolate there unsatisfactory, covered with a heat-induced white film which spoilt the taste. When I returned to Britain, my first move at Heathrow Airport was to go to a kiosk and buy myself a bar of chocolate. It became a symbol of return, a product that paradoxically acted as a marker of home. When I felt a touch of depression, I used to dash out to acquire chocolate – only later did I discover that some do indeed consider that cocoa contains an anti-depressant within its chemistry. Chocolate inspires cravings and can even seem life-enhancing. No doubt others in the privileged west will have many similar memories.

Beyond the experience of individuals, chocolate was essentially a discovery of empire, setting up one of the many economic chains of the imperial relationship. As such, it has attracted a great deal of attention. The historiography of empire has indeed been well served in three fields: the significance of just such colonial, generally tropical, products in the economic culture of the metropolis; the gendering of advertisements and consumption relating to such products; and the striking contrasts between the agricultural and manufacturing ends of the production chain. Yet Robertson's book carries all three of these into new and highly productive directions. Her analysis of the origins of cocoa in the deep past of western imperial expansion, of the multiple sources of the product in Africa, the Caribbean, South America and the East Indies, and of the manner in which an exotic product can create such major cultural waves goes further than any previous work. She examines advertising with a greater attention to gender and class, to cultural characteristics such as patriotism and national identity, and to concepts of health and nutrition. And she

[ix]

carries forward these analyses into the post-Second World War period, revealing the manner in which the symbols and selling points of empire survived into the 1950s. Only with decolonisation was there a shift in emphases from the nexus of empire towards the alluring prospects of distant foreign travel. Finally, perhaps her most important contribution lies in her remarkable unveiling of the role of women in both the production of cocoa and in the manufacture and consumption of chocolate. What has so often been seen as essentially a male preserve (except in respect of the consumers) has now been revealed as a world where women were more significant than previously recognised throughout the processes of cultivation as well as in the transformation of the bean into a drink and a sweet and tasty delicacy.

Robertson's other notable contributions include the manner in which she locates cocoa and chocolate in a comparative frame, both in relation to other products and with regard to a multiplicity of places of production. She compares the manufacturing approaches and advertising strategies of both Cadbury and Rowntree in the British chocolate cosmos, and she reveals the considerable significance of the latter company (together with its competitor, Terry's) to the economy and culture of the city of York. In doing so, she again demonstrates the ways in which imperial connections can emerge in the cultures of so many British cities and towns. Above all, using intriguing oral evidence, she examines – with great insight and sympathetic understanding – the lives of women cocoa producers in Nigeria and of women on the production line in York. These are not disconnected environments, but different ends of the production chain where interactions and gender connections are of key significance, some of them developed and promoted by Rowntree's own in-house magazine. The result is a varied and satisfying assortment of analyses that further illuminate the processes whereby a tropical product is turned into a western luxury item.

John M. MacKenzie

ACKNOWLEDGEMENTS

So many people have supported me in the research and writing of this book that it will be impossible to name them all here. Apologies to everyone I have been unable to thank individually, particularly to colleagues and friends at the universities of York, Loughborough, Leeds Metropolitan and Sheffield Hallam.

For their tireless and ever-patient assistance in my archival research, I would like to thank all the staff at the Borthwick Institute and Sarah Foden at the Cadbury UK Archive. I was also helped enormously by staff at the Nigerian National Archives, the History of Advertising Trust, York City Archives, York City Library, Joseph Rowntree Trust and the Birmingham University Archives. Joe Dickinson generously donated copies of the *Cocoa Works Magazine* and gave me a fantastic tour of his collection of Rowntree packaging. In the final stages of the book, Alex Hutchinson (Nestlé Confectionery Heritage Assistant) was an invaluable contact. For permission to publish material from their archives, I gratefully acknowledge the companies of Nestlé Rowntree and Cadbury UK.

My visit to Nigeria would not have been possible without the help and encouragement of Susan Pearson, Catherine Jinadu and family, Shirley Tarawali and family, Jim Gockowski, Chris Okafor, Insa Nolte and Josephine Ogazi. During my short stay, I became indebted to so many people, including: the staff at the International Institute of Tropical Agriculture and the Ikeja Guest House; the Farmers Development Union and Enterprise for Development International (thanks especially to Charles Akinola and Layo Awodipe from EfDI and to Yinka Adeleye from FADU); my translators Samuel Dele, Paul Adejunro and Tayo Sadare (in Ibadan), and Veronica Omowunmi Oladele (in Bamikemo); and last but not least, Kayode Farinloye and Tony Jonise. Of course the fieldwork would not have been possible without the good will of the Nigerian communities I visited. The women interviewed all gave freely of their time and I hope I have done justice to their narratives. The trip itself was partly funded by generous postgraduate travel grants from both the Royal Historical Society and the Economic History Society.

During my postgraduate research for the project I was helped enormously by the supportive academic community at the University of York: in particular the Centre for Women's Studies and the Department of History. Since arriving at York for my MA in 1999, Ann Kaloski-Naylor has been a special influence intellectually and politically, as well as a real source of support. For feedback on my work in its various stages, I would also like to thank Elizabeth Buettner, Joanna de Groot, Catherine Hall and Allen Warren.

For their enduring friendship and emotional support, as well as for their insightful comments on chapters (often at short notice), and for many challenging and inspiring conversations as fellow postgrads and beyond, I

ACKNOWLEDGEMENTS

would particularly like to thank Neil Armstrong, Rachel Farebrother, Helen Graham and Catriona Kennedy.

Thanks to Mum, Dad and to my partner Bryan for their constant support, and to Kate and the Powell clan for giving me a happy home during my Cadbury research trips. I am especially grateful to those members of my family, once Rowntree employees, who have taken part in the research itself and who were my inspiration for this project.

For their crucial contributions to this book I must thank all the women who were kind enough to give their time and their memories and to welcome me into their homes. I felt privileged to be able to record their oral histories and I hope that they will be happy with my interpretation of their narratives.

Finally, my deepest thanks must go to my PhD supervisor John Howard, whose support and vision has been crucial at every stage of this project. Without his encouragement and enthusiasm, I would never have had the courage to take this project forward from my MA dissertation. He inspired me to read, write and think in new ways.

ABBREVIATIONS

BI	Borthwick Institute, York
BWM	*Bournville Works Magazine*
CDM	Cadbury's Dairy Milk
CWM	*Cocoa Works Magazine*
EfDI	Enterprise for Development International
FADU	Farmers' Development Union
HAT	History of Advertising Trust, Norwich
JWT	J. Walter Thompson
NNA	Nigerian National Archives, Ibadan
RFC	Rowntree-Fry-Cadbury (Nigeria) Limited
YEP	*Yorkshire Evening Press*

Introduction

'There!' cried Mr Wonka, dancing up and down and pointing his gold-
topped cane at the great brown river. 'It's all chocolate! Every drop of
that river is hot melted chocolate of the finest quality.' (Roald Dahl,
Charlie and the Chocolate Factory (London: George Allen & Unwin,
1967), 57–8)

for paper

First published in the US in 1964, Roald Dahl's depiction of Willy
Wonka's chocolate factory tapped into a western fascination with the
commodity. The book and the original film achieved huge mainstream
and cult success.[1] In Dahl's vision, chocolate bars are manufactured
in a factory where instead of machines there are chocolate rivers and
waterfalls: 'No other factory in the world mixes its chocolate by water-
fall! But it's the *only* way to do it properly!'[2] Chocolate lends itself
well to such a fantasy, loaded with meanings of sensuality and excess
even as it is constructed as a wholesome, 'natural' product.

It is amongst the green meadows and buttercups of Willy Wonka's
'chocolate room', a rural idyll made entirely out of sugar, that we first
catch sight of the Oompa Loompas – Wonka's secret labour force.
In original versions of the story, the Oompa Loompas are explicitly
racialised: 'Their skin is almost black!' Indeed, the young white
working-class hero of the tale, Charlie Bucket, asks if they are made
of chocolate.[3] These black characters are used to add an exotic, magical and sometimes comic air to the factory. Rendered unthreatening
by their tiny stature, and safely (for white readers) contained within
the factory walls, they are the mischievous entertainers who sing and
dance their way through the book. Willy Wonka, meanwhile, is the
imperial explorer who discovered this tribe of 'pygmies': 'I found them
in the very deepest and darkest part of the African jungle where no
white man had ever been before.'[4] As I demonstrate in chapter two,
such raced and gendered narratives of discovery have been a common
trope in histories of chocolate as a commodity.

In later versions of Dahl's text, blackness was written out of the
story altogether and the Oompa Loompas are described as having 'rosy-
white' skin.[5] In the 1995 edition, with new illustrations by Quentin
Blake, any reference to Africa has also been deleted, to be replaced by
the fictional Loompaland. Even in the 1967 version, the illustrations
by Faith Jaques which accompanied the written descriptions of the
black Oompa Loompas actually depicted them as white. Although their

skin colour could change, their jungle home, tribal relations and lack of clothing placed them within a colonial Africa frame of reference for generations of British readers. The description of them in chapter sixteen of both the original and later versions resonates with stereotypes of the happy African worker: 'They love dancing and music. . . . They like jokes. They still wear the same clothes they wore in the jungle. They insist upon that. The men . . . wear only deerskins. The women wear leaves, and the children wear nothing at all.'[6] In the first film, the characters are more fantastical and are thus divorced from obvious racial categories: they have orange faces, green hair, and dungarees instead of deerskins. The 2005 remake used a British Kenyan Asian actor, Deep Roy, to represent all the Oompa Loompas.[7] Significantly, these chocolate workers are always 'racially' distinct from the white characters.

In her best-selling novel, *Chocolat*, Joanne Harris evoked a more adult, 'sophisticated' world of small-scale chocolate production and consumption.[8] Set in France, home of the chocolatiers, it is far removed from the fantastical factory setting of Willy Wonka and the mass production methods of British firms. It is thus able to revel still more deeply in the sensuousness and luxuriousness attributed to 'fine' chocolate. Vianne Rocher, the heroine, is an enigmatic single mother who moves to a small French town and sets up a successful 'chocolaterie artisanale', much to the consternation of the local priest. The villagers, including the villainous priest, are all eventually seduced by the rich chocolate on offer. The film of the novel, starring Juliette Binoche and Johnny Depp, further romanticised and sexualised the setting and the product.[9]

These two texts by Dahl and Harris, though very different in their intended audiences, convey some of the commonly held classed, raced and gendered understandings of chocolate. In Dahl's novel, chocolate as manufactured by the ingenious white male industrialist is the saviour of the decent, but starving, white working class – embodied by Charlie and his family. Chocolate is both a nutritious and magical food. In Harris's narrative, the white heroine, Vianne, is sensual, mysterious and attractive, like the product she sells. She is also a mother, crossing and undermining the boundaries between domestic and public production and consumption. Chocolate in Harris's novel may be simultaneously redemptive and damning, like the heroine herself.

Such romanticised narratives of chocolate may be pleasurable to those lucky enough to be able to consume them. However, they are largely divorced from the material conditions of production. This is further exemplified by the work of Marcia and Frederic Morton, who offer their own enraptured introduction to the commodity: 'Chocolate is divine, we all know that – divine as in delicious, delectable . . . a-a-ahhh.' The assertion of the Mortons that chocolate is the divine gift of the Gods ignores the history behind the creation of what is now known as 'chocolate' from the cocoa bean. Instead, they tap into popular western understandings of the commodity as luxurious, hedonistic and sensual.[10] This book begins with the romantic construction of chocolate, but will attempt to understand the actual human endeavours, and systematic exploitation, which have made such chocolate fantasies possible.

Cocoa and the imperial commodity chain

Historians such as Catherine Hall, Sidney Mintz and James Walvin have made explicit the imperial power dynamics behind the consumption of seemingly innocuous and quintessentially 'British' commodities.[11] Sugar, tea and tobacco, for example, first became widely available in Britain through the coercion of workers, predominantly African slaves, in the tropical world. Whilst recognising the exploitative labour practices and racial hierarchies behind the processes of production and marketing, imperial historians have also used commodities to explore the mutually constitutive relationship of Britain and its empire. As Joanna de Groot surmises, 'Whether unreflective (as in daily routines) or politically and culturally self-conscious . . . , consumption placed "British" homes in an imperial world.'[12] This book draws on and contributes to such scholarship, focusing on chocolate as an imperial commodity.

The history of chocolate corresponds to some extent with the more well-documented histories of tea, coffee and sugar: notably in the early dependence on coerced labour, and in the transformation of the product from luxury to everyday commodity. Nevertheless, chocolate is revealing of particular histories of colonial agriculture, western manufacture and consumption. Unlike tea and sugar, for example, it has never been successful as a plantation crop – for both agricultural and socio-cultural reasons. Since British West Africa became the chief supplier of cocoa to British firms in the early twentieth century, African smallholders have triumphed over European estates.[13] Chocolate has been invested with specific cultural meanings which are in part connected to such conditions of production. I analyse how chocolate has been produced by workers differently situated in Africa and Europe; how it has been imagined by producers and consumers in Britain; and how it has brought into question any neat separation of the metropolis and the peripheries of empire.

William Gervase Clarence-Smith provides a detailed study of cocoa and chocolate for the period 1765 to 1914, studying the journey of the product along the 'commodity chain' from cocoa pod to consumer product. Commodity chain analysis has become increasingly popular amongst economists, as illustrated by the 2003 edited collection by Clarence-Smith and Steven Topik on the global coffee industry.[14] Clarence-Smith's independent study of cocoa is an attempt to 'understand the wealth and poverty of nations, using the cocoa-to-chocolate commodity chain in the liberal era as a litmus test for theories of economic development'.[15] However, such theories of 'development' are problematic in privileging 'modern' western capitalism over so-called 'traditional' methods. Women, in particular, are often labelled as 'backward' in such approaches. My own work will not be a study of the macro-economics of commodity production (although the unequal distribution of wealth will be highlighted), but rather an analysis of its social and cultural consequences. I examine the ways in which the meanings of production and consumption have been created, controlled and contested, in gendered and raced ways, by those involved in the chocolate industry.

The commodity chain model is not ideal, then, creating a progress narrative in which western consumption is prioritised as a symbol of economic development and modernity. However, the process of following a product from so-called 'raw material' to consumable good has challenged researchers to cross national borders and to make connections between people.[16] A recent edited collection by John Brewer and Frank Trentmann brought together studies which aimed to reconnect consumption with production by examining the 'reciprocal' and 'multidirectional flows of goods and their meanings' across space and time. As Brewer and Trentmann emphasise:

> Thinking about the connections between different sites of consumption and between production and consumption requires attention to physical, material places as well as to virtual ones, to the forests in which labour gangs risk their lives in the making of tropical commodities as well as to the conceptual and discursive realms that produce labour and utility, as in recent brand management.[17]

It is the material and discursive connections between places, and particularly between people, as brought about through the chocolate industry, which will be my focus here.

Since commencing this study, the politics of commodity chains have gained wider popular currency as part of a shift in Britain towards a concern with the origins of food and other commodities. This shift is related to worries over health (the use of pesticides in agriculture for example), the environment (the carbon footprint of each product) and the exploitation of workers in a global economy. Ethical consumption, now an essential element of middle-class identity, depends partly on a sense of consumer responsibility for the conditions under which commodities such as chocolate are produced, and a guarantee of a fair price for the producer. In the light of recent marketing campaigns for luxury fairtrade chocolate such as 'Mayan Gold', it is important to recognise the ways in which ethical consumption today may smooth over the inequalities of the imperial past, and bypass an awareness of the processes of industrial manufacture, by drawing on ancient, mystical and exotic imaginings of the origins of cocoa. Here I bring an important historical dimension to the debate. As Brewer and Trentmann argue, we need to pay attention 'to the changing moral landscape of consumption'. The idea of ethical consumption is nothing new but instead represents 'a reconnection with older notions of civic consumers and socially responsible consumption'.[18] Moreover, ethical consumption today suggests how selective memories of the past can be harnessed at particular historical moments, to the benefit of western marketing agents and the companies they represent.

My work does not follow comprehensively the process of chocolate production from 'the bean to the bar'. I concentrate on three key stages: growing cocoa beans, manufacturing chocolate from these beans, and the marketing of chocolate products. These stages do not exist in isolation from each other; rather, they are deeply interconnected, as suggested above. The concept of a 'chain' is, then, useful to a certain extent in conceptualising how the agents and locations of production have been locked together through unequal relations of mutual dependence. Yet the narrative of the chain also needs to be subjected to scrutiny for the ways in which it has over-simplified complex webs of imperial relationships to construct raced and gendered hierarchies of producers/consumers.[19]

From the local . . .

This project began as a local study – a study inspired by the working lives of generations of family and friends, particularly women, in the chocolate factories of York. From the late nineteenth until the late twentieth centuries, this northern English city has been dominated by two industries: railways and chocolate. In 1951 and 1971, these accounted for two thirds of workers employed in manufacturing, with confectionery alone employing over half of this total.[20] The dominant chocolate-producing firms of Rowntree and Terry's, both founded by Quaker families, depended heavily on a supply of women workers, who usually made up over half the workforce. Although there was local rivalry between employees, Rowntree was undoubtedly the larger and more influential of the two companies.[21]

The name of Rowntree has been an almost constant presence in my own life. I was educated at the Joseph Rowntree School, saw plays at the Joseph Rowntree theatre, learned to swim in what was once the company swimming pool and fed the ducks in Rowntree's park. Every weekend as a child, I ate the waste chocolates purchased by my grandmother, who retired from the factory the year I was born. As an adult, I studied at the University of York, spending many hours in the library dedicated to J. B. Morrell (a Rowntree company director). I thus wanted to learn more about the place of Rowntree in the city of York, and its meanings for York residents.[22]

The Rowntree confectionery business was established in 1862 by Henry Isaac Rowntree, with his brother Joseph joining him in business in 1869.[23] Originally based at Tanner's Moat in the centre of the city, production moved to a more rural location in the 1890s. The Rowntree factory has since been a very physical presence on the northern outskirts of York, with its existence made known far beyond the factory gates through the wafting smell of chocolate.[24] From the 1930s, the company became nationally and internationally renowned for products including Kit Kat, Smarties, Aero and Black Magic. The influence of the Rowntree family, meanwhile, has been felt in numerous ways outside the field of industry: most famously through the establishment of the Joseph Rowntree charitable trusts.[25] Indeed, the Rowntrees are one of the celebrated families of non-conformist philanthropists and entrepreneurs in Britain, often considered alongside the Cadburys, Frys and Jesse Boot.[26] Existing histories of the company have thus tended to focus on the biographies of the Rowntree men (particularly Joseph Rowntree and his son Benjamin Seebohm), or they are a top-down study of welfare policies at the firm. The one extensive published company history, by Robert Fitzgerald, is an analysis of marketing techniques, with the lives of the workers necessarily a secondary consideration.[27] Women workers have been either neglected or trivialised as pretty but temporary employees, with the generic Rowntree worker constructed as implicitly white and male.

This book is rooted in thirteen oral histories with retired women workers, three of whom were members of my own family, conducted in the summer of 2000.[28] By focusing on women in these interviews, as well as in my archival research, I aimed to begin to redress the gender imbalance of many existing Rowntree histories and to value women's own interpretations of their working lives. I adopted a life history approach, encouraging each woman to narrate her own biography from childhood. Where appropriate, I used open-ended questions to ask them to expand in more detail on aspects of their working life at Rowntree. This allowed me to follow the concerns of the narrator whilst still covering a similar range of topics in each interview.[29] Although once treated sceptically by mainstream historians, oral histories have become widely accepted as rich and revealing sources. As Alessandro Portelli convincingly demonstrates, the apparent unreliability of memory actually offers key insights into the way historical 'events' are understood and discursively (re)created.[30] The narratives of these thirteen women were crucial in beginning to investigate in more depth some of the discourses of Rowntree as a 'good firm' to work for in the city, and in offering an insight into the everyday realities and understandings of chocolate manufacture.

However, in the process of conducting these oral histories, many more gaps in the official histories came to light. These women were all white women; where could I find the stories of non-white women who had been born in or who had migrated to York?[31] By focusing on life at the York factory, I also ran the risk of perpetuating the selective historical amnesia Catherine Hall has identified in relation to colonial products such as cocoa.[32] Growing up, I had come to understand the chocolate industry as a source of employment, of paternalistic philanthropy, and as a focus for local pride; I had seldom given a thought to the origins of the cocoa used in Rowntree chocolate or to the lives of cocoa farmers. In a city in which history, or at least a palatable version of it, has become a saleable commodity, the histories of colonial relations are tellingly absent.[33]

To the global . . .

This is still a local study in many ways, but one in which the 'local' is contested and redefined by histories of empire and colonialism.[34] The Rowntree industry and the city in which it was founded have never existed in isolation: chocolate manufacture depends on the supply of key ingredients from around the world; on the availability of labour locally, nationally and internationally; and on the purchase of finished goods by consumers 'at home' and 'abroad'. Perceptions of Rowntree and the other Quaker chocolate firms of Terry's, Cadbury and Fry as 'enlightened', 'model firms' may be held in tension with the imperial and colonial origin of key factors of production such as sugar and cocoa.[35] This book follows the cocoa bean on its historical and geographical journey from South America, to the West Indies, to West Africa, to York and to consumers across the British Isles, revealing histories of imperial exploitation, sexism and racism in which the Rowntree firm and the people of the city of York are deeply implicated.

Rowntree, like Cadbury and Fry, purchased cocoa from several countries. However, as I explore in chapters two and three, during the twentieth century these firms became heavily dependent on supplies from West Africa. The York company had a particular connection with Nigeria, as the factory became the headquarters of cocoa-buying operations there on behalf of themselves, Cadbury and Fry. Agents representing the three firms were sent out to the colony to supervise the purchase of cocoa directly from producers. The buying and selling of cocoa for use in 'British-made' products such as Kit Kat was thus clearly conducted under the inequalities of colonial rule and its consequences. It is important, however, not to focus purely on the impact of Britain on the colonies. People in Nigeria had agency within the structures of colonial rule and their actions had repercussions for life in the city of York.

The second geographical focal point for my study is, therefore, the cocoa-producing villages of Nigeria. I am particularly concerned with the lives and experiences of Nigerian women farmers, who are largely absent from existing academic studies. Driven partly by a lack of primary sources and partly by a desire to engage with women's own accounts of their experiences, I spent a month in Nigeria in 2002 recording fifteen oral history interviews and researching written documents in the National Archives. My decision to conduct my own fieldwork research raised some immediate problems. I am not an anthropologist or an expert in African history. And, as several people pointed out to me, I could not speak Yoruba; how could I possibly hope to interview Nigerian women in the cocoa-farming villages? However, this lack of knowledge, of connection, was also at the heart of my project. I wanted to confront the disconnection of women in York and Nigeria whose lives have in fact long been intertwined through the economics and politics of cocoa. Crossing the borders between countries, and between disciplines, enabled me to disturb and analyse the boundaries between women, including those between myself, my interviewees and those who assisted me in my research.[36]

Linking the chain . . .

From embarking on what had appeared the most local of studies, then, I was now confronted with the two seemingly disparate locations of York, England, and the numerous cocoa-producing villages and towns of Nigeria. As discussed above, I am not solely interested in these locations in their own right, but in the interactions which have connected them.[37] At the most basic level these are economic connections between the manufacturers of chocolate and the producers of its most essential ingredient. However, the Rowntree firm manipulated such connections to further its own self-image as the responsible manufacturer, constructing the ideal of a paternalistic and later – in the context of decolonisation – mutually beneficial relationship. Its presence in Nigeria was cited as evidence of its concern for the welfare of cocoa farmers and Rowntree aimed to occupy a special place in the institutions dealing with African cocoa.[38] I will explore these kinds of connections, and the connections between the women involved in production at both these sites.

The 'cocoa chain' has bound together women in York (including myself) and women working in former British colonies. But it is not the only means by which York has been bound to empire and to imperial ideologies. Within the process of manufacturing chocolate (just one stage in the chain), white women born in York have worked alongside white and non-white women migrating from the empire overseas, as well as with non-white women born in Britain. This is a reflection and culmination of complex movements of people throughout the British empire. Having established the connections of Rowntree and York with people producing cocoa in the British colonies, it is important to consider how relations of race and empire played out on the shopfloor itself, as well as in the local community outside the factory walls. Again, oral history, alongside official company records and publicity, has proved crucial in allowing some insight into such dynamics for women workers. Following the original thirteen interviews in York, I recorded life history interviews with three women of varied ethnic backgrounds who had migrated to the city from Liverpool, from Malta and from Uganda.

An analysis of the operations of just one apparently 'local' firm thus illuminates the complex networks and power relations of the globalised chocolate industry. The York factory is the location – the physical and symbolic space – which connects the numerous actors in this history. It is the site at which cocoa becomes transformed into chocolate. It is a mid-way point, therefore, at which many of the meanings of chocolate production and consumption come into being – and sometimes into conflict. I consider the ways in which the Rowntree management attempted to control the meanings of chocolate production through their actions at the factory, in the city and at the sites of cocoa farming in the British empire. Moreover, I explore how everyday commodities in the west have been produced through the labours of people on a global scale, binding them together in frequently exploitative relationships. The central figures will be the 'ordinary' women positioned at two key sites of production: the cocoa farms of Nigeria and the Rowntree factory in York. These women are not usually seen as the 'great actors' within the cocoa chain yet they are key to its operation at every stage.[39]

Chapter outline

The chapters in this book each examine a different stage in the cocoa commodity chain: from the farming of cocoa beans, to the site of chocolate manufacture, to the marketing of the finished goods. I have not confined myself to one historical period but will range widely over time and place in order to understand how the politics of empire (extending into the 'postcolonial' period), as well as ideologies of gender, race and class, have functioned in relation to chocolate from its earliest appearance in western society to late twentieth-century production and consumption. Whilst it is Rowntree that will be the focus of my study, I draw on the histories of Cadbury and Fry to suggest how the York case relates to the broader context of chocolate manufacture in Britain.

I begin my story of chocolate at the end of the cocoa chain, with an analysis in chapter one of chocolate advertising from the late nineteenth to the late twentieth centuries. Like the fictional accounts mentioned above, adverts have perpetuated western sexist and racist ideologies under a veneer of pleasurable consumption, and have divorced chocolate from the conditions of production. This chapter will make such meanings explicit, through a close reading of a range of advertising campaigns. Labour historians increasingly have called for analyses of consumption and of production to be integrated. Gary Cross, for example, asserts that we 'must recognise that wage-earners and their families are consumers at least as much as part of a work process'.[40] However, my aim here is not simply to reintegrate consumption practices into histories of labour. Rather, I want to combine an informed understanding of cultural constructions of the product with a shift in focus to the actions of the manufacturers and everyday working lives. Hidden behind popular marketing images lie the experiences of women at two key stages of production – the farming of cocoa and its manufacture into chocolate. Paying particular attention to such silences, my analysis of advertising establishes connections and tensions between the worlds of production and consumption, emphasising the dynamics of gender, class, race and nation.

Chapter two tackles imperial histories of chocolate and how British firms, including Rowntree, constructed their own romantic narratives of the 'discovery' and development of chocolate production. I study the early involvement of Rowntree in the purchasing of cocoa, including their ownership of plantations in the British West Indies. I then trace the expansion of cocoa farming in British West Africa; as a result of which, Rowntree, Cadbury and Fry stationed buying agents in Nigeria, putting the firms in direct relationship to the colony. In this and the following chapter I examine the ways in which Rowntree negotiated this relationship and how management represented it to cocoa producers and to factory workers in York. I argue that the history of Rowntree and cocoa was told through a romantic rendering of colonial exploitation and that this was in keeping with other historical narratives of chocolate.

Chapter three is devoted to women's experiences of cocoa farming in British colonies and former colonies. I outline the important role of women in the West Indies during the early period of chocolate manufacture, before turning to women's lives in West Africa. My focus is on women farmers in Nigeria and the ways in which they have conceptualised their roles in the industry. Whilst there has been relatively extensive work, in English, on women cocoa farmers in Ghana, Nigerian women have received little attention. Their labour is too often devalued as 'light' seasonal tasks on farms run by their husbands or male relatives. I argue that, within prescribed but contested limits, these women have always been active agents in cocoa production, despite having to struggle against the often intersecting structures and ideologies of colonialism, capitalism and patriarchy. I hope that this chapter will be a useful step towards reassessing the relationship between women in York and Nigeria, who have for too long been kept apart economically and conceptually.[41]

York, though it is often marketed as a medieval city, is inextricably tied to modernity and to colonialism through the confectionery industry. In chapter four, I explore the ways in which Rowntree created and reflected particular understandings of York and of empire, through media such as their in-house journal, *Cocoa Works Magazine* (*CWM*). First published in 1902, *CWM* was conceived by Joseph Rowntree as a means of maintaining communication between management and workers in an increasingly depersonalised industrial setting. Throughout its history the magazine contained a mix of serious articles on the state of the industry, reports of individual and group achievements both on and off the shopfloor, and a miscellany of items intended to be of interest to primarily York-based employees.[42] In this and other internal and external publicity, Rowntree was often complicit in creating a version of York seemingly divorced from the world of industry and colonialism. Yet it also produced narratives of cocoa farming in the West Indies and Nigeria, and even functioned as a space where representatives of both coloniser and colonised could meet. I examine the complexities of these co-existing discourses to see how gender, race and class function in different ways. I also study the ways in which white Rowntree workers may have come to understand race and empire through, for example, the minstrel shows held at the factory, or local church projects. I argue that such activities illustrate the multidirectional nature of imperialism. The British empire did not simply exist 'out there' in Nigeria; it took shape within the factory itself, informing the daily lives of women workers.

York's image as a relatively non-industrialised city, untouched by race politics, has masked the ways in which ideas about race were indeed present on the Rowntree shopfloor. An analysis of how race was a structuring factor in the lives of women in the York factory and how they conceptualised 'race' is long overdue. Chapter five studies the oral histories of women workers, both 'white' and 'non-white', and their experiences of gendered and raced labour in chocolate manufacture. Whiteness was the dominant racialised ideology of the factory, often articulated and legitimised through a discourse of cleanliness. The presence of non-white women challenged this hegemonic whiteness; yet for the three migrant women who took part in this study, racism was largely absent from their narratives, though it was sometimes implicit in individualised anecdotes. Whilst this certainly does not preclude the prevalence of racism at either an institutional or individual level, I argue that it speaks to the ways in which each woman was able to forge friendships across differences and to create new, hybrid yet localised identities. Given my emphasis on the histories of labour and exploitation masked by romantic discourses of chocolate, it is appropriate that this book culminates in the rich testimony of individual women whose lives have been intricately connected with the manufacture of some of Britain's best-known confectionery lines.

(Re)writing histories of chocolate

Chocolate has been a source of fascination in the west for centuries, inspiring diverse writers to pen both fictional and apparently non-fictional accounts. This book is in a sense simply one more partial version of the history of chocolate, rooted in my own particular investment in the commodity. However, existing narratives (both academic and popular) rarely include any recognition of the labour required to produce chocolate on a mass scale, preferring to focus on smaller scale 'craft' production, with its attendant values of male 'skill' and artisanship. They also consistently fail to address imperialism, except as a romantic backdrop to the co-option of cocoa for western consumption. By placing chocolate production by a particular firm, indeed by individual women, in the broader context of imperialism and popular culture in the twentieth century, I plan to disturb and overturn some of these histories. In so doing, I explicitly address the very nature of writing history: the politics of who is included/

excluded; the intended audiences; and the subjective construction of events which are then elevated to historical 'facts'.

An intrinsic part of this project will be to de-romanticise the cocoa bean, highlighting the power dynamics behind a product frequently understood in the western world only in terms of pleasure. This will have resonances and implications for existing understandings of the chocolate industry, of the Rowntree firm, and of the city of York. Moreover, I hope it will suggest broader critiques of the inequalities of gender and race and the 'innocuous' ways in which these are perpetuated in society. Chocolate marketing often encourages us to indulge in a depoliticised moment, to 'Have a Break'; this moment, as I shall demonstrate, is and has always been deeply political.

Notes

1 The book was published in Britain in 1967. The film, *Willy Wonka and the Chocolate Factory*, was released in 1971, directed by Mel Stuart. Nestlé Rowntree produced a line of confectionery under the Wonka name, trading on the association with magic and fantasy.
2 Roald Dahl, *Charlie and the Chocolate Factory* (London: George Allen & Unwin, 1967), 59.
3 Dahl, *Charlie* (1967 edition), 60. This equation of black people with chocolate will be discussed in chapter one.
4 Dahl, *Charlie* (1967 edition), 61. I have adopted a very broad definition of imperialism: to refer to ideologies of 'discovery', exploration, and ultimately exploitation and control of other territories, their people and their resources. I use 'colonialism' to refer to the occupation of territories, as in the Scramble for Africa in the late nineteenth century. In doing so I differ from Catherine Hall's more specific definition of imperialism as the particular historical moment 'when European empires reached their formal apogee'. Hall, 'Introduction: thinking the postcolonial, thinking the empire', in Catherine Hall (ed.) *Cultures of Empire: A Reader* (Manchester: Manchester University Press, 2000), 5.
5 Roald Dahl, *Charlie and the Chocolate Factory* (London: Puffin Books, 1995), 101.
6 Dahl, *Charlie* (1967 edition), 62.
7 *Charlie and the Chocolate Factory* was directed by Tim Burton and starred Johnny Depp. Ironically, the presence of Deep Roy brings yet another imperial legacy into the *Charlie* story by evoking complex histories of Indian migration in response to the growth and dramatic decline of the British colonies in East Africa.
8 Joanne Harris, *Chocolat* (London: Black Swan, 2000).
9 The film, *Chocolat*, was released in 2000, directed by Lasse Hallström. For an in-depth historical and ethnographic study of chocolate making in France, see Susan J. Terrio, *Crafting the Culture and History of French Chocolate* (Berkeley: University of California Press, 2000).
10 Marcia Morton and Frederic Morton, *Chocolate: The Illustrated History* (New York: Crown Publishers, 1986), 1. The term 'cocoa' can be confusing as it may refer to the cocoa bean (also referred to as cacao) or to processed cocoa powder. I will be using the term to refer to both the beans in their 'raw' state and the powder sold for use in drinks and in cooking. Although 'cacao' is often considered the correct term for the beans, it is not so widely understood.
11 Catherine Hall, 'Turning a blind eye: memories of empire', in Patricia Fara and Karalyn Patterson (eds) *Memory* (Cambridge: Cambridge University Press, 1998), 27–46; Sidney Mintz, *Sweetness and Power: The Place of Sugar in Modern History* (London: Penguin,

1985); James Walvin, *Fruits of Empire: Exotic Produce and British Taste, 1660–1800* (Basingstoke: Macmillan Press, 1997). Commodity histories have flourished in recent years. See for example, Brenda King, *Silk and Empire* (Manchester: Manchester University Press, 2005) and James Mills, *Cannabis Britannica* (Oxford: Oxford University Press, 2003).

12 Joanna de Groot, 'Metropolitan desires and colonial connections: reflections on consumption and empire', in Catherine Hall and Sonya O. Rose (eds), *At Home with the Empire: Metropolitan Culture and the Imperial World* (Cambridge: Cambridge University Press, 2006), 190.

13 See Gareth Austin, 'Mode of production or mode of cultivation: explaining the failure of European cocoa planters in competition with African farmers in colonial Ghana', in William Gervase Clarence-Smith (ed.), *Cocoa Pioneer Fronts since 1800: The Role of Smallholders, Planters and Merchants* (Basingstoke: Macmillan Press, 1996), 154–75.

14 In this useful collection, a cross-cultural approach is adopted which compares and contrasts the coffee commodity chain as it operates in different places and at different historical moments. William Gervase Clarence-Smith and Steven Topik (eds), *The Global Coffee Economy in Africa, Asia, and Latin America, 1500–1989* (Cambridge: Cambridge University Press, 2003). For an earlier example of the genre, see Gary Gereffi and Miguel Korzeniewicz (eds), *Commodity Chains and Global Capitalism* (Westport: Greenwood Press, 1994).

15 William Gervase Clarence-Smith, *Cocoa and Chocolate, 1765–1914* (London: Routledge, 2000), 1.

16 For an excellent example of this, see Stephanie Barrientos and Diane Perrons, 'Gender and the global food chain: a comparative study of Chile and the U.K.', in Haleh Afshar and Stephanie Barrientos (eds), *Women, Globalisation and Fragmentation in the Developing World* (Basingstoke: Macmillan Press, 1999), 150–73. In today's context of 'globalisation' such studies have particular political resonance; but global production and markets, and the exploitation of people and resources in non-western or less 'developed' nations, are not a new phenomenon.

17 John Brewer and Frank Trentmann, 'Introduction: space, time and value in consuming cultures', in John Brewer and Frank Trentmann (eds), *Consuming Cultures, Global Perspectives: Historical Trajectories, Transnational Exchanges* (Oxford: Berg, 2006), 3.

18 Brewer and Trentmann, 'Introduction', 4, 9. Clare Midgley, for example, documents the boycott of sugar by women in Victorian Britain, in protest at the treatment of slave labourers. Midgley, *Women Against Slavery: The British Campaigns, 1780–1870* (London: Routledge, 1992).

19 As Simon Potter points out, ideas of imperial 'webs' and 'networks' are proving increasingly popular, yet run the risk of glossing over the unequal power dynamics of empire and the role of institutions in systematising such relationships. Potter, 'Webs, networks, and systems: globalization and the mass media in the nineteenth- and twentieth-century British empire', *Journal of British Studies*, 46 (July 2007), 621.

20 The number working in manufacturing was on the decline by 1971. For detailed statistical analysis see Charles Feinstein, 'Population, occupations and economic development, 1831–1981', in Charles Feinstein (ed.), *York 1831–1981: 150 Years of Scientific Endeavour and Social Change* (York: The Ebor Press, 1981), 140–1.

21 The Terry's firm has now closed, following the announcement in April 2004 that production would move to Europe.

22 I believe, as do Karen Olson and Linda Shopes, that, 'By doing work where we have personal commitments, our academic contributions are more likely to come out of a . . . creative, politically engaged self, one that has a social – and not simply academic – purpose.' Olson and Shopes, 'Crossing boundaries, building bridges: doing oral history among working-class women and men', in Sherna Berger Gluck and Daphne Patai (eds), *Women's Words: The Feminist Practice of Oral History* (London: Routledge, 1991), 201. Gordon T. Stewart similarly begins his study of the jute industry from an autobiographical connection. Stewart, *Jute and Empire:*

The Calcutta Jute Wallahs and the Landscapes of Empire (Manchester: Manchester University Press, 1998), ix.

23 The Rowntree family had successfully established themselves as grocers in the city by the late nineteenth century. See chapter two for further details on the early history of the firm; also Gillian Wagner, *The Chocolate Conscience* (London: Chatto & Windus, 1987), 24–30; Ian Campbell Bradley, *Enlightened Entrepreneurs* (London: Weidenfeld and Nicolson, 1987), 140–7; Anne Vernon, *A Quaker Business Man* (London: George Allen & Unwin, 1958), especially chapters 8–12.

24 Like Charlie in Dahl's novel, I have been surrounded by the sights and smells of a chocolate factory: 'little Charlie Bucket had to walk right past the gates of the factory. . . . he would hold his nose high in the air and take long deep sniffs of the gorgeous chocolatey smell all around him.' Dahl, *Charlie* (1967 edition), 12.

25 Joseph Rowntree set up three trusts in the early twentieth century: one related to New Earswick village, the others to finance research.

26 For a celebratory account of non-conformist businessmen, including Joseph Rowntree and George Cadbury, see Bradley, *Enlightened Entrepreneurs*. Taking a more critical approach to the intersections of religion and business, Michael Rowlinson has challenged idealised histories of the 'Quaker' firms, particularly those which see Quakerism as the guiding principle of management. He emphasises instead their adoption of scientific management techniques. Michael Rowlinson, 'The early application of scientific management by Cadbury', *Business History*, 30: 4 (1988), 377–95; Michael Rowlinson, 'Quaker employers', *Historical Studies in Industrial Relations*, 6 (1998), 163–98.

27 Vernon, *Quaker Business Man*; Wagner, *Chocolate Conscience*; Robert Fitzgerald, *Rowntree and the Marketing Revolution, 1862–1969* (Cambridge: Cambridge University Press, 1995).

28 These interviews were conducted in women's own homes, usually on a one-to-one basis in a fairly private setting. Interviews with family members were challenging as they tested the boundaries of the conventional interview frame. It was difficult, for example, to know exactly at what moment to start the tape: when did a family visit end and a more formal interview begin? Shopes sees interviews as 'highly framed encounters, not governed by the rules of ordinary interaction'. Olson and Shopes, 'Crossing boundaries, building bridges', 195. However, I agree with Kristina Minister that it is important to 'discard idealized, andocentric concepts of the effective oral history interview', in order to formulate an interview strategy sensitive to the needs of individuals. Kristina Minister, 'A feminist frame for the oral history interview', in Gluck and Patai (eds), *Women's Words*, 39.

29 I did not use a question sheet but had a piece of paper with themes I hoped to cover scattered randomly over it. For this I adapted the model shown in Ken Howarth, *Oral History* (Stroud: Sutton Publishing, 1998), 140. There were problems with this method, however, as not all women felt comfortable in the position of narrator. Minister encourages the development of methods that value the ways in which women communicate amongst themselves. She advocates a more conversational approach and the interjection of personal anecdotes by the researcher. Minister, 'A feminist frame for the oral history interview', 35–6.

30 Alessandro Portelli, *The Death of Luigi Trastulli and Other Stories: Form and Meaning in Oral History* (Albany: State University of New York Press, 1991), 26.

31 I have struggled to find a language to write about 'race' as a historically constructed category of difference. 'Black' is an important political identity but may also obscure the experiences of those who do not identify with such a category. The term 'non-white', on the other hand, implies that there is a stable 'white' identity, when whiteness itself is shifting and contested. As Henry Louis Gates Jr insightfully remarks, 'we carelessly use language in such a way as to *will* this sense of *natural* difference into our formulations'. By using the constructed and dichotomous categories of 'white' and 'non-white' I do not want to suggest that these artificial descriptors can in any way capture complex identities and identifications. However, I do want to think about how whiteness and non-whiteness came into being, particularly through

the movement of people within the empire. Indeed, it is the fact of movement, of migration, which has in many cases determined how women are defined (and define themselves) in terms of race and ethnicity: whether as black, non-white, Asian, Chinese, Maltese or 'Yorkshire'. See Henry Louis Gates Jr (ed.), 'Race', Writing, and Difference (Chicago: University of Chicago Press, 1986), 5. On the construction of 'whiteness' see Theodore W. Allen, The Invention of the White Race. Volume One: Racial Oppression and Social Control (London: Verso, 1994); Noel Ignatiev, How the Irish Became White (London: Routledge, 1995).

32 Hall, 'Turning a blind eye', 37.

33 There is now a developing recognition of the connections between York and Africa, particularly since 2001 and the forging of links with the Ghanaian district of Fanteakwa. Fairtrade has also raised the profile of African farmers, with a visit to York in 2003 by two Ghanaian women cocoa farmers (members of the Kuapa Kokoo co-operative). Still, the long-standing connections of York with Ghana through cocoa are celebrated with no recognition of colonial exploitation. Nigeria remains unmentioned. See chapter four for a more detailed study of the politics of 'history' in York.

34 In theorising this relationship I am indebted to historians such as John MacKenzie who have challenged the separation of 'metropole' and 'colony' and the assumptions of a one-way stream of influence from the 'centre' to the 'periphery'. John M. MacKenzie, Propaganda and Empire: The Manipulation of Public Opinion, 1880–1960 (Manchester: Manchester University Press, 1984), 2.

35 Roger J. Southall, 'Cadbury on the Gold Coast, 1907–1938: the dilemma of the "Model Firm" in a colonial economy' (Ph.D. Dissertation, University of Birmingham, 1975).

36 On border crossings, see Gloria Anzaldúa, Borderlands/La Frontera: The New Mestiza (San Francisco: Aunt Lute, 2nd edn, 1999). Ruth Behar also uses Anzaldúa's concept of crossing borders in Translated Woman: Crossing the Border with Esperanza's Story (Boston: Beacon Press, 1993).

37 I have been influenced by calls for a transnational approach to women's studies, which sees 'the nation as inadequate for thinking about gender experience'. Transnational scholars do not simply compare experiences of women in different 'nations'; rather, they emphasise the constructed nature of the nation and focus instead on the ways in which national borders are shaped through gendered and raced processes of interaction and contact. Mary Louise Roberts, 'The transnationalization of gender history', in History and Theory, 44 (October, 2005), 456.

38 For instance, Rowntree demanded to be represented on the Cocoa Advisory Committee in 1947, claiming, 'this Company has done pioneer work in establishing a direct link between the actual consumer of cocoa in this country and the grower of cocoa in Nigeria'. However, they were excluded from the organisation as it was felt that they would be representing commercial interests rather than those of the farmers. Nigerian National Archives, Ibadan (NNA), CSO 26, 36148/S73A, T. Croft (Rowntree-Fry-Cadbury (Nigeria) Limited) to Mr E. Melville (Under Secretary of State, Colonial Office, Whitehall), 24 June 1947. See also chapters two and three.

39 The terms 'woman' and 'women' are problematic, disguising important points of difference in an assertion of an apparently stable and coherent category. Denise Riley, 'Am I That Name?' Feminism and the Category of Women in History (Basingstoke: Macmillan, 1988), 2. However, June Purvis asserts the necessity of the term in giving women 'a position from which they can speak'. Purvis, 'From "women worthies" to poststructuralism? Debate and controversy in women's history in Britain', in June Purvis (ed.), Women's History: Britain 1850–1945. An Introduction (London: UCL Press, 1995), 13.

40 Gary Cross, 'Consumer history and the dilemmas of working-class history', Labour History Review, 62: 3 (1997), 261.

41 The move towards comparative studies of women has been an important one but has not been without problems. It is important to avoid eliding cultural difference and, for western academics, using western cultural models as the 'norm' by which everything is measured against. This book has only two chapters that discuss the

lives of 'non-western' women but the research for these chapters has informed the rest of the project by highlighting the dangers of looking at the chocolate-manufacturing industry, York and white women in isolation. It is important to see connections between women, but also to recognise the inequalities that structure these connections. For committed analyses of global economies which make these kinds of connections, see Cynthia Enloe, *Bananas, Beaches and Bases: Making Feminist Sense of International Politics* (London: Pandora, 1989); Swasti Mitter, *Common Fate, Common Bond: Women in the Global Economy* (London: Pluto Press, 1986).

42 *CWM* was freely distributed to employees until 1970, when it was replaced by a factory newsletter.

CHAPTER ONE

'A deep physical reason': gender, race and the nation in chocolate consumption

In the cocoa chain model, consumption is the final stage, the definitive purpose of production. It is the privilege of those who can afford to consume, who are distanced geographically and economically from those at the very start of the chain. I want to disturb this hierarchy, critiquing and challenging the versions of chocolate produced in the domain of consumption. The focus in this chapter is therefore the texts and images of chocolate created by manufacturers and their advertising agents from the late nineteenth to the late twentieth centuries. Subsequent chapters will emphasise the histories of production behind these advertising motifs: returning first to the very start of the chain, and to the earliest western associations with cocoa, before tracing the cocoa bean's journey from farm to factory. Rather than being discrete, neatly ordered stages of the commodity chain, the processes of production and consumption are inextricable. Whilst consumer demand drives production, production motivates and to some extent defines modes of consumption. Moreover, women located at different points along the chain may be both producers and consumers (though in very different ways), undermining the logic of industrial commodity manufacture. My aim throughout this book will be to shift the focus away from the linear, finite movement of the cocoa bean, onto the ongoing interconnections between people (particularly women) and between places linked by the chocolate industry.

The inter-related processes of production and consumption have been facilitated and stimulated in the west by increasingly sophisticated marketing strategies. This chapter studies the meanings of chocolate consumption created in British advertising campaigns. It focuses on the marketing of Rowntree brands developed – with the exception of cocoa – in the 1930s. This decade was a turning point for the company, marking the launch of products such as Black Magic, Dairy Box, Kit Kat and Aero, and the start of their successful, if sometimes fraught, relationship with the J. Walter Thompson advertising firm (hereafter, JWT). Until this point, Rowntree had struggled to keep pace with their main rivals Cadbury, who had invested heavily in advertising from the late nineteenth century. Fitzgerald argues that it was the new emphasis on brands, supported by innovative market research, which came to distinguish the Rowntree company. Cadbury, in contrast, strongly promoted the company name on all their products: even embellishing each piece of Cadbury's Dairy Milk with the company logo.[1] The adverts of the two firms will be compared to reveal the similarities and differences in the versions of consumption they each construct.

The adverts here represent a range of products: cocoa powder, boxed assortments and individual bars. The versatility and malleability of melted chocolate allow it to be literally moulded to take on different forms, which are themselves endowed with different associations. Advertising has created, and reinforced, particular uses and identities for each type of product: so, whilst a chocolate bar may be consumed as a source of concentrated energy (to be carried on walking expeditions for instance), a box of chocolates may be bought as a gift (with all the social implications of the gift relationship).[2] In both situations the commodity is chocolate, but the attendant meanings are vastly different. Studying adverts for different products, I consider how chocolate consumption has been represented and how it has been encoded with meanings of gender, race and nation. Throughout this analysis, and in the chapters that follow, it will be crucial to ask in what ways such advertising represented, or failed to represent, the actual economic, political and social conditions in which Rowntree and Cadbury products, and ultimately profits, were produced.

Some of the earlier theories on advertising tended to underestimate the power and agency of the consumer. Judith Williamson contends that, 'We are trapped in the illusion of choice . . . [adverts] invite us "freely" to create ourselves in accordance with the way in which they have already created us.'[3] Diane Barthel, in contrast, highlights a more active reciprocal relationship between product and consumer which is facilitated by advertising: 'We are not passive recipients of goods, using them instead as a "cultural mode" to express our own sense of identity. Yet goods may also use *us* to "acquire social meaning".'[4] Adverts offer us ways of using commodities such as chocolate to say things about ourselves, our families, our social world. They also position us in relation to that product as gendered, classed and raced beings. Stuart Hall's work is useful here, as it allows for a level of negotiation of meaning within hegemonic ideologies.[5] Whilst I will not be looking specifically at the reception of adverts by women,

[19]

I do hope to maintain this sense of instability of meaning. A textual analysis of particular adverts will reveal some of the cultural attitudes and assumptions at work, but it cannot encompass all the possible readings and understandings of a particular advertisement.[6]

Representing gender

The consumption of chocolate in the west became feminised early in its history. From the male-dominated coffee and chocolate houses of the seventeenth century, chocolate became associated with luxury and leisure in the domestic sphere from the eighteenth century. With developments in industrial manufacturing processes and a reduction in duties, modes of consumption diversified. Luxury assortments remained for those who could afford them, but cocoa and chocolate also became available for the working classes from the nineteenth century. In this context, women were charged with providing wholesome cocoa for respectable consumption within the family.[7]

Given the importance of women to the chocolate industry as both producers and consumers, I focus in this section on the ways in which they were represented in marketing for a number of different confectionery products. I begin with a consideration of cocoa advertising and the images of housewives and mothers that dominate. I then examine briefly the occasions on which women feature outside the domestic context as paid workers. Next, I turn to the intersection of gender and class in marketing campaigns, particularly for chocolate assortments, and the portrayal of women within heterosexual courtship rituals. Finally, I consider adverts, mostly from the later twentieth century, in which women are increasingly individualised as consumers. By considering not just cocoa marketing but adverts for chocolate assortments and chocolate bars, I hope to demonstrate the ways in which images of women have been manipulated to suit particular brands.[8]

'My wife's a witch': the fetishisation of
women as housewives and mothers

The identities of mother and wife were closely intertwined in Rowntree advertising. The significance of women in these familial roles as potential consumers was reinstated in an advertising brief of 1951: 'We are selling to mothers and wives chiefly (because more cocoa is drunk in families with children than in families without, because the woman is the family's purchasing agent, and because she can be inspired to act in her husband's and children's interest when she might not do so in her own).' JWT were clearly prepared to exploit women's own self-doubt in converting them to the Rowntree brand: '_Any_ technique by which we can appeal to the mother's concern for the well-being of her family or her related anxiety about being a successful mother and winning the loyalty and gratitude of her husband and children might serve as a vehicle to make her think of Rowntree's Cocoa in the way we want her to think of it.'[9] Cocoa was shown to be the tool of both the devoted mother (a demonstration of maternal love), and the savvy housewife (economical, efficient, nutritious).

Targeting women buyers, Rowntree agents strove to find a medium which would appeal directly to women as consumers of advertising itself. Introducing the 'Special Mothers Campaign' of the 1930s, for instance, the advertising agency advised the Rowntree salesforce and retailers, 'Women read their magazines leisurely. They want pictures. They want a story. Here is a story told in pictures that will interest every mother. A story of natural, lovable children – just like her own.' 'Natural' in this case meant white, healthy, rosy cheeked and respectably dressed, and was therefore a classed and raced representation of children. This particular campaign, designed for women's magazines, showed children attempting to help their parents (usually the mother, particularly for girls) in gendered ways. Daughters attempt to bake and clean, for example, while sons try to polish their father's shoes. All these tasks are too exhausting for the young children and they abandon them in favour of drinking a nice cup of Rowntree's Cocoa. The caption reads: 'For growing children, there's no better drink at mealtimes.' Rowntree's is apparently 'more *bone and muscle-building* than ordinary cocoa'.[10] It is implicitly the mother who will provide this drink, thereby not merely safeguarding the health of her children but enhancing it.

The housewife is a dominant figure in postwar adverts for Rowntree's Cocoa. Although children continued to feature, JWT considered that too much emphasis had been placed on child consumers, ignoring the needs, desires and tastes of adult cocoa-drinkers, who in fact made up two-thirds of consumers in 1946.[11] There was, therefore, a subtle shift in cocoa advertising of the late 1940s and 1950s, from appealing to women as mothers, to appealing to them more broadly as housewives. In one set of adverts from 1946–47, the housewife is represented as a 'magical' figure. The awe-struck husband declares, 'My wife's a witch', as he marvels at the domestic bliss she creates. The wife, blond and youthful, is dressed in fancy-dress style witch's attire, with a pointy hat decorated with moons and stars. She is holding a tray with two cups and looking demurely, seductively at the viewer. This is in stark contrast to the previous campaign of 1946, which had acknowledged the stresses faced by women in the context of wartime and postwar shortages. Women were pictured apparently lashing out (though this was figured as within their imagination) in public places such as shops. One caption read, 'When you're so fed-up you could _hit_ someone.' The new campaign placed women firmly back in the domestic sphere, administering to their husband's needs.[12]

Mystical representations of women as angels and witches effectively made actual household work 'disappear'. As Anne McClintock notes of nineteenth-century advertising for household commodities, 'Housewifery became a career in vanishing acts. A wife's vocation was . . . to ensure the skilled erasure of every _sign_ of her work.'[13] In the 'My Wife's a Witch' campaign, both the woman and the product were fetishised. The wife in one advert is initially reduced to just one aspect of her physical appearance – her eyelashes. Yet, through using Rowntree's, she has exceeded all her husband's superficial expectations: 'I picked her for her eyelashes – I never dreamt she was so wizard at housekeeping. D'you wonder I'm spellbound?' The rational man has been seduced by the magical labours of his wife and by the 'magical' properties of the product.[14]

Knowledge about the benefits of Rowntree's Cocoa could be acquired through more mundane means, as illustrated by the 1946 advertising film entitled 'Tomorrow's Wives'. The film tapped into postwar optimism as it showed 'how schoolgirls of to-day are preparing to be useful and happy wives of tomorrow'. The commentary for the advert draws on a nationalistic discourse: 'Foreigners say the British housewife is a bad cook. It's not true, of course.' Indeed, these schoolgirls are not just good cooks, they also learn about nutrition and the 'food value' of drinks, particularly Rowntree's Cocoa. The cocoa takes on a socially useful role as a wholesome drink for the postwar nation. It is also implicated, once again, in the proper fulfilment of gender roles in British society. Through Rowntree's, women will prove their abilities as good housewives and maintain healthy British families. The final reference to the girls depicts their roles in quasi-military language: 'these eager young women troop off homewards'.[15] Rowntree's Cocoa will be a key weapon in their arsenal.

In a later campaign, beginning in the early 1950s, the mysteries of good housekeeping are revealed to the housewife who has been 'ignorant' in neglecting to consume Rowntree's Cocoa. Other women educate her in the art of consuming properly. Conspiratorially, in hushed tones, they point out inadequacies, drawing on notions of respectability and correct social behaviour: 'Mrs. Linton thought herself well up in household affairs until a simple hint from Mrs. Fyffe at the sale of work displayed her ignorance about a familiar item in the store cupboard.'[16] In a similar advert from the same year, 1952, 'Jill' learns about Rowntree's Cocoa following a TV party. Though she initially adopts

a critical tone regarding the hostess's housekeeping, she then exposes
her own ignorance:

> 'I always find that house like an iceberg. Really, Phoebe seems to have
> no idea . . .'
> 'Oh? But she was marvellous . . . gave us a lovely hot cup of cocoa before
> we left . . . that wonderful new Rowntree's. Have you tried it?'
> 'No.'
> 'But you must – straight away!'[17]

The unspoken rules of hospitality, and the role of food/drink in
such social practices, are here underscored. This campaign appeared
in connection with the 'new' Rowntree's – an attempt to increase
competitiveness with Cadbury in the postwar market. Packaging
their product in a new tin, and dropping the word 'cocoa', Rowntree
asked JWT to target a higher class of consumer, and to encourage more
aspirational consumption in their working-class customers.[18]

In contrast to the image of the innocent housewife is that of the
competent, 'clever' mum, who makes a prominent appearance in a
campaign of 1954. Mums who have Rowntree's Cocoa 'in stock' are
praised by other members of the family and by the authoritative voice
of the narrator. Possession of a tin of Rowntree's is possession of
superior women's knowledge of how to soothe children and stressed
husbands: 'it's clever of Mum to know that Rowntree's is so easily
digested . . . Cleverer still always to make sure there's a tin of
Rowntree's in the house.'[19] Women are clearly defined in these adverts
as the main shoppers of the family, or at least the coordinator of all
the family shopping. Their 'feminine' knowledge includes knowing how
to consume properly in a domestic context. Advertising agents used,
and continue to use, notions of 'clever' consumption to both persuade
and flatter women consumers.[20]

'Worry, worry, worry': female consumers
in the workplace

Despite encouragement from modernists in the 1930s to include representations of production on chocolate packaging, I found no evidence
of either packaging or advertising which depicted chocolate workers
at the York factory.[21] Rowntree advertising tended to avoid direct
associations of chocolate production and chocolate consumption. By
contrast, Cadbury regularly featured illustrations of workers as part of
their 'factory in a garden' campaign; male and female cocoa farmers
from the colonies also appeared in selected adverts. The skills of their
workforce, and the high standard of the environment in which they
laboured, were exploited by Cadbury to emphasise the quality of their

products. Still, neither firm chose to feature their own workers as consumers of the products they manufactured. Workplace consumption took place everywhere except the chocolate factory.[22] With so many female employees themselves, it is interesting to trace how, and when, the confectionery firms strategically deployed images of women consuming chocolate whilst working outside the home.

Depictions of women as paid workers were rare in cocoa advertising prior to the 1940s, except during wartime.[23] Chocolate bars, however, had never been connected to familial, domestic consumption in quite the same way and so allowed for more scope in the possible representations of women. Kit Kat adverts from the late 1930s suggested that the product was popular with female office workers, as well as with 'modern housewives'. Cadbury also evoked consumption of chocolate bars by women typists. In 1937, they advertised their Dairy Milk bar with the light-hearted slogan, 'At 11 a.m. do you FLIP or do you FLOP[?].' Two photographs displayed a young woman at a typewriter: in the first image she appears bright and alert; in the second she sits with her head in one hand, clearly exhausted. In the bottom left-hand corner, a chart illustrates 'just why Miss Flip flips', with a 'rising line' to show increased 'physical efficiency' after eating a bar of Dairy Milk.[24] As with cocoa, pseudo-scientific discourses of nutrition were invoked to persuade consumers that chocolate could be both healthy and a boost to productivity.

Cadbury were somewhat bolder than Rowntree in their use of images of working women prior to the Second World War. An advert appearing in 1938 suggested that Cadbury's Dairy Milk (CDM) was suitable for working women of all classes. It presented a testimonial from 'Britain's own prima ballerina' in the form of a newspaper article. Inset in the bottom left-hand corner of the advert was the rather more 'ordinary' tale of housekeeper Edith Matthias, who described eating CDM to get her through her morning's work. The advertising copy explained the connection: 'The part of *prima ballerina* demands heights of human effort that few can reach. But everything you do takes energy, and your ordinary job of work is quite tiring enough.'[25] As a 'handy' bar of chocolate, and indeed of *milk*, which was easy to transport, CDM was marketed to women and men working – and playing – outside the home from an early stage.

In the context of both world wars Rowntree featured women workers outside the home in its cocoa advertising. This reflected and reinforced contemporary patriotic notions of the whole nation working to fight a common enemy, as will be discussed in more detail later in this chapter. During the Second World War, photographs depicted women, and men, in diverse roles on the home front. Sustained by

[24]

Rowntree's Cocoa, women were productive workers in agriculture, industry, construction and specific wartime roles such as fire wardens.[26] Market research confirmed that consumption practices had indeed altered due partly to wartime conditions and advertising aimed to capitalise on such changes and to confirm cocoa's significance in the nation's diet.[27] Despite striking changes in the representation of women outside the home, they were still addressed as those responsible for providing and preparing cocoa through their roles as caring wives and mothers.

The 'stretching' of gender roles in wartime was expected to end with the onset of peace and this was broadly reflected in Rowntree adverts.[28] As Deirdre Beddoe illustrates with reference to cocoa adverts from the end of the First World War, female characters quickly make the transition from war work to housewife.[29] Following the Second World War, however, representations of women as workers and women as housewives and mothers were held in tension. With echoes of the Cadbury ballerina campaign, adverts depict women in high-powered, busy careers yet stress that women's work in the home is equally strenuous. Indeed, illustrations of women in difficult, professional jobs in the public sphere were used more as a simile for the hard work they were doing in the home than as a direct appeal to women in those jobs. One advert from 1945 shows a Continuity Girl in a film studio with the caption, 'worry, worry, worry'. This job would obviously have been far removed from the lives of most women in Britain, but the Continuity Girl finds comfort in Rowntree's Cocoa, 'and in this she is just like the hard-worked housewife, equally worried by details of rations, points, cooking, cleaning, and clothing'.[30] The targeted consumer is the housewife and mother, roles which women were being forcefully encouraged to adopt in the context of postwar reconstruction. Through advertising, Rowntree was (re)validating these domestic roles.

So, in adverts for Rowntree's Cocoa as a drink, women were represented predominantly as wives and mothers. Images of women as paid workers really only surfaced during wartime, although this changed somewhat in the post-Second World War period. Only in advertising for chocolate bars did women feature prominently in a workplace environment. It was women's labour in the home which was highly valued; domestic labour, and its subsequent stresses, was placed on a par with more 'high-flying' occupations in the 1940s and 1950s. This may have sent out contradictory messages to Rowntree workers themselves. In company adverts, as in the factory, Rowntree enforced a message of women as key workers in the home. A cookery class at the firm's Day Continuation School, for example, could well have been the setting for 'Tomorrow's Wives'. The school had been founded on factory premises in 1905 to ensure that young female employees learned the domestic skills necessary for their future roles as housewives.[31] However, the firm continued to need married women workers in order to produce the very products which would later be imbued with such 'domestic' values. As an employer, Rowntree constructed more ambiguous meanings about appropriate roles for women.

'The wonderful chocolates which Society is preferring': gendered discourses of class

In an early Rowntree advertising campaign from 1910, an elegant woman is asked to sample different kinds of cocoa whilst wearing a blindfold. The logic behind this experiment being that her sophisticated taste would recognise the superior flavour of Rowntree's Cocoa: 'It's the flavour which appeals to a refined taste.'[32] The emphasis is on identifying with, or aspiring to, high social status through consumption. Female consumers are invited to identify with this refined character and to demonstrate their own good 'taste' by choosing Rowntree's Cocoa.[33] Class, though inseparable from gender, was thus an important tool in marketing.

Cadbury drew explicitly on upper-class stereotypes to distinguish their 'Cup' brand of cocoa in the early 1930s. Adverts featured well-dressed, educated and well-travelled consumers pouring themselves a delicate cup of cocoa from an ornamental jug. The text urged consumers to 'DRINK *better* CHOCOLATE'. There is a clever slippage between appealing to upper- and upper-middle-class women and men, and encouraging other consumers to aspire to the social distinction afforded by drinking and serving the best cocoa: 'To offer one's visitors a fine cup of chocolate is a social distinction within everybody's reach.' To lend even greater sophistication to the product, the advertising copy then emphasised that this cocoa was on a par with that tasted on the Continent: 'Once it was a fixed belief that to drink chocolate at its best you had to drink it in Paris. Now . . . you can make at home a pot of chocolate worthy of a *cordon bleu*.' These adverts appeared in *The Times*, the *Daily Telegraph* and the *Morning Post* in the early 1930s, thus targeting a particular class of reader/consumer.[34]

Whereas the advertising of Rowntree's and Cadbury's Bournville brand cocoa from the 1920s mostly featured 'respectable' working- and lower-middle-class women as rational consumers in their ideal gendered roles as wives and mothers, other chocolate products drew on potentially more pleasurable, irrational and aspirational consumption. Marketing for the Rowntree Black Magic assortment, for example, (re)created discourses of chocolate as a luxury product for the upper classes. Black Magic adverts are immediately striking in their use of images of 'Society' women. One of the earliest examples includes a detailed painting of a woman horse riding. In the bottom right-hand corner is part of a letter written by the woman to one of her friends. The content and language signal that the woman is upper class: 'out with the hounds yesterday, and had a grand run. My new mare is a marvel!' At the bottom of the ad, the voice of 'the company' addresses the consumer: 'Let us explain: Black Magic are the wonderful chocolates which Society is preferring even to 5/- a pound chocolates.'[35] A Rowntree rhetoric of 'affordable quality' is evident here. Yet there is also an aspirational element to the advert. The non-Society female consumer may aspire to the romantic lifestyle of the leading character. As the recipient of the letter is absent, the female viewer is able to position herself as the friend and confidant of the author.

Cadbury took a rather different approach to their assortment advertising, as I will discuss in more detail later. Nevertheless, in the 1960s Cadbury also drew on images of high-class female consumers, though in a rather more playful style, to advertise their dark chocolate bar, Bournville. Women of conspicuously expensive tastes were photographed with captions listing their 'plain, simple' needs: 'A large simple bank-account. A few thousand Ordinary Shares. And plain chocolate.' These are not the 'Society' women of the Black Magic adverts, however; their consumption is individualistic and almost vulgar in its excess. One character is shown wrapped in leopard skin, stating her likes as: 'Plain chinchillas. Simple sables. A few ordinary leopard skins.' The joke in the adverts serves to elevate a 'plain' chocolate bar to a 'slim, elegant' luxury.[36]

By contrast to Black Magic, Cadbury's 'Cup' cocoa and the Bournville bar, the emphasis for Rowntree's Dairy Box was on its affordability rather than any pretensions of sophistication. Indeed, prior to the Second World War, adverts usually featured an image of a shilling to emphasise the point. They appealed much more directly to men as purchasers of chocolate for girlfriends: 'Half a pound of sweet content / That only costs a shilling: / DAIRY BOX are heaven-sent – / She'll find them simply thrilling!' The trite nursery-rhyme style of the adverts suggests cheap and cheerful chocolates, though quality is always emphasised: 'You couldn't get better chocolates at twice the price.'[37] For those men who could not afford the more expensive selections, Dairy Box allowed them to aspire to the gentlemanly practice of buying romantic gifts for a girlfriend. Despite the emphasis on 'cheapness', then, Dairy Box may still have offered the potential for upward social mobility.

Figure 1 White, upper-class, heterosexual femininity in advertising for Black Magic, 1937.

Alongside the shilling image, Dairy Box advertising adopted the character of a dairymaid carrying pails of milk.[38] Pastoral imagery such as dairymaids and shepherds created an idealised rural working class, rather than addressing industrial working-class consumers directly. The fantasy of the English countryside is evoked in implicit contrast to the industrial employment of many potential consumers. Once again, Rowntree's chocolate, with its origins in African agriculture, drew upon an exclusively white rural idyll where actual labour (such as the carrying of heavy milk pails) was romanticised and sexualised through representations of particular white women. In marketing their milk chocolate bars, Cadbury also emphasised the addition of English milk.[39] For their Milk Tray assortment, however, interwar advertising tended to stress the quality of the chocolates in a fairly straightforward style. As for Dairy Box, the emphasis was on affordable quality, but with a more individualistic motive: 'The Chocolates You Give Yourself'. A photograph of a business woman featured in one ad, with the following recommendation: 'As a business woman I consider Milk Tray a value-for-money proposition that's just too good to miss.'[40] It was not until the 1950s that Cadbury began to experiment with more romantic associations for this assortment, as we shall see in more detail later.

Ideas about social class were clearly a useful means of distinguishing between brands. Market research consistently claimed that dark chocolate was more popular amongst the higher social classes, with milk chocolate favoured amongst the working classes.[41] This is likely to have influenced the different advertising strategies adopted for Black Magic and Dairy Box, although such class preferences may themselves have been, at least in part, the product of early associations between nutritious milk chocolate and the needs of the working classes. Both Black Magic and Dairy Box had been originally conceived as providing a more 'affordable' chocolate assortment, where previously such collections of chocolate-covered centres had been the preserve of the rich. The assortments would still have a degree of luxury appeal but could be mass-produced.

The 'affordability' and value for money of both Black Magic and Dairy Box, though marketed in different ways, was thus predicated on the production processes and employment strategies of the Rowntree firm. The gradual breaking down of tasks into simple, repetitive moves supposedly facilitated greater productivity. This eventually became assembly line work, with consequences for women workers including decreased aesthetic satisfaction in chocolate production and increasing monotony. By employing women, particularly as dispensable seasonal staff, Rowntree were also able to keep production costs

[29]

down. The experience of women workers, working-class women on the shopfloor, must therefore inform our understanding of representations of class in advertising the products of their labour.

'Keep your "Sweetie" sweet': narratives of heterosexual romance

As will be discussed in more detail in the following chapter, chocolate has had long-standing associations with female sexuality. By the twentieth century, at least until the 1970s, the link between sex and chocolate had become circumscribed according to the *type* of chocolate being marketed. Cocoa retained its rather wholesome connotations. Luxury assortments, in contrast, tended to carry a flavour of courtship, romance and sex. Rowntree adverts for assortments placed consumption firmly within heterosexual courtship: chocolate was to be a gift from a man to a woman. Black Magic, as already mentioned, used letters apparently written by women to female friends, extolling the pleasures of receiving a box of Black Magic chocolates. The earliest examples are mere extracts; breaking off at interesting points, they echo the techniques of romance narratives which women (including women workers at Rowntree) may have been reading in books or women's magazines. Later letters are occasionally from men to women, displaying the conventions of the love letter. Black Magic advertising thus offered the potential of pleasurable consumption by women readers, just as the chocolates themselves offered pleasure and romance.[42]

Postwar adverts are at first glance far more cynical and ironic in their treatment of male/female relationships. Within Black Magic adverts from the 1950s onwards, women were often given a voice to complain about their man: 'He was so interested in his awful football match that he didn't seem to notice me.'[43] Even so, the sanctity of the monogamous couple is never completely undermined. Dissatisfaction is resolved through the gift of Black Magic. This narrative pattern fits neatly with Janice Radway's analysis of romance novels in which the hero is presented as flawed initially, giving the readers pleasure in watching the heroine overcome such 'faults' as a bad temper. Of course, the man is never really 'bad' and there is usually a reason for his moodiness. The heroine does not 'change' her man; she only brings out in him what was already there.[44] In chocolate advertising, it is the gift which signals this inherent goodness. Men are assured that their gift will symbolise their appropriateness as romantic partners. Female consumers, on the other hand, are told that Black Magic may be taken as evidence of the right type of man. As one female character writes in an advert from 1956–57, 'I think anyone who chooses Black Magic must be nice.'[45] This particular man is a university student, attired in

[30]

a black gown, 'hanging about the quad'. His good taste in chocolate is inextricably linked to his good education and good social prospects.

Early Dairy Box advertising was surely less appealing to women. As discussed, it was men who were explicitly addressed in these adverts as the likely purchasers. Women in the Dairy Box rhymes are frequently referred to as 'sweet' themselves, implying that they, as well as the chocolates, may be consumed following the courtship gifting rituals: 'Spend a lucky shilling/ On giving her a treat –/ A DAIRY BOX of lovely chocs/ Will keep your "Sweetie" sweet!'[46] The style and down-to-earth language of the advert suggest a working-class male consumer, in contrast to the aspirational romantic fantasies offered to women in Black Magic adverts.

Wartime adverts for Dairy Box departed from the seemingly innocent nursery-rhyme style of the 1930s to offer more explicitly sexual images. Dairymaids were now dressed in hot pants and other skimpy outfits – a far cry from the 'sophisticated' women of the Black Magic campaign. The rhymes dealt more directly with courtship, and some were tinged with innuendo:

Pat-a-cake, pat-a-cake, baker's man!
Loses his sweetie, discovers a plan;
Takes her some Dairy Box down to her farm,
And wedding-cake, wedding-cake is soon the order of the day
– in fact she leaves her cows immediately and the lucky baker's man
finds it *is* possible to have your cake *and* pat it, after all![47]

Chocolate marketing can be seen, here, to follow the cultural trends of the Second World War, in objectifying women as sexual objects to maintain male morale.[48]

Dairy Box advertising quickly moved away from this overtly sexualised, wartime campaign. Postwar adverts featured light-hearted but respectable courtship stories about two 'wholesome' young white couples: Mary and John, and Peter and Joan (later Jenny). They are usually depicted engaged in some form of worthy leisure activity: on hikes, cycle rides or railway excursions. Peter is always wooing Joan with Dairy Box, while Mary reprimands John for not doing the same. In a typical exchange, John wonders why Peter has 'Joan on a string'. Mary retorts, 'Not such a knotty problem, John. Look at those chocolates he's brought her!' Of course, it is not just the chocolates themselves that are important, as Mary points out, 'it's the thoughtfulness behind the gift that makes Joan feel so secure'.[49] John then produces some Dairy Box and Mary realises that he has always been in control of the situation: 'I do believe you've been stringing me along about them all the time.'[50] In contrast to cocoa advertising, then, it is men's knowledge which is valued and fostered in the marketing of assortments. Both Black Magic and Dairy Box advertising initially depict the women as dominant, only to be subdued by the gift of chocolate. The inequalities of heterosexual gender roles are thereby reinforced.

The model of chocolates as synonymous with romance persisted throughout the nineteenth and twentieth centuries. Yet the marketing of assortments through romantic associations was by no means inevitable. Cadbury tended to market their assortments, at least until the 1960s, as the products of the 'factory in a garden'. Illustrations of consumption practices emphasised the element of choice, and the potential for sharing. Cadbury assortments were presented as a suitable gift for women but the element of heterosexual 'romance' was neither as consistent nor as explicit in the 1930s and 1940s. In 1931, for example, an advert for Cadbury assortments as a Christmas gift was illustrated by a pencil sketch of a middle-aged man with a walking stick and bowler hat pondering over possible presents. He dismisses gloves, 'fancy goods' and stockings, concluding: 'but she'll love a lovely box of . . . [Cadbury's Chocolates]'. This is not a campaign for any particular brand of chocolates but establishes a general connection between buying Cadbury's as a Christmas gift. The buyer is assured that the name 'Cadbury' appears on '<u>every piece</u> of chocolate', thus emphasising a stamp of quality rather than suggesting the sensuous fillings of the assortments.[51]

Despite this different approach to assortment branding, it is Cadbury's Milk Tray that is perhaps now most famous for its romantic associations, thanks to the 'And all because the lady loves . . .' campaign, introduced in the late 1960s. These adverts depicted a dashing and enigmatic 'danger man' who would go to any lengths to secure a box of Milk Tray for his 'lady'. According to an article in the *Bournville Works Magazine* (*BWM*), the campaign was designed to raise the profile of Milk Tray from a 'good' to a 'special' assortment. The London Press Exchange, Cadbury's advertising agents, apparently suggested that 'a good way of making Milk Tray appear more special would be to show a man going to extraordinary lengths to give a box to someone'. The man is motivated by the desire of a beautiful woman, as the Assortments Product Group Manager explained in an interview: 'when asked why the mysterious hero goes to such lengths to give his lady Milk Tray, Ted Hirst replied: "Wait until you see what she looks like . . ."'.[52] The chocolates thus gain in value through association both with a dynamic adventure/romance narrative and with an imagined ideal of feminine beauty.

Consumed as part of courtship, or within the institution of marriage, chocolate could reinforce, by eliding, unequal relations between men and women. Of course, not all women would have accepted such gifts; others may have accepted the gift but not the implied meanings of gratitude and sexual submission. Associations of chocolates and romance would have been still less apparent in the shopfloor environment where they were produced, and sometimes consumed. Similarly, chocolate assortments purchased cheaply by Rowntree employees as waste bags from the factory shop would not have fitted so neatly into the image projected by the advertising. None of the retired women workers I interviewed voluntarily offered memories of receiving chocolates as a romantic gift, though some enjoyed consuming chocolate on the shopfloor, at home or in leisure settings such as the cinema. There is evidence that for working-class women gifts of chocolates from male partners are treated more pragmatically than the adverts suggest.[53] Nevertheless, the ideals of heterosexual marriage and monogamy presented in chocolate advertising are echoed in some of the oral histories of former Rowntree workers, who structured their life stories and indeed their working patterns, around their married lives. Moreover, links between chocolates and romance had a very real impact on the women as producers, with the increasing commercialisation of Valentine's Day, for example, leading to a surge in demand for chocolates and a corresponding demand for their labour.

'She's enslaved by Dairy Box': women as irrational narcissistic consumers

The young female characters in the Dairy Box stories are apparently obsessed by chocolates. As John comments at one point, 'Joan seems to *exist* on chocolates!' Mary refutes this: 'Naturally, she likes Dairy Box, John. . . . But what thrills Joan is that *Peter* brought them for her.'[54] Joan's passion for chocolates is reinterpreted as a 'natural' liking of the Dairy Box brand. Her real 'thrill' is the romantic significance of Dairy Box: female obsession and excess is thus contained within the heterosexual couple. That Mary uses the word 'brought' rather than 'bought' masks the economic dynamics of this courtship.[55] Other adverts from the late 1940s and 1950s shift the emphasis onto female characters so enamoured of Dairy Box that men literally fade into the background and the women are defined solely in relation to the chocolates.

This trend towards a narcissistic consumer begins with the character of Judy: usually depicted in a French-style costume of stripy top and beret with trousers.[56] There is a certain chic, modern femininity to this character and she appears independent of any male suitor. However, the commentary to the advert takes on a masculine tone of rationality and paternalism: 'Take no notice of Judy. Judy's always up

[33]

to her eyebrows in chocolates.' Judy is so 'scatterbrained' she forgets to tell us about all the different centres in Dairy Box. Instead, she is seduced by the chocolates themselves, which are like 'kisses'. The apparently independent female consumer continues to be contained within (hetero)sexualised narratives and gender relations where she is positioned as weak.

Judy's successor in the late 1950s was the young actress, Una Stubbs. Like Judy, Una's focus is usually on the chocolates, although a handsome male is often in attendance to provide them for her. Una's identity is now completely defined, in the words of her male partner, by the chocolates she consumes: 'She's enslaved by Dairy Box. She's a Dairy Box Girl.'[57] As a young, popular actress of nineteen, Una clearly embodied meanings that Rowntree wished to associate with this brand of chocolates: she was fun, cheeky, fashionable and modern. O'Donohoe points out how celebrities may 'bring with them identities from other performances'.[58] Stubbs had meaning for consumers in relation to these identities but also through the ways in which she was represented as a 'personality' in the media more generally. The 'girls' of Dairy Box are a complete contrast to the 'women' of Black Magic advertising. Rowntree chocolates are thus able to embody different, even competing modes of femininity.

Alongside chocolate assortments, which have long been strongly located within the rituals and meanings of heterosexuality, Rowntree was also marketing bars of chocolate such as Aero. As discussed earlier with reference to Kit Kat, the meanings attached to such bars were more varied. They have been conceived at different times as a food substitute, as a romantic gift, and as a pleasurable guilty treat to be enjoyed alone. Rowntree and JWT spent some months in 1938 deliberating over the best way to sell the numerous small bars Rowntree were producing, deciding on the 'Self-interest appeal': '2d blocks . . . are an essentially personal and selfish purchase, being neither a gift, something to share, nor something to buy for the household.' This principle could be applied in different ways for different products, 'just as Romance may sell both Black Magic and Dairy Box'.[59] In the late 1930s and the 1940s, Aero consumption was justified in the pseudo-scientific terms of nutrition: 'When you get a craving for a bit of chocolate, it's not just hunger – much less greed. It's an S.O.S. from your tummy that the energy reserves of your blood have fallen below the SAFE level.'[60] As a nutritional product Aero was shown to be suitable for men, women and children of all ages in a variety of situations, usually outside of the family home. Yet images of women tended to predominate in Aero marketing, drawing on and further maintaining the links between women, chocolate and sex.

Women consumers were often depicted in Aero adverts of the late 1930s being urged to listen to their desires in an implicitly sexualised discourse: 'Do you know that when you get an urge to eat chocolate, you shouldn't resist – there's a *deep physical reason* for it?' These urges are 'natural' and should be obeyed: 'When you resist the urge to eat chocolate you are ignoring one of Nature's most serious warnings.' In each advert a different woman is depicted taking a bite of an Aero bar. Some look a little guilty at being caught in the act, while others look sexily at the camera. The orgasmic pleasure brought about by their 'urges' being satisfied is revealed in the projected responses: 'You say, "A-ah, that was good" – and your whole body relaxes in utter satisfaction.'[61] The adverts are countering the guilt that supposedly arises from the selfish pleasures of consumption for women. But they are also suggestive of how women should project their heterosexual yearnings and fantasies onto chocolate consumption. Chocolate offers a safe (socially acceptable) and natural release of implicitly sexualised desires.

Women as consumers of chocolate have historically been depicted as obsessed by the product (see chapter two). This is in contrast to the portrayal in many Rowntree and Cadbury adverts, particularly for cocoa, of housewives and mothers consuming rationally in the interests of family health and domestic harmony.[62] Chocolate has supposedly addictive properties which women are unable to resist. Women's identities may thus become subsumed by their consumption habits, just as they may lose their identity in devotion to a man. Such loss of identity is represented as pleasurable. Women, particularly single women, are culturally constructed as constantly negotiating temptation; it is their responsibility to maintain a pure body by resisting male sexual advances except within marriage, and afterwards to remain monogamous. In the later twentieth century this has extended to maintaining 'beauty' by resisting the temptation of sweet and fatty foods such as chocolate. Succumbing to chocolate addiction momentarily allows the pleasurable surrender to such temptation.[63]

'Does you mean 'dis?': cocoa marketing and race

In 1946 and 1947 respectively, two new characters – 'Little Coco' and 'Honeybunch' – were created to sell Rowntree's Cocoa. They were both children, a common enough feature of many chocolate advertisements since the nineteenth century. However, unlike the boys and girls captured in Rowntree's 'Special Mothers Campaign' of the 1930s, these children were both black. Honeybunch was the girl character, whilst Little Coco was a young boy.[64] The two characters never appeared together and looked quite different. Coco had an oversized head, and large eyes, with the large lips associated with minstrels.[65] His baldness visually connected him to a cocoa bean, though this also distanced him from the golliwog character, which was at that time being employed by the Robertson's company as a mascot for their jam and preserves.[66] Like Coco, Honeybunch had a large head and eyes, but she clearly belonged to the 'pickaninny' stereotype, with bare feet, 'braids and spindly legs'.[67] Her features were not of the grotesque type of many nineteenth- and early twentieth-century images; rather, she was constructed as westernised and feminine through her light skin, blue eyes (in colour images) and hair ribbons. Despite their differences, the function of these two figures was essentially the same: to be the spokespeople for Rowntree's Cocoa. So why did Rowntree and their advertising agents choose to adopt black characters at this particular moment? And what ideologies of race and gender did they represent?

Commodity racism[68]

The use of black people in advertising has a long history. As Jan Pieterse demonstrates, products made available through the use of slave labour, such as coffee and cocoa, often used, and many still use, images of black people to enhance their luxury status.[69] Susan J. Terrio highlights how, in French adverts for chocolate in the late nineteenth century, 'the use of black men, women, and children . . . was ubiquitous'. She clearly connects the use of such figures to the construction of chocolate as an exotic commodity: 'Both the product and the race are marked primarily by their spatial, temporal, and cultural distance from Europe. The cultivation of this distance has always been a strategic component in the creation of demand for chocolate.'[70] In general, however, the use of black characters appears to have been both less common in Britain than in France and, at least in twentieth-century advertising, more complex in the construction of boundaries between black/white, colonised/coloniser. Cocoa, like other products from the colonies, was encoded with racialised meanings in the specific context of British imperialism.

According to Ramamurthy, in her impressively nuanced study of race in British advertising, support for indirect rule in West Africa (as being favourable to cocoa production) resulted in the Quaker chocolate firms adopting images of Africans as 'peasant producer[s] . . . with an appearance of potential development'. Furthermore, the São Tomé and Principe slavery scandal of the early twentieth century encouraged the Quaker manufacturers to use more 'positive' images of Africans. Soap advertising in Britain, in contrast, relied on derogatory images of black people, which Ramamurthy argues were informed

No country was too rough for Little Coco . . .

until the rope broke . . .

and left him stranded.

"You'll need your Rowntree's Cocoa, Coco!"

"You'se telling me!"

He could now face life's problems . . .

more resolutely.

Figure 2 Little Coco tackles a dangerous bear in
'Coco and the Cliff', 1947.

Figure 3 Honeybunch advising 'real' white consumers
to drink Rowntree's Cocoa, 1950.

by Lever's support for plantations in Africa (rather than for small-scale independent farmers). Making connections between imperial policy, company ideology and the need to sell products, Ramamurthy highlights the ways in which representations of black people were very specific in their ideological implications, and not simply reflections of a consistent racism. This is a convincing argument, though Ramamurthy perhaps underestimates the role of the advertising agents in constructing their own racist logics in relation to a particular product, or indeed a particular brand.[71]

Ramamurthy suggests that after about 1910, even though the cocoa companies were buying large amounts of cocoa from West Africa, 'Most of the images which predominate . . . are those of sugary-sweet white boys and girls.'[72] The Rowntree Cocoa Nibs, introduced in 1919, certainly appear to fit this pattern. The 'Nibs' were a white girl and boy (and occasionally their pet dog) who just loved Rowntree's Cocoa. Yet there was 'Another Cocoa Nib', a black boy in a straw hat and dungarees carrying an over-sized cocoa pod and tin of Rowntree's Elect, or sometimes a selection of Rowntree's Gums.[73] He appeared at the centre of shop window displays for Rowntree, as a rural child producer in amongst images of elegant white female consumers. The front cover of the *CWM* for March 1922 was also devoted to this figure, with his wide staring eyes and toothy grin. However, he seems to fade into the background in comparison to the other 'Nibs', and is not mentioned in the 1923 competition to name the two white children and their dog.[74]

Photo stories from the 1930s and 1940s returned the focus to white children as consumers, all growing stronger through drinking cocoa. These were the new generation of Britons being brought up on Rowntree products. Whiteness had also long been a dominant motif in adverts featuring adults. In 1891, the 'White Rose of York' label for Elect Cocoa featured a white woman, dressed in a white dress, carrying a pot of cocoa on a tray with white roses.[75] In the 1920s, consumers were introduced to Mr York, with his white top hat and waistcoat. Consumption, like the production process at the Rowntree factory, was here being supervised by an apparently benevolent, white paternalist figure. Moreover, Mr York was closely associated with both the city of York and the region of Yorkshire, thus effectively masking any connections of chocolate with the cocoa producers of West Africa.[76]

For Cadbury, the processes of chocolate production, and the environment in which these processes took place, were adopted as key selling points in some campaigns. As such, the firm continued to represent black cocoa farmers in the West Indies and West Africa even after the First World War. Black producers were represented positively in these adverts, though they were under the supervision, directly or indirectly, of white manufacturers in order for Cadbury to obtain only the best cocoa beans.[77] In 1930, for example, an advert explained, 'How to make chocolates as good as Cadbury's': 'Take the pick of the world's cocoa plantations. . . . Send your own buyers abroad and instruct them to follow the methods of Cadbury's experts who buy on the spot, rigorously rejecting all beans that fall below the high Cadbury standard.' This point was illustrated by an image of four faceless African women, carrying baskets of cocoa pods on their heads. As with Rowntree, it is whiteness which dominates in the end, though for Cadbury this is related explicitly to the cleanliness of the factory environment which purifies the ingredients. For example, another 1930s advert poses the question, 'What are "Ideal Conditions"?' The answer is 'a vast factory as clean as a dairy. White-tiled walls; . . . white-overalled workers. . . . [Visitors] see the purity of ingredients proved by a large staff of analytical chemists.'[78] Where the production process was not featured, the fictional characters in Cadbury adverts were exclusively white consumers.

The decision by Rowntree and their agents to use black cartoon characters to sell Rowntree's Cocoa in the late 1940s and into the 1950s appears to run against the dominant trends in British chocolate advertising. Indeed, in relation to British advertising more generally, Ramamurthy observes that, 'In the postwar period, as decolonisation became a reality, and immigration from the colonies began to change the face of Britain, consumer advertising stopped using the image of black people to sell products.'[79] The Rowntree case raises questions about this timescale.

Harnessing 'difference'

From correspondence and reports in the JWT archive, it is clear that the company saw the late 1940s as a crucial period in preparing consumers for the lifting of wartime measures and ensuring that Rowntree would be in a strong competitive position. Little Coco and Honeybunch were enlisted in this context. More specifically, Honeybunch appeared at a time when the continuation of wartime restrictions forced advertisers to rely on small-scale newspaper adverts to keep the brand name in the public view. She provided a simple but striking image, with single-frame cartoons depicting her adventures. Little Coco, meanwhile, was developed as a character suited to animated films, allowing JWT to overcome some of the restrictions on other forms of advertising at this time. In JWT records it is such concerns with advertising mediums which predominate; race is never explicitly discussed.[80]

At a time when Cadbury were using images of sturdy white youths to advertise their brand of cocoa, Honeybunch and Coco would have been visually 'different' and therefore potentially more memorable. Consumer research in 1948 tested the level of recognition for Honeybunch compared to the white children used in Cadbury adverts. The campaign certainly seems to have had some success. In the survey of 400 housewives, 200 were shown an edited version of 'Honeybunch and the Swordfish' and asked to identify the product and the firm being advertised; the remaining 200 women were shown a Cadbury advert showing three white children of different ages all growing stronger from drinking cocoa. Whilst 78 per cent of each sample were able to identify that it was cocoa being advertised, only 29 per cent correctly identified the Cadbury firm, compared to 42 per cent who associated Honeybunch with the name of Rowntree.[81] Advertisers, then, harnessed stereotypical 'blackness' for its visible difference, creating a strong identity for the Rowntree brand. Ramamurthy has highlighted the racialisation of brands in the late nineteenth and early twentieth centuries; clearly, distinguishing otherwise similar products by associating them with a distinct racial caricature remained a useful tactic in the postwar period.[82]

In the mid-1940s, Rowntree and JWT were searching for a campaign with the potential to create long-lasting brand loyalty. There was a clear belief that if only the children could be enlisted, their mothers would certainly follow. JWT noted that a 'merchandising idea' was needed which could attract children through stories involving lovable characters in different media, with associated merchandise to collect. They decided on the 'Adventure-Continuity Campaign': 'in the eyes of the children to whom the campaign is exposed, it adds a psychological value inseparable from Rowntree's brand of cocoa, to an extent that they will exert pressure on the mother'. There is nothing to suggest that they had envisaged a black character for this campaign. This may have been the idea of Coco's creator, David Hand. Yet even in 1945 the agents already had high hopes for the Little Coco films: 'it is feasible to think that we have got on to so outstanding a technique as to raise to some extent the basic value of cinema as a medium'.[83] Documents and correspondence from 1947 reveal Little Coco was indeed intended to have a life outside the films: 'a Press campaign using the "Coco" character is far in production, and supporting display material using the character is also contemplated'. Unfortunately for Rowntree and JWT, they had not considered fully the copyright claims on the character of the artist David Hand and the production company GB Animation and this appears to have hampered any meaningful extension of Little Coco merchandising.[84]

[41]

Although not discussed in official records, there were other, more disturbing logics at work in the figures of Honeybunch and Coco. Chocolate has been used as a 'euphemism for people of color' in many western cultures.[85] In the context of the Rowntree adverts featuring Honeybunch, and particularly those featuring Coco, the symbolic logic is reversed. The signifier and signified switch places as the black characters are made to serve as visual and – for Little Coco – linguistic metonyms.[86] In one advert from 1950, Honeybunch's body is replaced by a spring as she is shown bouncing, like a jack-in-the-box, out of a tin of cocoa.[87] She is being consumed by the product and losing her individual, physical identity. Ramamurthy cites other examples of adverts in which Africans effectively become cocoa – their head and feet sticking out of a cocoa pod. She sees this as typical of the 'equation of Africans with natural produce'.[88] Honeybunch's name, suggesting the 'naturally' sweet product of honey, is another way in which this association is achieved. In all the Rowntree adverts studied, it is significant that black figures are used to advertise cocoa powder rather than chocolate. Though processed by western industry, cocoa powder is closest to the 'raw', colonial material.[89] The two Rowntree characters only exist through their relation to the cocoa, effectively disempowering them. There is no recognition of the actual connections between the commodity and the labour of black people in the colonies. The following section will examine depictions of Coco and Honeybunch in more detail to see how, and to what effect, they correspond to contemporary black stereotypes, and how they deviate from such images.

Chocolate adventure(r)s

According to Rowntree sources, each short film starring Little Coco, their 'charming new salesman', was seen in cinemas across the country by 11,000,000 people.[90] In this role Coco fits clearly with the black stereotype of the 'entertainer', keeping white audiences amused while they waited for the main film to begin.[91] His nature and actions in each film also correspond with the Sambo stereotype: a happy-go-lucky male figure but with the potential for almost savage strength.[92] Though westernised and 'civilised' by virtue of his Boy Scout uniform, Coco battles with angry bears, fortified by Rowntree's.[93] Where the white Cocoa Nibs appeared largely in urban settings, Coco, as a black child, is more at home in the wilderness.[94] This does not prevent him getting into scrapes, however. Absorbed in activities such as angling, climbing and even bear trapping, he remains blissfully unaware of the dangerous animals lurking just around every corner. His seriousness in undertaking these tasks, and his innocence of the dangers, are intended to be amusing for the audience. From the privileged position of observer, the scene of the action is distant enough to be unthreatening.

Coco is not naturally heroic, his strength and bravery are located solely within the product. Like Popeye with his spinach, Coco needs his Rowntree's to give him the strength to fight off bears or to climb up rocks. He thus fits within a comic trope, at the margins of masculine adventure stories.[95] While the exotic, dangerous setting was meant to appeal to white children, they were presumably not supposed to identify too closely with Coco and his violent tendencies. Coco represented a safe version of black masculinity: as a child he was sufficiently desexualised, he was never put into contact with white people, and he was contained within a distant location. Unlike the black colonial migrants moving to Britain in the postwar period, he was right where white consumers expected him to be. Consequently the cocoa he advertised, indeed the 'Coco' he embodied, by association could be seen as neutralising fears as well as providing physical strength. The adverts themselves soothed postwar consumer anxieties, just as the product promised to do.[96]

Honeybunch exhibits many of the stereotypical features identified by Kern-Foxworth as typical of representations of black women: a happy-go-lucky nature, a desire to please, and folksy wisdom about food.[97] Her catchphrase description of Rowntree's Cocoa – 'So grateful, so genial, so good' – could also be assigned to her own character. Where Coco is active and occasionally aggressive, Honeybunch takes on a more persuasive role appropriate to her gender. The adjectives 'grateful' and 'genial' have connotations of supposedly safe female African American characters such as Aunt Jemima.[98] Yet Honeybunch, too, has adventures. She travels far and wide, meeting a variety of hungry wild animals and ravenous 'natives' who are usually in the midst of eating something 'comically' inappropriate. The adverts make use of grotesque racial stereotypes: an Eskimo, for example, whose in-turned feet suggest stupidity, attempts to eat a candle; in another image a cannibal, complete with a spear and a top hat, is about to cook a white explorer.[99] Honeybunch is unfazed by all her encounters. Perhaps the Cocoa Nibs would have been worryingly (for white consumers) out of place confronting a hungry Eskimo. Yet Honeybunch advises dangerous humans and animals alike to have a cup of Rowntree's Cocoa.[100]

Whilst much of the intended appeal of the Honeybunch and Little Coco campaigns relied on visual and situation comedy, racial 'difference' was also created through language. The dialect of both characters draws on long-standing stereotypes of black speech, influenced by imperialism, minstrel shows and other African and African American stereotypes.[101] Coco's, 'Yessah!', for example, is reminiscent of an 1899 advert for Fry captioned, 'Cocoa, Sah!' This featured a naturalist painting of a black boy wearing an apron and carrying a tray of cocoa.[102] The image and language are typical of the stereotype of obedient black people, sometimes constructed as 'Uncle Toms'. It could therefore be construed as unthreatening by white audiences.[103] Honeybunch's advice, meanwhile, is given in a 'folksy' dialect: 'Feelin' kinda hungry? Me, I'd have a cuppa Rowntree's.' There is an (African) American 'Southern hospitality' discourse at work here.[104] The use of such language by infantilised black characters was intended to amuse the white British audience: for instance, the pun on running 'roun' trees' and drinking 'Rowntree's' in one Coco ad. Of course, the use of non-standard English is amusing only to those who consider themselves able to speak it 'properly', a status primarily conferred by being white and born in England (though non-standard 'native' English dialects could also be the subject of parody). The adverts reinforce ideas about the supremacy of the English language, apparently spoken all over the world, and about the ignorance of those who do not speak it 'properly'.

Both Coco and Honeybunch have a degree of agency as active ambassadors for Rowntree. In later adverts, Honeybunch steps out of her cartoon world into the 'real' world of white consumers. She appears inset into photographs of white families, advising them to 'have a cuppa Rowntree's'. This fits with Ramamurthy's analysis of representations of the 'imperial family', in which black children serve cocoa to a paternalistic white consumer.[105] Honeybunch remains safely distanced by appearing in a different medium – that of animation. Her bare feet are a key marker of her inferior status in comparison to the well-dressed white families with whom she is often juxtaposed.[106] She is also smaller than the white characters, never positioned centre stage, and takes on a service role rather than actively participating in family life. As a black woman, she has some authority as regards what is good to eat and drink. Although she is not the 'mammy' stereotype of the US context, she does take on a knowledgeable role about food, which may well have its roots in such American representations.[107]

The characters of Honeybunch and Little Coco offered non-threatening images of blackness, reassuring in the postwar context of the collapse of empire and immigration. Nevertheless, I have found no references to Coco after his first series of films in the late 1940s. Only Honeybunch seems to have been acceptable in the context of the 1950s and even she does not survive the decade. In view of violent colonial uprisings, increasing racial tensions in Britain and the development of legislation against public expressions of racism in the 1960s, as well as the influence of the Civil Rights movement, Rowntree may have decided these characters were no longer so appealing.[108] However, as already discussed, issues over copyright payments for the use of Little Coco beyond the films themselves may also have played a part in thwarting plans for an extensive merchandising campaign featuring the character.

The civilising mission

Despite the racism inherent in the representations of Coco and Honeybunch, these characters were essentially cast in the role of civilising imperialists themselves. With the empire collapsing, it was 'civilised' black people who would be left to run the former colonies and to continue the civilising mission. Both characters appear in situations where they use cocoa, the product of African labour, to tame wild animals or to show uncivilised humans how to consume correctly – by consuming Rowntree's of course. Cocoa and chocolate are thus shown to be civilising forces (presumably of Honeybunch and Coco too, though Coco is given almost 'savage' strength).

Other campaigns drew on this civilising motif. A television animation from 1957 featured a group of cannibals, with bodies resembling cocoa beans, dancing around a cauldron.[109] A worried-looking white explorer (dressed in safari clothing, with a large white moustache) stands by the pot, flanked by two 'dusky guards'. He clearly fears he is about to be eaten. The advert begins with a witch doctor character, wearing a chef's hat, dancing around the steaming pot whilst waving a large bone. This is accompanied by a 'Background of beating drums' and a 'Chant sung by various natives'. The chief, sitting on a throne next to the cauldron, begins, 'What is it soothes the savage beast?' His words are accompanied by him 'smacking his lips' and 'rolling his eyes'. Preying on the racist fears of white audiences, these words and actions suggest that the explorer is about to be cooked. Then, by magic, the pot turns into a cup of Rowntree's Cocoa. The white explorer looks relieved and joins in the chanting: 'What is it all housewives request? ... Rowntree's, Rowntree's, Rowntree's, ... Cocoa.' White housewives are still the dominant consumers within this advert, despite their exclusion from the jungle setting. It is domesticity which prevails, neutralising the threat of savagery.

Cannibal jokes, according to Pieterse, were a clichéd staple of western humour in the twentieth century. However, he suggests a slight change in emphasis between the nineteenth and the twentieth century, with 'the ironization of the cannibalism motif' through the figure of the 'cannibal gourmand'. He sees this figure as the 'icon of the colonized savage and of a pacified Africa ... [A] cannibal with refined manners, with the attributes (chef's hat, implements) and attitudes of European cuisine'.[110] The witch doctor of the Rowntree advert conforms to this trope, complete with chef's hat. However, the advert goes further than Pieterse suggests by dispensing with cannibalism altogether. By essentially converting the cannibals, the power of Rowntree's Cocoa as a civilising force, and indeed as a food not just a drink, is stressed.

Considered with specific relation to Rowntree and cocoa production, this advert has the effect of erasing the labour of African farmers and of rendering women entirely invisible. Ironically, although these cartoon characters literally *are* cocoa beans, the processed cocoa they consume is owned by Rowntree. Africans are depicted first and foremost as savages and cannibals. Even when they turn away from cannibalism, they remain contained within the stereotype of 'the native' through their clothes and actions. Cups of cocoa appear by the magic of the witch doctor rather than as a result of the labour of farmers and factory workers. As detailed in the section on gender above, 'magical' consumption helps to obscure actual inequalities of labour. Here it also obscures inequalities of consumption and production faced by those in British colonies and former colonies. The product and the relations of production and consumption are exoticised, even as the civilising powers of cocoa are revealed. The histories of African cocoa farming, the cocoa trade, and the exploitations of British colonialism are forgotten.

By the latter half of the twentieth century, imperial conquest is treated almost as a joke. It is the white explorer who is made to look a fool, but only because of the success of Rowntree in penetrating even the depths of the African jungle.[111] Whilst there is an initial suggestion of resistance to white exploration, this is overturned by the friendly sharing of cocoa. The advert works because of collective white perceptions about savagery and cannibalism, even as these are comically undermined (though not entirely discredited). Mirroring but distorting the economic reality of colonial and postcolonial relations between Britain and Africa, British manufacturers magically send raw materials back to producers in the final irony of the cocoa chain.[112]

'The biggest little meal in Britain': consuming place and patriotism

So far, the majority of the advertising discussed has been designed to appeal to consumers within a broad framework of personal and familial satisfaction: people eating or drinking chocolate experience positive benefits of both nutrition and pleasure. This has implicit advantages for society as a whole. However, Rowntree and Cadbury also configured consumption explicitly as for the good of the nation, particularly in wartime. In chapter four I discuss in some detail the rhetoric of local, national and imperial pride pursued in packaging and advertising. This section will look more generally at how chocolate adverts drew on ideas about 'place' to exploit nationalistic feeling.[113]

Producing and consuming Britishness

With ingredients for chocolate products necessarily sourced at a global level, it is significant that so much advertising emphasised national, even local, narratives of production and consumption. Cadbury did, at times, strategically employ images of cocoa farming in the West Indies and Africa to market their products. However, this was achieved within a British imperial frame of reference. Thus, cocoa beans were explicitly 'Empire beans' from British farms in the colonies.[114] In 1932, an advert considered how Cadbury had been able to reduce prices once again thanks to 'Ever-growing public demand'. Consumers had been attracted by the high-quality ingredients: 'The milk . . . is full-cream *British* milk. The cocoa beans – again a 100 per cent. British product – are of the highest grade.'[115] The Cadbury slogan '100% British' reinforced a coherent narrative of *British* chocolate which successfully blended African beans with English milk, at a very reasonable cost to consumers. Prior to the Second World War, it was Cadbury who adopted the strongest appeals to nationalistic consumption through narratives of 'local' production of ingredients. The addition of one and a half glasses of *English* milk to every bar of CDM harnessed the goodness of the British countryside, whilst Cadbury and their consumers were directly supporting the nation's agriculture: 'The whole of the milk used . . . comes from the rich pastures of Shropshire and Gloucestershire, and every purchase . . . is a direct aid to British agriculture.'[116] Cadbury's patriotic relationship with their suppliers, and their consumers, became a key selling point.

The emphasis on chocolate and cocoa as being manufactured *within* the British Isles was strong in both Rowntree and Cadbury advertising. Rowntree used the name of York, the location of their factory, as a marketing tool in a number of ways. Whether or not this was successful is hard to assess but there is certainly evidence from market research that Rowntree had the edge over Cadbury in the north of England.[117] For Cadbury, however, the actual site of their factory was linked much more explicitly to pleasurable and healthy consumption practices. It was rural Bournville, rather than industrial Birmingham, which was consistently emphasised as the site of manufacture and the ultimate source of the goodness of Cadbury products.

To make 'chocolates as good as Cadbury's' it was necessary to 'leave the smoke and the grime of the city behind and secure a tract of pleasant, English countryside'.[118] It was at this 'factory in a garden' (as the slogan ran), that local and global ingredients were transformed by skilled workers in scrupulously clean surroundings into nutritious chocolate. For Rowntree, the company name and the location of the factory itself never took on the same resonance in marketing campaigns. Advertising agents at JWT created specific meanings in relation to the individual brands. In effect, as I demonstrate below, this allowed for, indeed almost demanded, a greater diversity of approaches to the patriotic message.

'Beat the Boche': wartime nationalism

As we have seen, mothers and children featured heavily in advertising, particularly for cocoa. Rowntree and Cadbury claimed to provide important nutrients, thereby urging mothers to buy their brand of cocoa through a discourse of 'rational' science and an appeal to maternal love. For most of the twentieth century, such adverts targeted individual families rather than appealing to a concern with national well-being. However, claims reached a new pitch in the war years. A series of Rowntree films featured 'Blitz Babies' fed on Rowntree's Cocoa. Born during the Blitz, these children survived the war and became healthy young white Britons, 'sturdy specimens of our island race'. Buying Rowntree's was thus conceived as a duty for patriotically minded mothers.[119] Such advertising was inward looking, rather than drawing on images of an imperial family as had been encouraged by the Empire Marketing Board in the interwar period.[120] Other companies adopted similar wartime tactics, adapting to and even exploiting government policy on food shortages and rationing. Cadbury, for example, marketed Dairy Milk as a source of the goodness of milk for children, though the nationalistic rhetoric was less explicit: 'So if you see it on sale, please leave it for the children – or, if you buy any, see that the children have it.' They were later forced to stop manufacture of CDM as milk was in ever-shorter supply.[121]

For the nation's adult workforce in wartime, cocoa could provide nutrition, sustenance and strength. Both Cadbury and Rowntree emphasised the food value of their product. A simple advert for Cadbury, for example, printed the word 'FOOD', with the two 'O's formed by the rims of a cup of cocoa and the top of a cocoa tin. Another Cadbury image was of a women worker in wartime service sleeping peacefully. The slogan ran: 'For Sleep and Energy Cadbury's Bournvita.'[122] In Rowntree campaigns, women workers, who had been something of a novelty in cocoa adverts prior to the war, became potent nationalistic symbols of mythic proportions. An advert from 1941, featuring female demolition workers drinking mugs of cocoa, bore the headline, 'And That's What Amazons Are Made Of.' Instead of 'sugar and spice and all things nice', these strong women are made of '10 stone of cheerfulness, grit and hard work', the 'ingredients for a British demolition worker, 1941 model'. The photograph depicts a group of women, dressed in trousers and heavy boots, with their sleeves rolled up ready for a good day's hard work. As British women they are 'naturally' strong mentally – 'cheerfulness and grit are qualities they are born with' – but their physical strength comes from cocoa.[123] Rowntree's enhances the health of the nation's women and makes a real contribution to the war through them.

Figure 4 Amazonian wartime femininity in cocoa advertising, 1941.

The most explicitly patriotic adverts during the Second World War were those for the product bearing the name of York itself. Consumption of Plain York could bolster national as well as local pride. As with cocoa, Rowntree added vitamins to their chocolate in an apparently patriotic move to aid the war effort: 'In this war, the side that wins/ Must be full of Vitamins./ This profoundly serious fact/ Made the firm of Rowntree's act.'[124] The claims were excessive, but grounded in apparent endorsements by mothers themselves: 'And, delighted mothers say,/ Plain York now checks tooth decay.' Dyer notes how manufacturers of bed-time drinks cashed in on wartime nerves on the home front to sell their products.[125] Plain York similarly capitalised on such wartime complaints as 'night blindness' during the blackouts. The rhymes in each advert relate the health of the nation specifically to victory and to the maintenance of national superiority, with its imperial overtones: 'Britain in this conflagration/ Must remain an A1 nation.' Consumption is presented as the moral obligation of every good Briton, rather than as a personal choice: 'Citizens, your bounden duty/ Is to guard your health and beauty'. Despite the pacifist heritage of the Quaker firms, Rowntree adverts were explicit in their populist, jingoistic language: 'We can help to beat the Boche.'[126]

A national habit

Following the Second World War, the coronation of Elizabeth II provided an opportunity for renewed pride in the nation and the British Commonwealth. The success of the Everest expedition, announced to coincide with the coronation, was a triumph of the British conquering spirit at a time when colonial 'conquests' were slipping away.[127] Firms and their advertising agents were quick to capitalise on any associations between their products and the expedition. In a campaign running during the early months of 1954, consumers were instructed to 'make sure it's Rowntree's . . . the Everest expedition did!'[128] Cocoa becomes the driving force behind the conquest, an 'agent of history', as McClintock describes, writing 'the inevitable legend of commercial progress across the colonial landscape'. This was not a new motif. McClintock illustrates how commodities featured as actors in all kinds of imperial adventures from the nineteenth century.[129] In the postwar context of the declining British empire, however, far-off, treacherous corners of the globe became the new field of imperialist conquest. Rowntree's Cocoa was positioned as central to this quest for supremacy in exploration.

In the late 1940s, Rowntree decided to market one particular product, Kit Kat, as a 'national habit'.[130] Kit Kat would unite Britain by appealing to young and old, rich and poor, men and women, all of whom would incorporate the bar into their daily routines. Interestingly, advertising of the 1930s had focused on London as the centre for consumption, claiming Kit Kat to be, 'the biggest little meal in London'. As the nation's capital and the heart of the British empire, London was the standard to be measured against. Even when depicting the 'discovery' of Kit Kat by women in Scotland, this caption was maintained: 'Aberdeen Typists Discover The Biggest Little Meal In London.' Kit Kat consumption was portrayed in December 1937 as a thoroughly 'modern', '1938 idea' with its roots in the fashionable capital. The ad, appearing in the *Radio Times*, featured upper-class women being brought Kit Kat by a maid. A delicate tea service is on the table. The caption reads, 'Modern housewives serve Kit Kat Chocolate Crisps for Tea.'[131] Consumers are invited to aspire both to higher social status and to ideals of 'modernity'.

In the context of the Second World War, the product was no longer just a snack but became 'the biggest little meal in Britain'.[132] In contrast to the leisurely, feminised setting of the 1937 image, wartime campaigns emphasised that the bar could be carried around at work. An advert from January 1941, for example, portrayed a busy female nurse with the accompanying line, 'Active people carry with them a block of concentrated staying-power – Chocolate Crisp.' Defined as a nutritional food, and given the status of a 'meal' rather than simply a luxury, Kit Kat would build up the nation's strength and would maintain productivity in the context of postwar reconstruction.[133] A 1948 advert proclaimed, 'this particular type of chocolate block produces a *slower* absorption of sugar – which gives you longer staying power – so that's why we call Kit Kat the biggest little meal in Britain.'[134] Consumption was once again framed as patriotism.

In marketing Kit Kat, Rowntree made calculated associations with another well-established product of empire: tea. 'Have a Cuppa ... Have a Kit Kat' became the new slogan of 1962, although the connections between tea breaks and Kit Kat consumption had their origins in the 1930s.[135] The association was intended to locate Kit Kat within an existing 'national habit', a habit which had been formed on the back of British imperialism (though this was never acknowledged in the adverts).[136] Like cocoa, tea has been largely divorced from its origins in imperial trading and exploitation in order to function as an expression of national identity. However, in advertising for tea itself, exotic images of tea plantation workers have been adopted by some British firms. The Kit Kat adverts constructed tea drinking solely within the bounds of the British Isles.[137]

Relying on western notions of industrial time, tea breaks are understood in Kit Kat advertising as sanctioned, controlled lapses in productive activity (whether work or rational leisure). 'Ordinary' people are shown taking a break from their gendered roles, whether the ironing or shop work for women, or building work for men. These events take place within a localised framework of the workplace or the British countryside. Rowntree announced the campaign to those in the confectionery trade as combining 'the biggest-selling chocolate biscuit line with Britain's most famous national habit'.[138] Even as the emphasis on tea faded, Kit Kat continued to be sold as the perfect accompaniment to everyday working routines: 'Have a Break, Have a Kit Kat.'

'The ends of the earth': representing the global

Whilst certain imperial commodities, like cocoa and tea, became divorced from their 'exotic' origins in Rowntree advertising, other products were made to retain a certain mystique. Assortments became repositories for a collection of foreign, exotic ingredients. The use of 'oriental sweetmeats' in selections such as Dairy Box became the specific focus of some advertising. For instance, the Judy character declares:

> If I could go to Turkey, now,
> I'd rush and ask them 'xactly how
> The Turks, and DAIRY BOX, combine
> Ripe raspberries, honey, sugar fine,
> To make a sweet so good to bite!
> It isn't just the *Turk's* Delight![139]

Turkish Delight is an exotic product, sensuously consumed by Judy. She cannot go to Turkey but the Rowntree firm becomes the imperial explorer, sourcing ingredients from the 'ends of the earth' for the privileged white British consumer.[140] Cadbury also used the exotic to market certain assortment brands, suggesting their suitability as a 'special' gift for a friend. In the 1930s, Cadbury's Golden East Chocolates were elaborately packaged to give them an air of opulence associated with the 'East': 'Lacquer red, green and gold lend a touch of the Colourful East to the rich casket.'[141] Cocoa powder was never presented in this way.

Assortments, then, through both their ingredients and their packaging, could offer consumers exotic fantasies of far-off lands. With expanding possibilities for worldwide travel from the 1960s, Rowntree tried to tempt consumers with images of tropical sandy beaches. In a competition connected to Dairy Box, winners would have the chance to pick their own Dairy Box orchid while on their free holiday in the Bahamas.[142] For Black Magic, too, adverts of the 1960s and 1970s increasingly came to depict characters in foreign locations, or hinted at exciting possibilities for travel. An advert from 1974 displayed tickets to Lyon-Perrache sent with the box of chocolates.[143] The fantasy of heterosexual romance became intertwined with aspirations of exotic travel.[144]

As discussed in the previous section on race, Rowntree products could be represented as being consumed by racial 'others'. In an Aero campaign from the late 1930s, people from 'foreign' lands were shown to be ignorant of the joys of Aero chocolate. For instance, when faced with an advert for Aero on the side of the Pyramids, the people on the camels passing by ask, 'What ees dat?'[145] This use of language reassures white English-speaking consumers that everyone in the world speaks English (therefore English people do not need to bother learning other languages) and that they speak it poorly (implying a lack of education, or natural stupidity). As in the Honeybunch adverts, chocolate travels around the world on a globalising, essentially imperialist mission. Loeb offers a more positive reading of representations of 'foreign' consumers in the Victorian advertisement as 'redefin[ing] community for a mass society. Through the fantasy of consumption it offers to unite those unknown to each other even from the most distant land.'[146] Aero adverts from the twentieth century do have elements in common with Loeb's Victorian examples: the use of images of Earth for instance. In May 1938, the Aero slogan 'Eat More Milk' was pictured on the side of planet Earth, with people viewing the sign from the Moon asking, 'What on earth does that mean?' Loeb, however, tends to downplay the power dynamics of imagined global communities.[147]

Conclusion

Rowntree and Cadbury advertising employed a variety of strategies in striving to find brand identities for the different forms of chocolate each firm was producing. Rowntree's Cocoa, for example, was encoded with very different meanings from assortments such as Black Magic. Although necessarily distinct, each advertising campaign drew on gendered, classed and raced discourses which reflected and reinforced dominant contemporary ideologies. In relation to cocoa, this involved positioning white women as mothers and housewives, the guardians of the family's health and welfare. That cocoa itself was a product of women's labours *outside* the home, and of colonial exploitation, was conveniently written out of this domestic picture of 'respectable' white women. The consumption of assortments, meanwhile, was a white woman's ticket to the ideal relations of heterosexuality and the institution of marriage. In contrast to the rational feminine purchasers of Rowntree's Cocoa, these women were irrationally overwhelmed and rendered slaves to the chocolates. By a process of association they would be seduced by the male giver, who was placed in a position of power through the dynamics of the gift relationship.

Whilst chocolate advertising by Rowntree was certainly conservative in its portrayal of gender roles, female characters did occupy a powerful space within the frame of the ad. Women could be increasingly independent and outspoken, although this was usually contained within heterosexual relations which relegated them to the role of submissive partner in the face of romantic gestures. From the 1950s, consumption was increasingly being framed as an individual, even narcissistic pleasure to which women are, apparently, particularly prone. Whilst there may be power in claiming the identity of a chocolate addict (or 'chocoholic') to the rejection of social norms, such adverts circumscribe the actual social, political and sexual liberation of women.

Understandings of gendered consumption patterns were disturbed during wartime. Women in adverts, as in everyday life, were increasingly visible working outside the home, whilst luxurious romantic gifts were acknowledged to be practically impossible due to shortages of raw materials.[148] Chocolate could now be shown being consumed as food in the workplace by women and men working towards national goals. This kind of patriotic consumption, like the imagined harmonious gender relations which accompanied it, was only 'for the duration'. Yet chocolate conceived as a 'British' product drew on, and created, national identity even in peacetime. Such consumption was seen to unite white British citizens across the nation.

Overall, both Rowntree and Cadbury adverts created a world of white consumers in which the black producers of cocoa beans and the black consumers of chocolate were at best pushed to the margins, if not excluded completely. Nevertheless, cartoon stereotypes of black children and uncivilised 'natives' were occasionally deployed in the creation of brand identities for Rowntree. This was not in recognition of African labour or a reflection of the increasing presence of black people within the metropole; such figures worked within contemporary white western cultural understandings of 'blackness', part of cultural traditions such as minstrelsy which were still popular in Britain at the time. The infant characters of Honeybunch and Little Coco were thus intended as amusing novelties contained within cartoon worlds. Racism and prejudice also infused images of ignorant foreign consumers in Aero advertising and representations of 'exotic' ingredients.

Textual analysis of chocolate advertising has, then, been useful in illuminating contemporary understandings of gender, race and the nation. The institutions of the British confectionery firms and their advertising agents perpetuated their own vision of the world – with which they hoped consumers would identify – within the campaigns they developed. Whilst the need to differentiate between brands allowed for inconsistencies and ambiguities in the vision of society put forward, it was a world in which the actual processes of production were to be erased. The cultural construction of chocolate in marketing has thus relied on and produced hegemonic narratives of gender, class, race and empire. This discursive trend is echoed in chapter two, though the empirical focus shifts from commercial marketing campaigns to broader popular and company histories of chocolate – the 'romance of the cocoa bean'. What I demonstrate in this and subsequent chapters is that such romantic narratives, like advertising tropes, depended on the unequal political and economic structures of empire, as well as on the daily labours of working women and men in Nigeria and York.

Notes

1 Fitzgerald, *Rowntree*, 6.
2 Allison James discusses how a box of chocolates may be an appropriate gift – 'a highly decorated and festive symbol' – but also how as a 'traditional gift' it can 'depersonalise' the gift relationship. James, 'The good, the bad and the delicious: the role of confectionery in British society', *Sociological Review*, 38: 4 (1990), 678. For more on the gift relationship, see Marcel Mauss, *The Gift: The Form and Reason for Exchange in Archaic Societies*, trans. W. D. Halls (London: Routledge Classics, 2002), 4.
3 Judith Williamson, *Decoding Advertisements: Ideology and Meaning in Advertising* (London: Marion Boyars, 1978), 42.
4 Diane Barthel, *Putting on Appearances: Gender and Advertising* (Philadelphia: Temple University Press, 1988), 1–3.
5 Cultural consumption is not necessarily a straightforward 'decoding' of the meanings intended by the author of a text. Hall's concept of 'negotiated' meanings remains extremely useful in theorising the ways in which dominant ideologies may be accepted, subverted and modified, within limits, by their intended audiences. Stuart Hall, 'Encoding/decoding', in Stuart Hall *et al.* (eds), *Culture, Media, Language: Working Papers in Cultural Studies, 1972–1979* (London: Routledge, 1992), 128–38.
6 Marieke De Mooij has highlighted the different possible interpretations of the 'Have a break' Kit Kat campaign according to culturally specific understandings of time and leisure. Marieke de Mooij, *Global Marketing and Advertising: Understanding Cultural Paradoxes* (London: Sage Publications, 1998).
7 On the gendering of consumption in early histories of chocolate, see chapter two.
8 Masculinity has also been used strategically in the marketing of confectionery. In the 1920s, for example, Rowntree's Pastilles were specifically constructed as 'The Sweets That Men Like' and were cleverly associated with other masculine accessories: 'Thousands of men now carry a little packet of Rowntree's Pastilles just as they carry their tobacco pouch or cigarette case.' The male consumer was appealed to as being particularly discerning: 'Men who eat sweets *must have the best*: they may not eat many but they do like them good.' Borthwick Institute of Historical Research, York (BI), Rowntree Company Archive, A1, 'Rowntree's Associated Papers Advertising 1927'. More recently, in a campaign launched in 2002,

the Rowntree Yorkie bar has been explicitly labelled as 'not for girls', being only appropriate for consumption by sufficiently masculine men.

9 History of Advertising Trust, Norwich (HAT), J. Walter Thompson Archive (JWT), Box 294, A710, copy of brief sent to Peter Rowntree, 29 January 1951.

10 BI, Rowntree Company Archive, N29, 'Cocoa (Women's Magazine Campaign) December 27th 1935–April 4th 1936'.

11 HAT, JWT, Box 294, A710, memorandum, 'Proposed Campaign for Rowntree's Cocoa', 28 August 1946.

12 BI, Rowntree Company Archive, N44, 'Cocoa 1946–50'.

13 Though her focus is on the nineteenth century, McClintock's use of a magical metaphor for women's work is relevant here. Anne McClintock, *Imperial Leather: Race, Gender and Sexuality in the Colonial Contest* (London: Routledge, 1995), 162.

14 BI, Rowntree Company Archive, N44, 'Cocoa 1946–50'. Raymond Williams describes advertising as a 'system of magical inducements'. But magic can operate within individual adverts, as this example demonstrates. Even more explicitly, adverts for Black Magic evoke magical associations. Williamson suggests that the Black Magic box 'has a mystical aura quite out of proportion to its actual contents'. See Raymond Williams, 'Advertising: the magic system', in Simon During (ed.), *The Cultural Studies Reader* (London: Routledge, 1993), 335; Williamson, *Decoding Advertisements*, 150.

15 BI, Rowntree Company Archive, N44, 'Cocoa 1946–50'. These quotes are taken from literature explaining the usefulness of the film to salesmen and retailers.

16 BI, Rowntree Company Archive, N45, 'Cocoa 1952–59'. This advert was featured in the *News of the World*, 16 March 1952.

17 BI, Rowntree Company Archive, N45, 'Cocoa 1952–59'. TVs would still have been rare in most lower-middle-class and certainly in working-class households at this time. The TV party both reflects a cultural moment before the widespread ownership of televisions and taps into a fashionable new phenomenon. The attendance at the party suggests an aspirational dimension to the ad.

18 HAT, JWT, Box 298, A40, memo, 21 June 1949.

19 BI, Rowntree Company Archive, N45, 'Cocoa 1952–59'.

20 Iceland supermarkets consistently adopt this strategy, with slogans such as 'because mums are heroes' (2003–4).

21 On modernism in chocolate box design, see Diane Barthel, 'Modernism and marketing: the chocolate box revisited', *Theory, Culture and Society*, 6 (1989), 435–6.

22 See chapter five for women's memories of eating chocolates whilst working on the shopfloor.

23 Men did feature as workplace consumers of Bournville Cocoa. A 1937 advert, for example, depicted a group of railwaymen. They expressed their appreciation for the product through the masculine language of the railways: 'This Bournville Cocoa's grand stuff for stoking up on.' Such gendered images of workers consuming chocolate as a 'food-drink' became commonplace for Rowntree during the Second World War. Cadbury UK, 520/003579, 'Cadbury: Loose Cocoa and Chocolate Adverts, 1886–1977'.

24 BI, Rowntree Company Archive, T8, 'Kit Kat, Black Magic and Plain York, 1936–38'; Cadbury UK, 196/520/003377, 'Cadbury's Dairy Milk Advertising, 1928–'. Later market research confirmed that consumption of Rowntree Kit Kat was indeed more popular with office workers than with housewives. BI, Rowntree Company Archive, R/DD/MT/OMR/11a, 'Investigation into the Market for Chocolate Crisp', February–March 1939.

25 Cadbury UK, 196/520/003377, 'Cadbury's Dairy Milk Advertising, 1928–'.

26 BI, Rowntree Company Archive, N41, 'Cocoa 1941–42'.

27 Research concluded that where cocoa consumption had risen to more than 20–25 per cent of the level of a 'Basic Year', this was due to specific wartime factors such as Fire Guard duties. Other increases were related to factors which continued after the war, such as food shortages. HAT, JWT, Box 293, 'An Estimate of the Civilian

Demand for Cocoa in General, During and After the 1939–1945 War', December 1946.

28 On the concept of 'stretching' gender roles, see Philomena Goodman, *Women, Sexuality and War* (Basingstoke: Palgrave, 2002), 158.

29 Deirdre Beddoe, *Back to Home and Duty: Women Between the Wars, 1918–1939* (London: Pandora, 1989), 12–13.

30 BI, Rowntree Company Archive, N44, 'Cocoa 1946–50'.

31 See also chapter five.

32 BI, Rowntree Company Archive, N2, 'Cocoa Advertising January–April 1910'. Flavour became less important in later years as an advertising tool (probably as the methods of each company grew closer), although manufacturing processes continued to be featured as creating a particularly high quality, user-friendly cocoa powder.

33 As Bourdieu describes, 'Social subjects . . . distinguish themselves by the distinctions they make.' According to Williamson, advertising uses such social distinctions 'to create distinctions between products' at the same time as *'things* are used to differentiate groups of people'. Pierre Bourdieu, *Distinction: A Social Critique of the Judgement of Taste*, trans. Richard Nice (London: Routledge, 1984), 6; Williamson, *Decoding Advertisements*, 27.

34 Cadbury UK, 196/520/003552, 'Cadbury's Special Ads: From, May 1930 to, December 1932'.

35 BI, Rowntree Company Archive, B22, 'Black Magic. September–December 1937 and Onwards – 1953'.

36 Cadbury UK, 520/003379, adverts published in *Punch*, c.1963.

37 BI, Rowntree Company Archive, B23, 'Dairy Box. September–December 1937'.

38 *Ibid.*

39 Catherine Hall suggests that milk from the English countryside added the 'vital white ingredient' to the colonial raw material of cocoa. This made Cadbury's Dairy Milk an essentially 'English' product. Hall, 'Turning a blind eye', 39. See also later in this chapter. I discuss the raced dynamics of chocolate production in more detail in chapter five.

40 Cadbury UK, 520/003579, 'Cadbury: Loose Cocoa and Chocolate Adverts, 1886–1977', advert from *Daily Express*, April 1938.

41 See for example, BI, Rowntree Company Archive, R/DD/MT/OMR/33, A. H. L. Johnson, 'Consumer Testing Department. A Note on Some Aspects of the Assorted Chocolate Market. London, April 1940'.

42 In the late twentieth century women tended to disappear from the frame of the advert, leaving only the letter. Judith Williamson observes how this technique allowed an 'elision between you as absent looker and the absent subject'. When women reappeared in the adverts, the letters had vanished, effectively silencing the female characters. Williamson, *Decoding Advertisements*, 79, 138–40, 150.

43 BI, Rowntree Company Archive, AB4, 'Specimens of Advertising in Great Britain 1959'.

44 Janice A. Radway, *Reading the Romance: Women, Patriarchy, and Popular Literature* (London: Verso, 1987).

45 BI, Rowntree Company Archive, AB2, 'Specimens of Advertising in Great Britain 1956–57'.

46 BI, Rowntree Company Archive, B23, 'Dairy Box. September–December 1937'.

47 BI, Rowntree Company Archive, O12, 'Wartime Adverts 1944–45'.

48 Goodman believes that wartime versions of femininity and masculinity 'created a heightened sense of heterosexuality'. Goodman, *Women, Sexuality and War*, 13, 16.

49 Chocolates are made to signify, even stand in for, real emotion. Williamson uses the example of a diamond 'which has come to "mean" love . . . Once the connection has been made, we begin to translate the other way and in fact to skip translating altogether: taking the sign for what it signifies, the thing for the feeling.' Williamson, *Decoding Advertisements*, 12.

50 BI, Rowntree Company Archive, AB1, 'Specimens of Advertising in Great Britain 1948–1956'.

51 Cadbury UK, 196/520/003552, 'Cadbury's Special Ads: From, May 1930 to, December 1932'.
52 *BWM*, April 1969, 50–1.
53 See also Nickie Charles and Marion Kerr, *Women, Food and Families* (Manchester: Manchester University Press, 1988), 67.
54 BI, Rowntree Company Archive, AB1, 'Specimens of Advertising in Great Britain 1948–56'.
55 See also Janice Winship on the ways in which adverts tend to '[gloss] over the capitalist moment of exchange'. Winship, 'Sexuality for sale', in Hall *et al.* (eds), *Culture, Media, Language,* 217.
56 BI, Rowntree Company Archive, AB1, 'Specimens of Advertising in Great Britain 1948–56'. There are no exact dates given for the 'Judy' adverts.
57 BI, Rowntree Company Archive, AB3, 'Specimens of Advertising in Great Britain 1957–58'.
58 Stephanie O'Donohoe, 'Leaky boundaries: intertextuality and young adult experiences of advertising', in Mica Nava *et al.* (eds), *Buy This Book: Studies in Advertising and Consumption* (London: Routledge, 1997), 264.
59 HAT, JWT, BOX 294, A710, memo from W. Tisbury, 'Self-Interest Appeal', 28 January 1938.
60 BI, Rowntree Company Archive, S.10, 'Press Advertising AERO 1938, 39 and 40'. Advertisers, and indeed scientists, still occasionally remind us of chocolate's beneficial chemical properties. Despite the continuity of a medicinal discourse, advertising in the late twentieth century was more likely to emphasise narcissistic pleasures.
61 BI, Rowntree Company Archive, S.10, 'Press Advertising AERO 1938, 39 and 40'. Myers has studied the semantics of the Aero campaign. However, he does not unpack the potential sexual reading of 'makes you go O!' Greg Myers, *Words in Ads* (London: Edward Arnold, 1994).
62 It is this familial mode of consumption which was more in tune with the oral histories of the women interviewed for this project, though it is impossible to say how far this is related to individual preference, their status as workers or generational factors.
63 The guilt of consuming chocolate has become related to the guilt of putting on weight, especially for women. Chocolate has been labelled a 'bad' food by health experts who cite its high fat and sugar content, although this is shifting again as chocolate with a high cocoa content is seen to be beneficial to health. As James argues, in the discourse of food 'morality', 'bad' food often becomes more pleasurable. James, 'The good, the bad and the delicious', 680.
64 Jan Pieterse observes how ageism and racism may go hand in hand. Jan Nederveen Pieterse, *White on Black: Images of Africa and Blacks in Western Popular Culture* (New Haven: Yale University Press, 1992), 171. Similarly, Marilyn Kern-Foxworth notes that 'advertisers have always felt more comfortable using black children in advertising than black adults'. Kern-Foxworth, *Aunt Jemima, Uncle Ben, and Rastus: Blacks in Advertising, Yesterday, Today, and Tomorrow* (Westport: Greenwood Press, 1994), xx. The addition of the diminutive 'Little' to Coco's name is part of this tradition.
65 Pieterse discusses facial features such as large eyes in terms of rendering black people as 'lap dogs'. Pieterse, *White on Black,* 193.
66 Pieterse cites the golliwog as 'England's most popular black type'. *Ibid.,* 156. As late as 1999, Robertson's were still getting more than 340,000 requests for their Golly badges. See David Pilgrim, 'The golliwog caricature', *Museum of Racist Memorabilia* (November 2000), www.ferris.edu/news/jimcrow/golliwog (accessed 19 June 2004). The figure was eventually removed from jars in 2001.
67 Kern-Foxworth, *Aunt Jemima,* 41.
68 McClintock employs the term 'commodity racism' to describe the ways in which the advertising of commodities appealed to 'imperial jingoism' in the nineteenth century. She sees it as distinct from scientific racism in its capacity to reach beyond

the educated few to the mass market. McClintock, *Imperial Leather*, 207–31. Adverts continued to draw upon racist ideas and imperial discourse well into the twentieth century, making the concept appropriate for my own research.

69 Pierterse, *White on Black*, 193.

70 Terrio, *Crafting the Culture*, 248–9.

71 Anandi Ramamurthy, *Imperial Persuaders: Images of Africa and Asia in British Advertising* (Manchester: Manchester University Press, 2003), 63, 68–70, 89–91. Ramamurthy does not include any Rowntree advertisements in her study, which may be related to the late, and cautious, entry of the firm into advertising. However, she presents convincing examples of advertising by both Cadbury and Fry.

72 *Ibid.*, 91. Ramamurthy does not highlight the irony of her metaphor of 'sugary' sweetness in relation to white children. Sugar was added to cocoa thanks to slave labour on the plantations of the British Empire. Like milk, it was believed to make the bitter cocoa more palatable.

73 This character is very similar to the stereotyped child 'sambo' producers Ramamurthy identifies in Cadbury and Fry advertising from the early twentieth century. Ramamurthy, *Imperial Persuaders*, 73–4.

74 BI, Rowntree Company Archive, N10, 'Rowntree Cocoa Nibs Names Competition, Autumn 1923'. Cocoa nibs are crushed cocoa beans. Rowntree Advertising Inspectors and Travellers also came to be affectionately referred to as 'Cocoa Nibs' (*CWM*, August 1920, 94). This 'other' Nib was therefore not only a part of the cocoa bean and connected visually and linguistically to the white Nibs, but he was also a Rowntree employee. Thanks to Alex Hutchinson for bringing my attention to this character.

75 Whiteness has an important regional association here. Since the fifteenth-century Wars of the Roses, the White Rose as symbol of York and Yorkshire implicitly evokes the Red Rose of long-standing rival Lancashire. For a reprint of the image, see Fitzgerald, *Rowntree*. Plate 1. Although Fitzgerald dates the image from 1881, the original painting is dated ten years later. Thanks to Alex Hutchinson for this information.

76 For more on Mr York, see chapter four.

77 Although Ramamurthy does not deny the existence of such images, she affirms that images of 'the black boy and "peasant producer" recede[d]' after 1910, to be replaced by images of white children. She also notes that images of adult producers were rare after 1900, although she does find one advert from 1906, which depicts adult women workers on the Cadbury plantation in Trinidad. Interestingly this does not include a white overseer. Ramamurthy, *Imperial Persuaders*, 90–1, 77.

78 Cadbury UK, 196/520/003552, 'Cadbury's Special Ads: From May 1930 to December 1932'.

79 Ramamurthy, *Imperial Persuaders*, 215.

80 HAT, JWT, Box 294, A710, 'Study of the Long-Term Prospects for the Cocoa Powder Market', 28 August 1945, 6.

81 BI, Rowntree Company Archive, R/DD/MT/OMR/28f, 'Cocoa Advertisement Recognition Test Report. November 1948'.

82 Ramamurthy, *Imperial Persuaders*, 15.

83 HAT, JWT, Box 294, A710, 'Study of the Long-Term Prospects for the Cocoa Powder Market', 28 August 1945, 4, 6.

84 HAT, JWT, Box 297, A61, 'Summary of "Little Coco" Copyright Negotiations'; letter from G. J. Harris to J. D. Watson, re. ' "Coco" Copyright', 10 March 1947.

85 See Terrio, *Crafting the Culture*, 248. Also Ramamurthy, *Imperial Persuaders*, 64–5. 'Chocolate' has sometimes been used by black people themselves to differentiate based on skin tone.

86 Pieterse similarly notes that, 'In Germany a chocolate cake . . . is referred to as the "edible negro".' The racist histories behind the association of black people and chocolate in advertising raise questions about Williamson's analysis of colour in advertising as 'simply a *technique* . . . to make correlations between a product

and other things'. Pieterse, *White on Black*, 193; Williamson, *Decoding Advertisements*, 24.

87 BI, Rowntree Company Archive, N44, 'Cocoa 1946–50'.

88 Ramamurthy, *Imperial Persuaders*, 75.

89 Chocolate in its more processed form became increasingly divorced from its origins. However, this trend is currently being reversed, particularly in the marketing of 'organic' and 'fairtrade' products. Companies now make a selling point of the areas from where they source their cocoa beans. Ironically, such marketing campaigns often construct a more exclusive commodity, harking back to the earliest adverts for chocolate as a luxury, because exotic, product.

90 BI, Rowntree Company Archive, N44, 'Cocoa 1946–50'.

91 Pieterse states that, 'The first role blacks were permitted to perform in white society, after that of slave or servant, was that of entertainer.' Pieterse, *White on Black*, 136.

92 On the Sambo stereotype, see Kern-Foxworth, *Aunt Jemima*, 79–80.

93 As a Scout, Coco may be 'contained' within a western imperialist mission. Terrio puts forward this argument in relation to the French adverts for Banania, in which a black African character is depicted as 'a disciplined and contained member of the French military'. Terrio, *Crafting the Culture*, 250. For an analysis of the connections between empire and the Scout movement, see Allen Warren, 'Citizens of the empire: Baden-Powell, Scouts and Guides, and an imperial ideal, 1900–40', in John M. MacKenzie (ed.), *Imperialism and Popular Culture* (Manchester: Manchester University Press, 1986).

94 On stereotyped settings, see Kern-Foxworth, *Aunt Jemima*, 95. David Hand's involvement may well be the key to the American tone of the films in terms of both setting and language.

95 The extraordinary alter-egos of Popeye and Little Coco do not occupy a place in 'normal' society, but only appear when necessary. The 'ordinary' characters are themselves marginal figures. As a sailor, Popeye (created in 1929) exists at the margins of society, in the liminal spaces between land and sea. Coco, meanwhile, is positioned between western civilisation and the wilderness.

96 As Terrio comments in relation to postwar France, 'The presence of large numbers of Africans tended to blur the line between the metropolis and the colonies, the dominant and the dominated, creating profound anxiety.' This led to a shift in the image of the black soldier used to advertise Banania chocolate; the figure 'became progressively stylized, abstract, and incidental to the marketing of the product'. Terrio, *Crafting the Culture*, 250–1.

97 Kern-Foxworth, *Aunt Jemima*, 79–80.

98 Under the conditions of slavery, and indeed imperialism, black women could adopt survival strategies such as acquiescence, silence and secrecy which were then interpreted as 'natural' traits. See Deborah Gray White, *Ar'n't I A Woman? Female Slaves in the Plantation South* (New York: W. W. Norton & Company, 1987), 24. Kern-Foxworth relates this to representations of Aunt Jemima, the mammy character used to market a brand of pancake mix in the US from the late nineteenth century. Modern, non-commercial, artistic representations of the figure have imagined Aunt Jemima's anger being released more overtly. Kern-Foxworth, *Aunt Jemima*, 101–4. Terrio notes that images of black women tended to displace those of black men in lending an 'exotic' element to chocolate advertising in postwar France. Terrio, *Crafting the Culture*, 251.

99 BI, Rowntree Company Archive, N44, 'Cocoa 1946–50'. This advert is dated 1948. It should be compared with the 1957 TV advert featuring 'cannibals', as discussed in the following section.

100 Pieterse argues that, 'Africans and crocodiles together within a single frame appear to be the European counterpart to the morbid American myth that crocodiles are particularly fond of black flesh.' Although Honeybunch is not obviously in danger of being eaten at any time (the characters she confronts are all engrossed in eating something else), the adverts may have been understood in this framework

by consumers. Instead of eating the 'chocolate' girl, the animal and savage human characters in the adverts should consume real cocoa. Pieterse, *White on Black*, 44.

101 Kern-Foxworth, *Aunt Jemima*, 93.

102 See Ramamurthy for this image. She interprets this as the earliest example of a 'shift from the image of a black plantation worker to the image of a domesticated, yet "freely" subservient "sambo" producer and server of chocolate'. Ramamurthy, *Imperial Persuaders*, 68. Little Coco does not fit directly into the transition she describes. He is answering to an omniscient narrator but he consumes the cocoa independently.

103 Harriet Beecher Stowe's *Uncle Tom's Cabin* (1852) had been widely read in Victorian Britain, as well as performed on the stage. An article in the *CWM* of July 1902 suggests the continuing popularity of the story: '*Uncle Tom's Cabin* has made us all more . . . acquainted with the horrors of slavery.' *CWM*, July 1902, 54. There was a film adaptation of the novel in 1903. As discussed in chapter four, postwar consumers were familiar with the mechanisms of minstrelsy, which continued to employ such stereotypical figures.

104 Kern-Foxworth has identified the connections between African American speech and the speech patterns of the white American South, suggesting that the presence of slaves (particularly as nannies within the white household) would have had an impact on white children. Kern-Foxworth, *Aunt Jemima*, 95. The 'hospitality' of the American South, meanwhile – the genteel practices of a white elite – was built upon the labour of slaves.

105 Ramamurthy uses a much earlier advert which portrays a male African child (visibly linked to cocoa production in this case) offering 'Massa Fry' (depicted as a 'John Bull' character) the best cocoa pods. Ramamurthy, *Imperial Persuaders*, 84–5. Although divorced from even such a cursory acknowledgement of the conditions of production, Honeybunch is a more modern incarnation of a similar figure: the black child 'serving' the best cocoa to white consumers.

106 Ramamurthy discusses a Cadbury advert from the early twentieth century in which a black boy and white girl sit together on a rug. However, this apparently mutually beneficial relationship 'is based on the notion of difference'. She notes, for example, the black child's bare feet in contrast to the elaborate clothing of the girl. *Ibid.*, 72.

107 Whilst it is important to keep in mind the different political and cultural contexts of the US and Britain, certain stereotypes had resonance in both countries thanks to their close relationship.

108 Unfortunately I have found no references to management discussions concerning the demise of these characters.

109 BI, Rowntree Company Archive, W24, 'Rowntree Cocoa – Television'. See also BI, Rowntree Company Archive, TV1, 'Television Guard Book 1955–60'. The visual connection between the cannibals and cocoa beans echoes my earlier point about the conflation of African producers with their product.

110 Pieterse, *White on Black*, 114, 119.

111 On the treatment of imperial masculinity as a joke in the postwar period, see Wendy Webster, *Englishness and Empire, 1939–1965* (Oxford: Oxford University Press, 2005), 184, 186. On the connections between the end of empire and the 'satire boom' in Britain from the 1960s, see Stuart Ward, '"No nation could be broker": the satire boom and the demise of Britain's world role', in Stuart Ward (ed.), *British Culture and the End of Empire* (Manchester: Manchester University Press, 2001).

112 The Nigerian cocoa farmers interviewed for this project had been consumers of Cadbury's Bournvita chocolate and other western imports. However, such items were expensive.

113 Associations of consumption and nationalism have a long history. See Loeb on advertising during the Boer War. Lori Anne Loeb, *Consuming Angels: Advertising and Victorian Women* (Oxford: Oxford University Press, 1994), 152.

114 Cadbury UK, 196/520/003377, 'Cadbury's Dairy Milk Advertising, 1928–', advert from 1934.

115 Cadbury UK, 196/520/003377, 'Cadbury's Dairy Milk Advertising, 1928–'.
116 Cadbury UK, 196/520/003377, 'Cadbury's Dairy Milk Advertising, 1928–', advert from 1929. As will become clear throughout this book, distinctions between 'British' and 'English' are often blurred and can be difficult to disentangle. Although Rowntree and Cadbury operated as British firms and employed the language and imagery of 'Britishness' in representing themselves and their products, they could also evoke 'Englishness' in official narratives. The latter was frequently, though not always, associated with a more inward-looking, localised version of national identity (see chapter four). For similar strategic elisions between British/ English beyond the world of confectionery, see Emma Robertson, 'I get a real kick out of Big Ben: BBC versions of Britishness on the Empire and General Overseas Service, 1932–1948', Historical Journal of Film, Radio and Television, 28: 4 (October 2008): 459.
117 HAT, JWT, Box 293, 'Rowntree & Company Limited. Market for Cocoa, January 1938'. See also chapter four on the use of 'York' in advertising.
118 Cadbury UK, 196/520/003552, 'Cadbury's Special Ads: From May 1930 to December 1932', advert from 1930.
119 BI, Rowntree Company Archive, N44, 'Cocoa 1946–50', Number 3 in the Blitz Babies film series. On the imperialist rhetoric of motherhood, see Anna Davin, 'Imperialism and motherhood', in Frederick Cooper and Ann Laura Stoler (eds), Tensions of Empire: Colonial Cultures in a Bourgeois World (Berkeley: University of California Press, 1997), 87–151.
120 Stephen Constantine, ' "Bringing the empire alive": the Empire Marketing Board and imperial propaganda, 1926–33', in MacKenzie (ed.), Imperialism and Popular Culture, 192–231.
121 Cadbury UK, 196/520/003377, 'Cadbury's Dairy Milk Advertising, 1928–', undated newspaper clipping. David Clampin sees commercial advertisers as more attuned to the practical, daily difficulties of wartime life than the Ministry of Information. Clampin, ' "The war has turned our lives upside-down": the merit of commercial advertising in documenting the cultural history of the British Home Front in the Second World War', Visual Resources, 24: 2 (June 2008), 147–8.
122 Cadbury UK, 196/520/003377, 'Cadbury's Dairy Milk Advertising, 1928–', undated clippings.
123 BI, Rowntree Company Archive, N41, 'Cocoa 1941/2'.
124 BI, Rowntree Company Archive, T8, 'Kit Kat, Black Magic and Plain York, 1936–38'. This file also contains adverts from the 1940s.
125 Gillian Dyer, Advertising as Communication (London: Routledge, 1996), 50. See also Clampin, ' "The war has turned our lives upside-down" ', 148.
126 Both these adverts were from 1941. See BI, Rowntree Company Archive, T8, 'Kit Kat, Black Magic and Plain York, 1936–38'. Such an explicit jingoistic message runs counter to Clampin's claim that advertisers relied on credibility and engaging with everyday worries rather than the propagandistic messages of the Ministry of Information. Clampin, ' "The war has turned our lives upside-down" ', 147, 155.
127 See also chapter four.
128 BI, Rowntree Company Archive, N45, 'Cocoa 1952–59', adverts dated January– March 1954.
129 McClintock, Imperial Leather, 219.
130 BI, Rowntree Company Archive, T10, 'Choc Crisp/Kit Kat – 1941/1964'.
131 BI, Rowntree Company Archive, T8, 'Kit Kat, Black Magic and Plain York, 1936–38' (this folder includes adverts from 1941).
132 BI, Rowntree Company Archive, T8, 'Kit Kat, Black Magic and Plain York, 1936–38'. See also BI, Rowntree Company Archive, T7, 'Kit Kat Chocolate Crisp 1940'.
133 Where women were unable to prepare a wholesome 'meal' for their family or themselves, Kit Kat was a substitute. Labelled as a 'meal', it evokes the feminised tasks of cooking and food preparation as well as consumption in a familial domestic context. Ann Whitehead has discussed the meanings of a 'proper meal' in more

detail. Whitehead, 'Food symbolism, gender power and the family', in Barbara Harriss-White and Raymond Hoffenberg (eds), *Food: Multidisciplinary Perspectives* (Oxford: Blackwell, 1994), 123–4.

134 BI, Rowntree Company Archive, T10, 'Choc Crisp/Kit Kat – 1941/1964'.

135 BI, Rowntree Company Archive, AB18, 'Specimens of Advertising in Great Britain 1962'.

136 See Roy Moxham, *Tea: Addiction, Exploitation and Empire* (London: Constable & Robinson, 2003). Early biscuit advertising drew associations with the tea break in an explicitly imperial setting, with images of white British explorers stopping for tea and biscuits in the jungle. Such adverts empowered commodities with maintaining 'British' traditions at all times, thereby keeping control. See the advert for Huntley and Palmers' biscuits in McClintock, *Imperial Leather*, 221.

137 On images used in tea advertising, see Ramamurthy, *Imperial Persuaders*, 216–17. However, as discussed in chapter four, brands such as Yorkshire Tea rely on overtly localised, 'English' imagery.

138 BI, Rowntree Company Archive, T10, 'Choc Crisp/Kit Kat – 1941/1964'. On the social meanings associated with tea and the tea break, see de Groot, 'Metropolitan desires and colonial connections', 175, 179–80.

139 BI, Rowntree Company Archive, AB1, 'Specimens of Advertising in Great Britain 1948–1956'.

140 See BI, Rowntree Company Archive, W6, trade advertising for Black Magic, 'We Still Go to the Ends of the Earth . . .', 1971.

141 Cadbury UK, 196/520/003552, 'Cadbury's Special Ads: From May 1930 to December 1932'.

142 BI, Rowntree Company Archive, AB21, 'Specimens of Advertising in the United Kingdom 1969'.

143 BI, Rowntree Company Archive, B44, 'Black Magic 1974–79'.

144 Adverts for the Bounty Bar, manufactured by Mars, also draw on exotic locations. Allison James notes that, ' "Bounty" still . . . provides you with a "taste of paradise".' However, James sees this solely within her thesis of the 'specialness' of chocolate and its complex place in the 'morality' of food. She does not consider the exoticism of the Bounty adverts, only their exclusivity. It is the coconut in Bounty, rather than the chocolate, which is presented as 'exotic' in this case. James, 'The good, the bad and the delicious', 678.

145 BI, Rowntree Company Archive, S.10, 'Press Advertising AERO 1938, 39 and 40', advert dated June 1938. This intrusion of western capitalism through advertising hoardings should be seen in the context of widespread looting of the Pyramids by western archaeologists. In both cases the Pyramids have been effectively colonised by the west.

146 Loeb, *Consuming Angels*, 157.

147 BI, Rowntree Company Archive, S.10, 'Press Advertising AERO 1938, 39 and 40'. Benedict Anderson's concept of 'imagined' communities works equally well on this global scale. No one knows everyone within the world community but an attempt is being made to create an imagined sense of connection and common identity. Anderson, *Imagined Communities: Reflections on the Origin and Spread of Nationalism* (London: Verso, revised edn, 1991).

148 This was one time when the global labour needed to produce chocolate was actually recognised. Adverts explained that raw materials were stuck at their source. See BI, Rowntree Company Archive, O12, 'Wartime Adverts 1944/5'.

CHAPTER TWO

'The Romance of the Cocoa Bean': imperial and colonial histories

there is much to be told on the romantic side of chocolate, of its divine origin, the bloody wars and brave exploits of the Spaniards who conquered Mexico and were the first to introduce cocoa into Europe, tales almost too thrilling to be believed. (R. Whymper, *Cocoa and Chocolate: Their Chemistry and Manufacture* (London: Churchill, 1912), 327)[1]

Cacuatl, cacao, Theobroma cacao: the etymology of the words cocoa and chocolate reveals an imperial history. For the Mayans, usually alleged to be the first people to have used cocoa, it was 'ka-ka-wa'; for the Aztecs the bean was 'cacuatl'. But the Spaniards, in conquering the Aztecs and exploiting their resources, apparently found their words difficult to pronounce and called the bean 'cacao'.[2] Imperial conquest is clearly not just the possession of land and people; it is the possession of language, the power of naming. In his adoption of cocoa into a European frame of reference in 1735, Linnaeus's 'scientific' classification 'Theobroma cacao' (translated as 'food of the Gods') captures the air of myth that surrounds the cocoa plant, particularly in western histories.[3] Yet if cocoa was the food of the Gods, it was also the food of empire.

It is vital not to obliterate the imperialist histories of chocolate. As Catherine Hall urges, 'unless the legacy of the British Empire is re-remembered it will continue to disrupt and unsettle our present'.[4] This chapter aims to put chocolate into its imperial context, and to recognise the position of British confectionery companies such as Rowntree within this context. I begin by studying the ways in which the early history of chocolate has been written in the west and the ideologies underpinning these narratives. As a feminist historian, what should be my version of chocolate's past? Moving on from these academic and popular histories of chocolate, I examine archival evidence and secondary literature to assess the nature of British firms' involvement in the purchasing of cocoa. I explore the daily operations of the Rowntree-Fry-Cadbury buying agency in Nigeria and offer some insight into the experiences of staff employed by the British chocolate manufacturers. These histories, rarely told, must inform our understanding of the romantic popular narratives set out earlier in the chapter. Finally, I turn to the ways in which cocoa farming itself has been represented. This will bring me back to the question posed in the following section: how has the history of cocoa production been told through assumptions about race, class, gender and sexuality?

(Re)creating chocolate histories

In my own narrative of the origins of chocolate, I must necessarily draw on stories already told. There is little primary material to study for, as John West observes, 'conquistadors and Catholic missionaries in Latin America destroyed records wholesale in their haste to erad-icate native religious and social systems'.[5] Despite this destruction of evidence, details of the origins of cocoa have become cemented through numerous re-tellings. From academic texts such as James Walvin's *Fruits of Empire*, to popular histories such as the Mortons' *Chocolate*, to versions produced by chocolate manufacturers themselves, the same evidence is presented again and again, often with no indication as to its source.[6] Sophie Coe and Michael Coe, though unashamedly calling their own work *The True History of Chocolate*, complain that much of chocolate's written history 'falls into the cat-egory of Voltaire's "accepted fiction"'. They make the comparison with a game of Chinese Whispers: 'the story, of course, becomes increasingly less faithful to the original'.[7] The imperial history of cocoa thus becomes stabilised, not to be disrupted by the violence of imperial conquest. My aim here is not simply to add my own reworking of a mythologised set of events to a grand narrative but to analyse and hopefully destabilise some of the existing representations of cocoa's history.[8]

The cocoa tree is indigenous to South and Central America; more specifically, to the region between the Amazon and the Orinoco. It is the Mayans who have been widely identified as the first consumers. West, for example, relates the discovery of 'a well-preserved pottery container at Río Azul, Guatemala, which contains cacao residues and bears a Mayan glyph for *ka-ka-wa*, from which the Spanish word *cacao* is ultimately derived'.[9] However, Mayan history is usually swiftly glossed over in favour of the Aztecs.

Most writers focus on the Aztecs as consumers of cocoa at the time of European conquest, thereby defining Aztec heritage solely within a Eurocentric framework. Some historians do look back a little further into Aztec history. A. W. Knapp, writing in the 1920s, imagines how cocoa beans were first discovered to be edible:

> doubtless the beans were always thrown away until . . . someone tried roasting them. One pictures this 'someone,' a pre-historic Aztec with swart skin . . . The name of the man who discovered the use of cacao must be written in some early chapter of the history of man, but it is blurred and unreadable: all we know is that he was an inhabitant of the New World.[10]

In Knapp's vision the Aztec man, and it must have been a man, rendered exotic by the description of his skin, is beyond the bounds of history. Yet he is simultaneously part of a 'new' world and must, therefore, have been written about; if we cannot read the man's name, it is not because it has been destroyed by the conquistadors but because it is blurred. It is this man who discovered the only use imaginable for cocoa – that of consumption. John West, writing seventy years on, constructs his history not through romantic imagination but using the limited quantifiable evidence available to him through palaeontology and archaeology. Still, the emphasis is on reading the privileged written evidence of the past: 'recent strides toward decoding Mayan hieroglyphics hold out hope for a more complete and accurate picture in the future'.[11]

The Aztecs apparently believed that 'Quetzalcoatl, the feathered serpent god, had planted the chocolate tree in the region of southern Mexico'.[12] They used this divine gift both for consumption and as a currency: several secondary sources assert that one could buy a 'tolerably good slave' for 100 beans.[13] I have yet to discover the origin of this anecdote, although W. H. Prescott's *Conquest of Mexico* (1843) is the source most often quoted. A similarly persistent tale is given to illustrate the early popularity of drinking chocolate: the Emperor Montezuma reportedly had 'no less than fifty jars or pitchers . . . prepared for his daily consumption: two thousand more were allowed for that of his household'.[14] It is Montezuma's excessive love of chocolate that apparently inspired Cortés to take cocoa back to Spain.

'Discovery', as Hall shrewdly observes, is the 'code word' of colonialism, and in western histories it is the Spanish who are credited with the 'discovery' of cocoa.[15] Columbus is occasionally acknowledged as being the first to introduce cocoa to Spain in 1492 but it is Cortés who becomes the key player, bringing both cocoa beans and the technology to produce chocolate to the Spanish Court in 1528.[16] The supposed encounter between the reigning Aztec emperor and the Spanish conquistador tends to be presented unproblematically, with no sense of the 'bloody wars' highlighted in the epigraph to this chapter. However, Richard Cadbury's publication on cocoa (published under the pseudonym 'Historicus') does recognise the brutality of colonial conquest and the resistance of Montezuma: '[it is] difficult to realise the brutality and treachery of Cortés in seizing and holding captive the generous and noble Emperor'.[17]

Having glossed over the turmoil of imperial conquest, the story moves quickly on to the expanding consumption of chocolate within Spain. For around 100 years the Spanish Empire had a monopoly on production and trade. Indeed one episode, related in several works, details the throwing overboard of cocoa when the English captured Spanish galleons. This is largely attributed to the secrecy with which the Spanish guarded the value of the 'new' plant.[18] Knapp places the event in a more political context: 'It is not impossible that the English, with the defeat of the Armada fresh in the memory, were at first contemptible of this "Spanish" drink.'[19] Gradually, knowledge of chocolate did spread, though consumption was initially confined to elite society.

One final imperial ingredient was necessary to ensure chocolate's success in the west: the addition of sugar made chocolate more palatable to the Europeans. As Walvin observes, this was 'thanks to the emergent slave-based sugar cane economy of the Americas'. The story of chocolate subsequently becomes increasingly intertwined with that of European imperial politics. Cocoa growing expanded from South America to regions such as the West Indies 'on the back of European exploration, trade and settlement'. As territories changed hands, so did the power of chocolate production: for instance, when England took control of Jamaica from the Spanish in 1655. Walvin explains, 'chocolate first made its name in England as a West Indian product. This was perfectly understandable – but again only in the context of empire.' Chocolate thus first gained meaning in England as a product of imperialism.[20]

Richard Cadbury's publication, *Cocoa: All About It*, took as its frontispiece a painting of 'A Casket of Chocolate being handed to Neptune to make known to all the Countries of the World.'[21] In this picture, men are the mythical bearers of imperial wealth. Indeed, it is men who have been largely credited with the dissemination of chocolate production and consumption across the globe. The merchant Antonio Carletti apparently took the commodity to Italy in 1606.[22] Spanish friars, meanwhile, were responsible for taking their taste for chocolate to France and Germany in the early seventeenth century.[23] Disrupting this Eurocentric narrative of the transmission of chocolate is the African figure of Tetteh Quarshie. Although several sources emphasise the role of European missionaries in taking cocoa to mainland West Africa in the nineteenth century, others attribute the arrival of cocoa beans to the now legendary Tetteh. Cited alternately as a carpenter[24] or a blacksmith, Tetteh appears to have brought the beans from Fernando Po to Ghana in around 1881, where he is now honoured as a national hero.[25] Tetteh has become a focus for celebrating the significance of African enterprise, rather than European involvement, in establishing West Africa's successful cocoa industry. However, this still keeps the expansion of the chocolate trade firmly within a male frame of reference.

Whilst men may be the bearers of chocolate, women are positioned as consumers early in the narratives. In the 'Cadbury World' exhibition, as Hall recounts, it is the indigenous woman as consumer who first gives Cortés knowledge of chocolate:

> the colonial encounter between Cortés and an Aztec woman Marina meant that he heard tales of the riches of Quetzalcoatl. . . . Thus the 'native' woman, both the feeding mother of infancy and the sexual woman, gave the European man access to the New World and its delights.[26]

McClintock has analysed the ways in which women became the boundary markers of empire: 'Female figures were planted like fetishes at the ambiguous points of contact'.[27] The anxieties McClintock identifies surrounding the penetration of imperial borders are seemingly still present in the late twentieth century. A more common anecdote of transgressive feminine consumption relates how the women of Chiapas in Mexico would interrupt Mass to have their hot chocolate brought to them.[28] When the bishop excommunicated them, they simply moved to another church. The bishop was later poisoned. Chocolate becomes explicitly associated with sinful temptation in this tale, with women ruthless in its pursuit.

The most famous 'chocoholic' of this early period in European consumption – Maria Theresa, the Spanish Infanta – is likewise the object of scandal. Legend has it that Maria gave birth to a black child because she consumed so much chocolate. There are complex intersections here of chocolate, sexuality and race. Walvin's explanation is rather more prosaic, suggesting that the African slave who brought Maria her chocolate each morning may have had more bearing on the nature of this tale.[29] Wagner, meanwhile, plays on the modern notion that chocolate is a 'comfort' food: 'It is to be hoped that she found the sweet warm drink consoling, for the king, preoccupied by affairs of state, intrigues at court and his succession of powerful mistresses, had little time for his queen.'[30] Here the mythologised history of chocolate allows the author to digress into other tales of sexual and political intrigue.

Despite the place of women in these narratives, when chocolate first arrived in England it seems to have been confined to the masculine space of the coffee and chocolate houses. The most renowned consumer in this context is Samuel Pepys, whose diary entry of 1664, describing 'jacolatte' as 'very good', is quoted in virtually every history of the commodity. Chocolate becomes a prop in narratives of seventeenth-century male bonding and political manoeuvrings. According to Knapp, 'In the sixteen-sixties there were no strident newspapers to destroy one's equanimity, and the gossip of the day began to be circulated and discussed over cups of tea, coffee, or chocolate.' However, Walvin hints that chocolate, like tea, was 'soon relegated to the social dominance of coffee' and thus 'became the focus for a distinctively female sociability'.[31] Still, chocolate remained for a long time the privilege of elites, ensconced in the expensive paraphernalia one needed to prepare it.

Chocolate was, and remains, the site of many different meanings, largely thanks to its imperial past. In Spain, its 'alleged medicinal benefits and its aphrodisiac qualities were paraded as part of that broader social and medicinal discourse about new tropical commodities'.[32] J. Othick posits that the continuation of this medicinal discourse into the nineteenth century was partly due to chocolate's unpleasant taste prior to technological developments such as the Van Houten process: 'since the product must almost certainly have tasted like medicine, it was only logical to pretend that it had medicinal properties'. As the taste improved (according to European palates), the emphasis changed and manufacturers marketed cocoa as 'a wholesome foodstuff which should form a regular item of diet'.[33] Indeed it formed an important part of Royal Navy rations, which accounted for half of Britain's cocoa imports in the mid-nineteenth century.[34] With a reduction in duties during the mid- to late nineteenth century, chocolate consumption became increasingly democratised. At this juncture, at least in British histories, the Quaker manufacturers begin to be truly successful and chocolate is made to harbour new associations of temperance and social advancement. I now turn to the Quaker firm that will be the focus of this history, Rowntree & Co., to determine how and in what ways it became involved in the cocoa trade.

Rowntree's early involvement in the cocoa trade

The Rowntree factory officially has its origins in the Walmgate grocer's shop established by Mary Tuke in 1725. Mary – an orphan who, as an unmarried woman, successfully rebelled against the trading restrictions of the Merchant Adventurers Company – has taken on a mythic status in company histories.[35] Her nephew, William, joined her as an apprentice and took over the shop in 1752. Like fellow Quakers the Cadburys, the Tukes began to deal in the products of the flourishing British empire: tea and cocoa. Although they would have stocked chocolate produced by other manufacturers, they also became involved in making chocolate themselves. They had a small factory in Castlegate, producing the very successful 'Tuke's Superior Rock Cocoa'. This was rebranded as 'Rowntree's Prize Medal Rock Cocoa' after Henry Isaac Rowntree took over manufacture in 1862.[36]

In the days of Henry Isaac, cocoa beans were purchased from London and Liverpool markets.[37] However, there were early moves to become more directly involved with the producers. Southall suggests that Cadbury involvement in Ghana from the early twentieth century was precipitated by the scandal over working practices in the Portuguese-owned islands of São Tomé and Principe, in which the firm faced accusations of having knowingly purchased cocoa grown by slave labour. He claims that before this, 'they had had no direct contact with . . . primary producers . . . The San Thomé affair constituted a formidable challenge to this innocence.'[38] Yet both Cadbury and Rowntree were already owners of their own estates in the West Indies by this point, motivated as much by profit, and a desire to control quality, as by the welfare of cocoa workers. The Rowntree company became the owner of estates in Jamaica and Trinidad in 1899 for £9,000. These estates were, however, largely unsuccessful and were up for sale by 1914.[39] The West Indies were declining in importance as cocoa producers by this time. Nevertheless, the archives show that Rowntree still had their Dominican estates until the early 1930s.[40]

Whilst most histories of Rowntree pass over their involvement with cocoa from the West Indies, there is some archival evidence to help us more fully understand how the firm was involved. Rowntree were the owners of several estates: Blenheim, Picard and Moore Park (all in Dominica);[41] Bonny, Hatton Hall, Mount Jewel and Bois Chandelle (in Dominica).[42] There was also the Dover estate and Vinery estate in Jamaica.[43] Managing an agricultural workforce at such a distance from York was a new challenge for the Rowntree industrialists. Hamilton Law McDonald was appointed overseer of Vinery estate in May 1899. His origins are not clear but it is significant that his contract should demand that he 'solemnly promise during the continuance of this agreement to abstain entirely from all intoxicating liquor or alcoholic beverages of any kind whatsoever'.[44] This clause is not contained in any of the agreements with staff appointed as Trading Managers or Attorneys and could be related to assumptions about both class and race. Certainly, there were non-white overseers on the estates. On the

Picard estate in 1929, for example, 'Winston – a coloured man – lives in and has charge of Ti-bay.' A list of staff at Picard includes Mr Bruney who, in a move that immediately sets him apart from the implicitly white employees, is given the racial signifier of 'coloured'.[45]

Aside from those in charge, there is little information in the archives concerning workers on the estates. The *CWM* gives a useful early indication of the labour force in Jamaica and Trinidad in 1904, organising statistics by gender and race. From just a handful of employees in the 1890s, there were now nine 'White Managers and Overseers', 100 'East Indian Coolies' (seventy-five men and twenty-five women), and 343 'Negro Cultivators' (of whom the majority, 178, were women).[46] These workers were not only producing cocoa; limes, coconuts and bananas were also cultivated. The brief for the overseer of the Vinery estate included, 'The planting, cultivating and gathering of . . . BANANAS PIMENTO and other produce.'[47] Photographs in the *CWM* from 1904 show women on the Blenheim estate in Dominica involved in carrying limes to the Works Yard for pressing, as well as working with cocoa.[48] By 1926, the approximate number of 'coloured people' employed per week on the Dominican estates was 100–200. Ironically, by this time, the cocoa produced in Dominica was not being used in the Rowntree factory at York.[49] The estates there were sold to Messrs Rose & Co. in 1934.[50]

Although Rowntree ceased to own estates in the West Indies, they still purchased West Indian cocoa. In a 1958 report, K. Haslinger (from the purchasing department) set out from where Rowntree was buying cocoa and how this altered according to external events such as the Second World War:

> During the war and the following ten years our choice of cocoa was very much limited, first by direct Government control which ended in 1950, and second by strict currency regulations, which generally meant that 'flavour cocoa' could in the main be obtained only from Stirling sources, e.g. West Indies, Samoa and Ceylon.[51]

Before the war, Rowntree had blended cocoas from Trinidad and Venezuela. Prevented from buying from Venezuela until the lifting of currency restrictions in 1954–55, the firm turned to Grenada. This became an increasingly important supply as the quality of Venezuelan cocoa deteriorated, whilst New Guinea cocoa also became an ingredient in Black Magic. Worries that the quality of cocoa from Trinidad was worsening led to a visit in 1955 whereby arrangements were made 'that we might get more of the "cream" of Trinidad than hitherto'.[52] Tracking these fluctuations in supply highlights the variety of means by which Rowntree sourced their cocoa but does not render visible the chaos that international events and the whim of the manufacturer may have caused for the workers and farm owners. Of course, Rowntree could not only withdraw their buying agents from a particular country, they could also actively encourage the production of cocoa. Fears about swollen shoot disease in West Africa, coupled with increasing consumer demand during the postwar period, led to research into potential areas of cocoa cultivation. This was again a colonial enterprise as, in 1951, a report was produced into the 'Prospects of the growing of cocoa in the British Solomon Islands'.[53] The project is presented as beneficial to the country concerned, diversifying their economy, yet it is clear who were to be the ultimate beneficiaries.

West African cocoa production

From plantation to smallholding

Early involvement by British manufacturers in the African cocoa trade was highly controversial. The so-called 'Cocoa Scandal' of 1908–9 centred on the Cadbury firm, who sued the *Standard* newspaper for libel following accusations of hypocrisy over the issue of slavery in West Africa. The paper alleged that Cadbury, despite their public anti-slavery stance, knowingly bought cocoa grown by slaves on the Portuguese-owned islands of São Tomé and Principe. Although Cadbury eventually won the high-profile case, they were awarded minimal damages of just one farthing.[54]

Vernon attempts to exonerate Rowntree from this scandal: 'Rowntrees were not, in fact, purchasers of cocoa from the Portuguese islands of San Thomé and Principe.' Instead, she emphasises Rowntree's role in changing the system. However, Fitzgerald asserts that all three of the major firms (Cadbury, Rowntree and Fry) 'had obtained supplies from this source'. In his detailed study of the scandal, Satre also notes the involvement throughout of Rowntree and Fry. He provides evidence from the Cadbury archive that J. B. Morrell, one of the Rowntree directors, wrote to Cadbury in 1904 regarding the difficult question of how to investigate the issue and how to proceed once the results became known. From this letter it is clear that the Rowntree firm were concerned with the 'very serious pecuniary loss' which would be suffered by the manufacturing firms in the case of a boycott.[55]

Cadbury, Rowntree and Fry had certainly been aware for many years of accusations against the Portuguese of exploiting African workers. J. B. Morrell, in a notebook from the late nineteenth century detailing the characteristics of the major cocoa exporting countries, included this short but telling extract under the heading 'Africa': 'St Thomas (Portuguese) an island . . . having Guchona coffee cacao and other plantations, cultivated to a large extent by negroes undergoing a forced apprenticeship.'[56] This recognition that working conditions were not all that they might be did not initially stop Rowntree or the other Quaker firms from buying cocoa from this region on the open market. Instead, Cadbury, Rowntree and Fry, joined by Stollwerck of Cologne, commissioned their own agent, Joseph Burtt, to investigate conditions on the islands.

Burtt's report took several years to produce, during which time the English journalist, Henry Nevinson, had published graphic accounts of the horrendous treatment of plantation workers. Nevinson documented how people were being forcibly taken from Angola, and were shipped to the islands under appalling conditions. Once on the plantations, they would never return to the mainland and many died within the first few years. Although Burtt confirmed suspicions of slavery, the firms decided not to cease buying immediately as this would end any influence they might exercise on working practices. Hall concludes that this was in keeping with the Quaker's anti-slavery stance, merely reflecting the difficult choices that had to be made.[57] Nevertheless, the firms were still profiting from chocolate sales. They did not boycott São Tomé and Principe cocoa until 1909, following a visit by William Cadbury to West Africa which confirmed that insufficient progress had been made. Although plantation owners subsequently asserted that labour practices had improved, Knapp was able to write in 1920 that, 'the mortality of the plantation labourers has generally been very heavy, one large and well-managed estate recording on an average of seven years an annual death rate of 148 per thousand'.[58] Conditions were still far from satisfactory. However, the Quaker firms were now able to source the majority of their cocoa from the mainland British colonies of Nigeria and the Gold Coast.[59]

The early twentieth century saw Nigeria and Ghana, particularly the latter, make startling progress in the production of cocoa. Although a very minor producer in 1901, Ghana's exports had risen to over 40,000 metric tons by 1911. The two colonies were clearly emerging as the principle producers, overtaking Venezuela and other South American exporters.[60] This was indeed a 'rich historical irony' considering the use of West African slave labour in the cocoa plantations of South America and the West Indies.[61] The establishment of the Nigerian cocoa industry has been interpreted as either a consequence of western capitalism, supported by structures of colonialism, or as the result of indigenous enterprise. Accounts which stress the hard work and innovation of indigenous entrepreneurs are particularly convincing, if highly gendered.[62] However, as Gordon Stewart concludes in his study of jute and empire, it is important to study the 'interplay' of indigenous and colonial factors.[63] The earliest cocoa farms are thought to have been the work of Creole merchants in Lagos. Identified as the 'true pioneers' of the cocoa industry, they occupied a position on the borders between Yoruba and British society (thus illustrating the 'interplay' of factors Stewart suggests).[64] The industry was then taken over by Nigerian farmers (always generically male in academic accounts) on smallholdings.

Despite West African success, the Rowntree company maintained an attachment to those regions which they perceived to be producing the highest quality cocoa, particularly Equador.[65] Haslinger, discussing the flavours needed for Black Magic chocolates in the late 1950s, reported, 'What we do not want is the mild neutral flavour of West African cocoa.'[66] However, it was not only 'flavour' which was at issue; there were other prejudices at work, particularly in relation to who owned the cocoa farms. This is apparent from a company-produced history of chocolate, 'The Romance of the Cocoa Bean': 'The best qualities of cocoa come from the West Indies, South America and the East Indies, where the production of cocoa is largely in the hands of white planters.'[67] Here the discourse of quality, so often deployed by the firm, conveniently intersects with racial prejudices and colonialist economics. Rowntree's York rival, Terry's, emphasised their ownership of cocoa plantations in South America as evidence of the high quality of their cocoa beans, using a motif of palm trees in their company logo throughout the twentieth century.[68] However, by 1958, less than 10 per cent of the world's annual cocoa crop was 'flavour' cocoa, with the largest proportion of imports being from West Africa.[69] In view of the importance of the West African crop, it is appropriate at this juncture to chart the increasingly formalised involvement of Rowntree, Cadbury and Fry in the cocoa economy there under British rule.

Taking control: setting up a buying agency in Nigeria
In response to the problems of buying cocoa during the First World War, Rowntree attended a conference with Cadbury and Fry in 1919. It was clear by this point that West Africa would become their main source of cocoa. Besides, under British colonial rule (Lagos was declared a British colony in 1851, Ghana became a colony in 1874), the area could be relied upon to continue exporting to Britain.[70] This meeting subsequently led to the founding of Cocoa Manufacturers Limited (later renamed Rowntree-Fry-Cadbury (Nigeria) Ltd).[71] The three companies had equal shares in this enterprise but its headquarters were at York. Meanwhile, Cadbury, who had had their agents stationed in Ghana since 1907, were to coordinate the purchase of Ghanaian cocoa on behalf of the British firms.[72] The basic remit of the agencies

was to supervise the purchase of cocoa from the producers, arrange for its transportation to the port and to ensure it was shipped safely to its destination. It is the specific workings of the Rowntree-Fry-Cadbury (hereafter RFC) firm in Nigeria which will be the focus of the following paragraphs.

Buying agents had initially been stationed at the port of Lagos to supervise the purchase of cocoa. With the formation of the joint buying agency and the construction of road and rail networks (encouraged by colonial officials but made possible by Nigerian labour) the three Quaker firms were able to expand their operations into the 'interior'. They leased additional stores, other buildings such as labourers' quarters, and transport links, thereby establishing a very physical (though not necessarily permanent) presence in Nigeria.[73] Moving further inland allowed the agency increased and potentially preferential access to supplies of raw cocoa as well as a position from which they could monitor the processes of cocoa farming being adopted. The expansion thus facilitated, indeed it demanded, increased contact with the producers themselves, along with the employment of 'native' Nigerians. Rowntree were now engaging directly in colonialist relations of production in British West Africa; they were no longer distanced as they could be when buying cocoa on the open market or at the local port. So how did the operations of the buying agency align with the self-image of the Quaker companies as 'model firms'? What were relations like between the agency and the indigenous population of Nigeria, and between the agency and the colonial government? How did relations change between Rowntree and Nigeria when the colony became independent?

Rowntree-Fry-Cadbury (Nigeria) staff

In 1920, Percival Howard Soper was appointed Trading Manager for the Nigerian agency. He was also to serve as attorney for the company, being their chief representative in the colony. His assistant, also appointed in 1920, was Harold Noble. These two men were responsible for overseeing the entire operation in Nigeria, with duties ranging from purchasing cocoa and hiring workers, to doing the accounts and renting properties. Initially they were also responsible for setting up the buying stations. By 1930, seven members of 'white staff' were working in Nigeria.[74] Information for 1938 to 1941 lists eight men (including Soper), suggesting that around seven to eight men was average. This would correlate with the eight residential properties listed in the company records: Agege, Agbado, Ibadan Old Bush House, Ibadan New Bush House, New House Ibadan, Otta House, Ife House and Ondo Bungalow. Numbers did increase slightly as by 1953 there were ten members of 'European staff' (they are not explicitly gendered as male).[75]

Whilst I have not found any evidence of women employed as British West Africa staff, white British women were certainly present in Nigeria as part of the RFC enterprise. Accounts ledgers detail the fares paid to bring wives to and from Nigeria; women are also present on group photos. Although 'Mrs Slack was the only wife in Nigeria during the 1930 season', between 1938 and 1941 several wives were present.[76] Material held in the Cadbury UK archive provides a more personal insight into the experiences of, and relationships between, husbands and wives in Nigeria. On a visit to the colony in 1924, Mr Iredale of RFC reported his misgivings about Mr Noble as 'rather harsh in his treatment of native labourers'. He was reassured by

Figure 5 A formal group photograph in honour of Seebohm Rowntree's visit to the Nigerian buying agency, 1933. P. H. Soper, one of the original agents, is seated to the right of Seebohm and Mrs Rowntree.

Mr Soper: 'From what Soper told me Noble is much more tolerable since he has had his wife out with him.' As for Mrs Noble herself, she 'seems to have settled down very well and to like the life in Nigeria'. Women could exercise a key influence on the behaviour of their husband but they also engaged with Nigeria on their own terms.[77]

Photographs and a surviving architectural plan offer evidence of the type of housing in which RFC staff made their homes.[78] Some were certainly living in an urban environment, based in Ibadan. The urban residential system had been highly regulated since Lugard's Townships Ordinance of 1917. As Anthony D. King points out, the urban environment was segregated into a European Reservation and 'non-European or Native Reservation', divided from each other by 'a non-residential area 440 yards broad'.[79] Archive photographs illustrate that European residences were not simply segregated from the indigenous population, they were also distanced from each other. This was in direct contrast to both the urban environment experienced by Nigerians and to traditional ways of living in which connecting huts facilitated the creation of thick walls to keep the interior cool. It was thus yet another means of emphasising, in physical terms, the cultural distance between coloniser and colonised.[80]

By the 1950s the company had buying stations in the Agege, Agbado, Ibadan and Ife districts. In his 1953 report, Blitz details sixty such stations in Western Nigeria. This would make each RFC agent responsible for around six stations, assuming they were divided equally. The work of supervising the purchase and shipping of cocoa is presented as difficult and time consuming: 'In the height of the season, this is a responsibility which occupies over 12 hours a day and every day, without exception, of the week.'[81] The agents were expected to visit their buying stations in person from time to time, entailing difficult travel in order to reach some of the more distant stations, even with the developing road networks. However, individual stations were, at least by 1953, run entirely by African staff under the supervision of an African buying clerk.

The experiences of Nigerian staff of the buying agency should not be neglected. It is, unfortunately, very difficult to find primary source material. Nevertheless, from the wage statistics available one can discern that there were indeed 'Native Clerks', 'Native Drivers' and 'Native Brokers'.[82] The problem is that the wages are only ever detailed collectively, allowing us no clue as to how much individual workers were being paid. Although Cadbury, for example, were paying slightly higher wages to their Ghanaian staff than other buying agencies, Southall shrewdly observes that the complacent labour framework of the colonial economy allowed them to maintain their self image as a model firm by paying marginally better wages . . . at little cost to themselves; and their own complacency was fed by racial attitudes inherent in the colonial situation which saw the African as leading a simpler life, and therefore one which needed less material support.

The evidence on relations between African and European staff at RFC is limited. Southall has outlined some of the tensions around the issue of employing indigenous West African staff. For instance, 'In 1918, although the Bournville management wished to involve the European staff in training African clerks to act as buyers, the former were strongly resistant to any such ideas.'[83] Clearly RFC had a hierarchical structure in which a handful of white agents supervised the operations of an entirely African staff. Nevertheless, the distances involved meant that day-to-day tasks would have been carried out without constant supervision.

Relationships with producers and their intermediaries

Besides dealing with Nigerian staff employed directly by the firm, RFC also had to build up a working relationship with the producers of cocoa. R. Galletti, K. D. S. Baldwin and I. O. Dina, who made a study of Nigerian cocoa farmers in the 1950s, found that RFC was the only major firm which 'made it the rule to buy at its own depots through salaried employees dealing directly with producers'.[84] Evidence as to the specific dynamics of the producer–agent relationship is limited. In 1950, a Cadbury representative, Mr Norman Edwards, visited Nigerian villages where RFC had cocoa stores. His patronising depiction of the Nigerian 'bushman' – 'still the same cheery, courteous, apparently carefree fellow' – nevertheless suggests that the villagers were not unwelcoming to RFC agents: 'he does not show any signs of wanting to be rid of his European friends and colleagues'. For the producers their chief concern was with the prices they would receive for their crop: the farmer 'realises that he is better off because of the much higher postwar prices for his product, but he does not seem to trouble overmuch whether these prices have resulted from the setting-up of Marketing Boards or from some other cause'.[85] This article, published in the *Bournville Works Magazine*, painted a reassuring picture for Cadbury readers in Britain of friendly relations with happy, productive colonial subjects.

Galletti, Baldwin and Dina credit RFC with improving farming techniques through paying premium prices from the early 1920s for high-grade cocoa.[86] The boom in the cocoa trade immediately following the First World War would have allowed RFC to pay relatively high prices, although Galletti, Baldwin and Dina seem to be suggesting that they also managed this during the depression of the 1920s. If so, it is likely that relations between RFC and their suppliers were fairly healthy. However, the depression of the 1930s was particularly drastic for cocoa farmers: 'So depressed was the inter-war period . . . that the *highest* average annual price in the 1930s was only slightly above the *lowest* pre-1914 price.'[87] In 1937, the major cocoa buying firms entered into a market-sharing agreement, or 'pool', which prohibited competition amongst them. As Miles recognises, 'a buying agreement took away the farmers' only shield and defence – competition'.[88] Moreover, pooling tended to take place at times of low prices world-wide, so that the buyers could be sure of making some profit when they sold their chocolate in world markets. This led the farmers to blame the pools for low cocoa prices. The formation of such a comprehensive pool of firms in 1937 led the Ghanaian farmers to take their most concerted action so far: they refused to sell their cocoa. The cocoa hold-up of 1937 to 1938 illustrates that farmers did indeed hold some of the power in the colonial system.[89]

The Second World War in many ways cemented the pooling arrangement, for the British government was to purchase the entire cocoa crop in order to ensure that British firms did not suffer.[90] Representatives from Cadbury and the United Africa Company held important positions, first in the Ministry of Food (which purchased the first crop of the war), then in the newly created West African Cocoa Control Board of 1940 and also in its replacement of 1942, the West African Produce Control Board. The Nigerian government protested against such arrangements as being prejudiced against Nigerian cocoa cooperatives; the Colonial Office rejected their comments. The politics of indirect rule thus favoured British business interests such as those of Rowntree.[91] As Meredith puts it, 'The behaviour of the Colonial Office . . . shows that the permanent officials had both a clear grasp of business principles and . . . a strong predilection to regard what was good for the firms as being good for the colonies.'[92]

Following the war, the standardisation of marketing practices continued with the formation of the cocoa marketing boards in 1946–47. Such organisations allowed the Colonial Office to exercise their 'paternalistic trusteeship' whilst perpetuating the discrimination against African enterprise.[93] Nigerians were not allowed, for example, to manage their own marketing board. Rowntree, though admittedly in an article written post-independence, present the board as a positive influence: 'safeguarding the farmers against steep falls in world prices'.[94] By the 1970s, however, Rowntree were complaining to the board over the deteriorating quality of cocoa beans.[95] There is not room here to discuss the decline of the Nigerian cocoa industry but the failure of cocoa boards to address the needs of farmers was a significant factor.[96]

Rowntree actions in Nigeria were clearly responses to a highly complex business environment. Like Cadbury in Ghana, their reputation of being a 'model firm' was almost inevitably going to come under attack in the context of colonial economic exploitation. Nevertheless, RFC were relatively enlightened in their commitment to 'developing' African enterprise (making the assumption that the West African people needed help in this respect) and encouraging good practice in cocoa farming by paying high prices for better grades of cocoa. Certainly, company publicity was keen to stress the role of cocoa in improving the quality of life in producing countries: 'The world-wide trade in cocoa is playing an important part in the rapid advances now being made by the farming communities which produce its essential raw material.'[97] This rhetoric of social advancement for the newly independent colony conveniently interlinked with encouraging a more 'efficient' workforce and, therefore, with increasing profits for the company as a whole. In anticipating the move towards independence, however, the firm had distanced itself from the difficult problems to be overcome:

> Aside from politics, Nigeria has immense economic problems to tackle; but it is probable that within the lifetime of most of us, Nigeria and the nearby Gold Coast will become the first all-negro self-governing Dominions of the Commonwealth of Nations.[98]

The author of this extract, Mr J. F. Blitz, emphasises Nigeria's problems without placing them in the context of the consequences of imperialism.[99] Still, he had at least entered into a dialogue with the Nigerians themselves, meeting with Nigerian officials as well as Europeans during his visit of 1953. Blitz was merely a temporary visitor to Nigeria; several members of Rowntree staff and their families, as well as colleagues from Cadbury and Fry, were stationed for months at a time in British West Africa. For the Nigerians, then, it was surely these men and women who came to personify the Quaker manufacturers.

The discourse of cocoa farming

Thus far I have examined imperialist discourses of the 'discovery' of cocoa and have studied in more detail the colonial context in which Rowntree and the other British confectionery manufacturers were embroiled. I now turn to western representations of cocoa farming and farmers: from book-length texts produced for the general reader, such as Knapp's *Cocoa and Chocolate*; to government documents surveying the industry; to company reports from the field. The focus will be on resources produced for consumers and for industry, rather than on academic studies (which will be addressed in chapter three). How did broader conceptions of race and gender function in these officially produced narratives?

In response to the very specific, tropical conditions required, the growing of cocoa became exoticised and romanticised in contemporary literature. Tropical outposts of the British empire already held a fascination in the imagination of those resident in the metropolis, thanks to their manifestation in British culture 'back home'. Knapp plays on these expectations: 'Many a young man, reading in some delightful book of travel, has longed to go to the tropics and see the wonders for himself.'[100] The cocoa tree, with its unusual way of growing fruit on its trunk rather than its branches, became symbolic of the strangeness of these 'unexplored' regions. Rowntree's own publication, 'The Romance of the Cocoa Bean', emphasised the 'beauty' of the cocoa tree. The Bois Immortelle, a tree often used to provide shade for the growing cocoa, appears to have added to the aesthetic appeal of the farm: 'the large undulating fields of cocoa are a gorgeous sight when the Bois Immortelle is in flower'.[101]

Observers were fascinated by the multiplicity of colours at play on cocoa farms, particularly in the plantations. Such 'colour' was provided by both people and plant. Describing a group sitting extracting cocoa beans from the pods, the anonymous author of 'The Romance of the Cocoa Bean' comments, 'Colour and brightness have a fascination for the West Indian girls.' This colour is located in the pods themselves, in the 'highly-coloured costume and headgear' of the girls and, implicitly, in the skin of the workers.[102] Cocoa farms, particularly the more well-ordered plantations, could be a site of leisurely contemplation for Europeans:

> One can spend happy days on a cacao estate. 'Are you going into the cocoa?' they ask, just as in England we might enquire, 'Are you going into the corn?' Coconut plantations and sugar estates make a strong appeal to the imagination, but for peaceful beauty they cannot compare with the cacao plantation.[103]

Knapp makes many such conflations with English culture. The purpose of this may well be to familiarise and domesticate foreign enterprise, making it all part of a British industry. In looking in detail at a cocoa pod, for example, he emphasises its whiteness, situating himself as a familiar character from nursery rhyme: 'The inside of the rind and the mass of beans are gleaming white, like melting snow . . . Like little Jack Horner, I put in my thumb and pull out a snow-white bean.'[104] The emphasis on snow is absurd in this tropical setting, yet it demonstrates clearly the Eurocentric framework in which Knapp's narrative has meaning.

Knapp was well aware in the 1920s of the labour required to produce both cocoa and chocolate: 'our liking for these delicacies has set minds and bodies at work all the world over!' His worldview is highly segregated and an essentially racist division of labour is rationalised through elevating the hard work of non-white peoples: 'To the black and brown races, the negroes and the East Indians, we owe a debt for their work on tropical plantations, for the harder manual work would be too arduous for Europeans unused to the heat of those regions.'[105] Physical capacity for cocoa farming was one of the many discourses used to justify the power structures inherent in chocolate manufacture. Others could function negatively to stress the need for European supervision of cocoa production. Ironically, it was West African enterprise which triumphed in Nigeria and Ghana, leading to much troubled speculation as to why European plantations failed.[106]

Despite the invisibility of female labour in so many recent academic accounts of cocoa farming, earlier works do describe female workers, if in an exoticised way: 'graceful, dark-skinned girls, who gather one by one the fallen pods from the greenery'; 'She trips through the trees, her bracelets jingling, and tumbles the pods on to the heap.'[107] Within a Rowntree narrative, the work of cocoa farming is quite specifically gendered: 'A man takes the pod in one hand and deftly cuts through the tough shell . . . Girls then remove the sticky beans . . . [baskets of cocoa] are transported on the backs of donkeys or carried on the heads of girls to the fermentory.'[108] Men are portrayed as skilled workers, able to handle machetes and 'deftly' cut open the cocoa pods; they are also the planters of cocoa. Women take over during harvesting, taking out the beans from the pods. In photographs from the Cadbury and Rowntree archives, male workers are frequently posed standing, holding the tools used for cutting pods down from the trees. Women are most often depicted carrying baskets of cocoa on their heads, or seated round heaps of cocoa pods. These stilted images are studies in exoticism, rather than of labour processes. One surviving Cadbury photograph does present perhaps a more 'realistic' image of work: it depicts over twenty-five Indian women, of varying ages, sitting on a dirt floor sorting through bags of cocoa. Two Indian men stand over them. This overview of women at work is very different to images of individuals which allow the viewer to see in greater detail their clothes and jewellery.[109]

Colonial officials expected women to be involved in cocoa farming at particular stages. In order to allay fears that cocoa would take labour away from copra production in the British Solomon Islands, D. H. Urquhart (former Director of Agriculture in Ghana) commented, 'When the cacao trees come into bearing, women and children can assist in most of the operations required in preparing cocoa for the market.'[110] Visiting Nigeria in 1953, Mr J. F. Blitz concluded that 'much of the hard work' is done by women. This was in keeping with stereotypes of the 'lazy' West African male, though it did at least recognise the labour of women. However, Blitz had other motives in describing Nigerian women, using them to berate the standards of Europeans: 'As a consequence of head-loading, the African women walk beautifully, swinging elegantly from their hips; and their erect carriage and deportment would put most European women to shame.'[111] In descriptions of gendered work in the colonial context, then, other ideologies of the colonisers (particularly concerning race and economics), as well as a desire for the exoticised other, are in evidence.

Whilst exploiting the romantic discourse of cocoa, particularly in their advertisements, Rowntree were also perpetuating an increasingly scientific approach to cocoa farming. Disease could wipe out a cocoa crop and new trees took many years to bear fruit; manufacturers were therefore concerned with how to prevent such diseases occurring and to limit their impact. Whilst the farmers had their own means of coping with disease, the aim was to use western technological advances to make cocoa growing a more scientific operation. Colonial authorities, manufacturers and scientists were clearly frustrated at the way in which the cash crop industry had developed independently of their attempts to control and regulate it. Paul Bareau, in a book published by Cadbury in 1953, lamented that, 'In its earlier stages the industry developed without guidance from scientists and administration, in circumstances which considerably magnified the difficulties of modernising it.' Although European farming techniques had failed in the West African context, perhaps through science they could regain a degree of control. Agricultural colleges in the colonies were to disseminate Western-developed methods to 'native' farmers. Bareau, however, patronisingly believed it would be no easy task to educate 'thousands of simple and mostly illiterate small cultivators'.[112]

Stereotypes of the illiterate Nigerian farmer were used to bemoan problems such as crop disease and low yields. He was identified in the racist discourses of official literature as both congenitally lazy and morally deficient. In the 'Proposals for the Reorganisation of the Nigerian Cocoa Industry by the Registrar of Cooperative Societies, 1944–5', Captain Haig, Director of the Registrar, wrote that cocoa had

had the effect of 'rendering the farmers averse to manual labour, and of consolidating habits of indolence already induced by the climate'. Haig believed there was a need for medical research on the farmers as 'there is a torpidity of mind and body about many southern Yoruba farmers noticeable enough to suggest that its causes are physical as well as temperamental'. Contemporary ideas of biological racism are here intertwined with an insinuation of the corrupting force of cash crops and, therefore, of capitalism. The apparently 'illiterate' farmers are said to have received 'no guidance whatever as to the proper use of money' and to be squandering their profits. Thus, 'the financial increment had no civilising value, since it was spent on simple but quite unimproving luxuries such as more drink, more gowns, more wives, more labourers'.[113] Capitalism without a western education or western guidance is portrayed as corrupting and encouraging the male Nigerian farmer to pursue his already uncivilised ways.

In the late 1950s, the cocoa farmer's indigenous knowledge was idealised as the pretensions of scientists came under attack. The period of decolonisation posed a challenge to colonial racism, shifting the emphasis in racial discourse onto the capacity of Africans for development and eventual independence within the Commonwealth. At the Cocoa Conference held in London in 1957, D. H. Urquhart used the 'simple skill' of the cocoa farmer to humble the scientists in attendance:

> I would like to remind the scientists present that the world cocoa industry was very largely developed without their aid. The great cocoa industry in West Africa was developed by the skill of the farmer. That skill – you might call it the simple skill of the simple man – was great skill.[114]

The figure of the 'simple' male cocoa farmer is retained, but his wealth of experience in the local context is finally being recognised and valued. There is, however, no mention of family labour. The male farmer is constructed using the western concept of the lone 'breadwinner'; he needs to be given increased scientific knowledge in order to better support his family:

> The majority of the world's supply of cocoa comes from small growers, usually with very limited scientific knowledge, but with a sound understanding of their local conditions and a personal awareness that he, the grower, has to make a living and usually support a family on the proceeds from his work.[115]

Women and children are to be passively supported whilst their contribution to the cocoa crop is rendered invisible. Hence, a purportedly scientific report is able to convey colonialist, patriarchal ideologies of gender and work.

Women appear in colonialist narratives as property to be bought by the new wealth but also as a means of influencing the male farmer. The wives of cocoa farmers are generally portrayed as extremely conservative, even more so than the male farmers themselves. In a discussion of the possibility of establishing Young Farmer's Clubs in schools in 1934, Mr C. F. Strickland, representing the cooperative societies, put forward the view that, 'The instruction of women and children in the co-operative idea [is] of prime importance. There is no hope of really converting the men if women are adverse, and I believe that the way to approach the women is through the children.' However, the Director of Education at the time felt that Strickland did not 'know much of the conservative nature of the African woman. But the child is father of the man and it is in the second generation that we find progress. . . . We must look to the education of women to break down harmful prejudices.'[116] The Director of Education believed that educating the next generation of women, in western-influenced schools, was the solution. Yet he still clung to the notion of a male lineage, claiming that the 'child is father of the man'. In reality, women were rarely the beneficiaries of improved education.

Conclusion

Whilst it was through imperialism that Britain first had a taste of chocolate, it was colonialism which enabled the mass manufacture of this increasingly popular luxury food. The colonisation of the West Indies and West Africa facilitated the economic exploitation of cocoa farmers by the British firms, whilst allowing representatives of chocolate manufacturers in Britain a degree of power in influencing farming practices. These unequal relations were lived out on a daily basis by male and female RFC representatives. Their personal contact with Nigerian men and women was an important element of the everyday connections between York and empire, which need to be re-established empirically and conceptually. An examination of the involvement of British firms in cocoa-producing colonies thus illuminates the gaps, discrepancies and omissions in the 'romance' of the industry espoused in popular and company discourse.

In the mythology of chocolate the power relations of production and consumption are subsumed by a more attractive narrative of exotic peoples and their surroundings, and by historical anecdote. Chocolate seems to generate a particular type of history writing – even in purportedly 'academic' texts – one which delves unashamedly into the realms of fantasy and romance. Writers eulogise their own relationship to chocolate, relating memories of childhood delight or adult indulgence. Yet this apparently harmless element of fun in writing of what is, after all, a luxury product for many consumers, masks the more sinister ideologies at work in most chocolate histories. Looking back to the ancient origins of cocoa, many historians have participated in a glorification of western 'exploration' and 'discovery'. The violence of imperial conquest seemingly has no place in the past of such a pleasurable commodity. Ancient civilisations are admired from the safe distance afforded by their extinction, a distance increased by tactics of exoticisation and even amusement at the seeming excesses and eccentricities of the people of the 'New World'. This is a gendered history in which women have little place except as markers of sexual excess or transgressive figures at the boundary of old and new worlds. The dissemination of chocolate is conceived as the achievement of men: Jesuit missionaries, friars, courtly taste-makers. Women are positioned early as consumers, yet men consume visibly in public spheres such as the chocolate houses, where consumption is inextricably linked to the 'worthy' pursuits of politics and literature.

Studying these chocolate mythologies, then, sheds light on some of the broader trends of history writing over the years. History penned by western male historians, with a vested interest in the institutions of imperialism, has too often rendered invisible the problematic of empire. The women historians of chocolate I have encountered, with the important recent exceptions of Sophie D. Coe, Catherine Hall and Gillian Wagner, have most often been working in a popular genre such as cookery books, where the history of cocoa is secondary and thus necessarily (for reasons of time and resources) draws on existing histories written by men.[117] History is here, as in so many other cases, bolstering and creating afresh dominant ideologies of race, class, gender and sexuality. The texts I have studied work to legitimise rather than destabilise existing power relations. Hopefully, by making visible the dynamics of gender and race at work in histories of chocolate and in the chocolate economy itself, I have fractured these implicitly imperialist, sexist and racist narratives. In particular, I want to give women a central place in this history, emphasising their significant contribution at all levels of the chocolate chain but without resorting to the sexualised, exoticised images of women employed in existing chocolate narratives. It is the experiences of the most undervalued group involved in this enterprise, the women cocoa farmers of the West Indies and West Africa (particularly Nigeria), which will be the focus of the following chapter.

[86]

Notes

1 As quoted in A. W. Knapp, *Cocoa and Chocolate: Their History from Plantation to Consumer* (London: Chapman and Hall, 1920), 5. Despite the scientific nature of his title, Whymper draws on tropes of romance and adventure to seduce the reader.

2 Wagner, *Chocolate Conscience*, 8. Wagner describes how the word chocolate itself comes from 'chocolath', which originally referred to a drink: 'lath' means water and 'choco' is likely to be an adaptation of 'cacuatl'.

3 Patricia Fara highlights the sexual and imperial politics behind Linnaeus's system. Fara, *Sex, Botany and Empire: The Story of Carl Linnaeus and Joseph Banks* (Cambridge: Icon Books, 2003).

4 Hall, 'Turning a blind eye', 31.

5 John A. West, 'A brief history and botany of cacao', in Nelson Foster and Linda S. Cordell (eds), *Chilies to Chocolate: Food the Americas Gave the World* (Tucson: University of Arizona Press, 1992), 105.

6 Morton and Morton, *Chocolate*; Walvin, *Fruits of Empire*. For a critique of the trend towards popular commodity histories, see Bruce Robbins, 'Commodity histories', *PMLA*, 120: 2 (March 2005), 454–63.

7 Sophie D. Coe and Michael D. Coe, *The True History of Chocolate* (London: Thames and Hudson, 1996), 12.

8 Susan Terrio has conducted a similar study of histories of chocolate in France. She demonstrates the continuing role of exoticised chocolate histories in creating the cultural context for luxury chocolate production by French chocolatiers. Terrio, *Crafting the Culture*.

9 West, 'A brief history', 106.

10 Knapp, *Cocoa and Chocolate*, 5.

11 West, 'A brief history', 106.

12 Walvin, *Fruits of Empire*, 89.

13 See, for example, Knapp, *Cocoa and Chocolate*, 8; Wagner, *Chocolate Conscience*, 8.

14 W. H. Prescott, *Conquest of Mexico* (1843), quoted in Knapp, *Cocoa and Chocolate*, 7.

15 Hall, 'Turning a blind eye', 34.

16 Knapp, *Cocoa and Chocolate*, 7; West, 'A brief history', 105.

17 Historicus, *Cocoa: All About It* (London: Sampson Low, Marston and Company, 1896), 40.

18 Wagner, *Chocolate Conscience*, 8.

19 Knapp, *Cocoa and Chocolate*, 10.

20 Walvin, *Fruits of Empire*, 90, 91, 93, 95.

21 See Wagner, *Chocolate Conscience*, 143.

22 West, 'A brief history', 110.

23 Knapp, *Cocoa and Chocolate*, 11.

24 Anon., 'The cocoa chain', *New Internationalist*, August 1998, 24.

25 West, 'A brief history', 116–17.

26 Cadbury World is situated close to the factory at Bournville. It opened in 1990. Hall, 'Turning a blind eye', 34.

27 McClintock, *Imperial Leather*, 24.

28 Walvin, *Fruits of Empire*, 90.

29 *Ibid.*, 94.

30 Wagner, *Chocolate Conscience*, 9.

31 Knapp, *Cocoa and Chocolate*, 12; Walvin, *Fruits of Empire*, 98.

32 Walvin, *Fruits of Empire*, 95.

33 J. Othick, 'The cocoa and chocolate industry in the nineteenth century', in Derek Oddy and Derek Miller (eds), *The Making of the Modern British Diet* (London: Croon Helm, 1976), 87. The Van Houten process allowed cocoa butter to be extracted from the cocoa bean.

34 West, 'A brief history', 113–14.

35 See, for example, *CWM*, Christmas 1932, 862.
36 These details are taken largely from Vernon, *Quaker Business Man*, 70–2. On Mary Tuke, see also Bennett Alan Weinberg and Bonnie K. Bealer, *The World of Caffeine* (London: Routledge, 2001), 174.
37 Fitzgerald, *Rowntree*, 514.
38 Southall, 'Cadbury on the Gold Coast', 130. The scandal will be discussed in more detail later in this chapter.
39 Fitzgerald notes that John Wilhelm Rowntree (son of Joseph Rowntree) was instrumental in arguing for the competitive advantage to be gained from owning estates. Fitzgerald, *Rowntree*, 515–16.
40 BI, Rowntree Company Archive, R/DF/P/3/5, 'Annual Reports, 1932. 1. Dominica'.
41 BI, Rowntree Company Archive, R/DF/PW/10, plan of Picard estate, Dominica, 1917.
42 BI, Rowntree Company Archive, R/DH/SC/1/2, correspondence regarding West Indian estates, 1899. The exact location of these estates is not clear from the correspondence.
43 BI, Rowntree Company Archive, R/DF/PW/22, agreements with overseers of estates in Jamaica.
44 BI, Rowntree Company Archive, R/DF/PW/22, 'Agreement with Hamilton Law McDonald', Clause 11.
45 BI, Rowntree Company Archive, R/DF/P/3/5, 'Report on J. B. Morrell's Visit to Dominica: November 2 to December 24, 1929', 4, 14.
46 *CWM*, February 1904, 147.
47 BI, Rowntree Company Archive, R/DF/PW/22, 'Agreement with Hamilton Law McDonald', Clause 4b. See also, BI, Rowntree Company Archive, R/DF/PW/10, plan of the Picard estate, 1917.
48 *CWM*, May 1904, 26.
49 BI, Rowntree Company Archive, R/DF/P/3/3, 'Report for Year 1926 on Dominica Estates', 16, 6.
50 BI, Rowntree Company Archive, R/DF/P/3/5, letter from Solicitor's Department to Mr H. Giles re. Transfer of Dominica estates to Messrs Rose & Co. Ltd on 23 April 1934.
51 BI, Rowntree Company Archive, R/BY/2/1, K. Haslinger, 'A Report on Flavour Cocoas', March–April 1958.
52 *Ibid.*
53 BI, Rowntree Company Archive, R/DF/P/20, D. H. Urquhart, 'Prospects of the Growing of Cocoa in the British Solomon Islands', 1951.
54 For an excellent, detailed study of the scandal, see Lowell J. Satre, *Chocolate on Trial: Slavery, Politics and the Ethics of Business* (Athens: Ohio University Press, 2005). The historical details in the following paragraphs are taken from this work.
55 Vernon, *Quaker Business Man*, 176; Fitzgerald, *Rowntree*, 107; Satre, *Chocolate on Trial*, 27–8.
56 BI, Rowntree Company Archive, R/DF/P/8, J. B. Morrell, 'Export of Cocoa from the Various Cocoa Producing Countries', no date, 17. Morrell was quoting from *Chisholm's Commercial Geography* (1894).
57 Hall, 'Turning a blind eye', 44.
58 Knapp, *Cocoa and Chocolate*, 104.
59 Satre notes that Cadbury may have delayed the boycott until they were able to guarantee other sources of cocoa beans. Satre, *Chocolate on Trial*, 147, also 258–9 (footnote 115).
60 See John Miles, 'Rural protest in the Gold Coast: the cocoa hold-ups, 1908–1938', in Clive Dewey and A. G. Hopkins (eds), *The Imperial Impact: Studies in the Economic History of Africa and India* (London: Athlone Press, 1978), 153.
61 'The cocoa chain', 24.
62 See Sara S. Berry, 'The concept of innovation and the history of cocoa farming in western Nigeria', *Journal of African History*, 15: 1 (1974), 83–95; A. G. Hopkins, 'Innovation in a colonial context: African origins of the Nigerian cocoa-farming industry, 1880–1920', in Dewey and Hopkins (eds), *The Imperial Impact*, 83–96.

63 Stewart, *Jute and Empire*, 24.
64 The Lagos Creoles were Yoruba slaves who had been freed by the British while in transit, settled in Sierra Leone and given a British education. Hopkins, 'Innovation in a colonial context', 88.
65 Fitzgerald, *Rowntree*, 513.
66 BI, Rowntree Company Archive, R/BY/2/1, K. Haslinger, 'A Report on Flavour Cocoas', March–April 1958, 2.
67 BI, Rowntree Company Archive, R/DD/SA/27, 'The Romance of the Cocoa Bean', August 1944, 3.
68 In 1927, Terry's had purchased an estate from a widow in Venezuela (indicating the significant, yet largely unacknowledged, role of women in the industry). BI, Terry's Company Archive, Box 27.
69 BI, Rowntree Company Archive, R/BY/2/1, K. Haslinger, 'A Report on Flavour Cocoas', March–April 1958, 2.
70 At least, this was the assumption. The Ghanaian cocoa producers demonstrated their own power to resist exploitation in the name of colonialism by withholding cocoa, particularly in the late 1930s. See Miles, 'Rural protest in the Gold Coast'.
71 See BI, Rowntree Company Archive, R/DH/SC/71, for papers relating to the formation of the Nigerian branch.
72 See Southall, 'Cadbury on the Gold Coast', 249–50.
73 The archives contain records of the buildings, railway sidings and so on which were on lease to RFC. They tended to be leased rather than bought as Nigerians retained their ownership of land during colonial rule. See BI, Rowntree Company Archive, R/DH/R/59–60.
74 BI, Rowntree Company Archive, R/DF/P/3/2, 'Cocoa Manufacturers Ltd. Report for Year Ending September 30th, 1930', 9.
75 Mr J. F. Blitz (Purchasing Department), 'Impressions of Nigeria', *CWM*, Autumn 1953, 11.
76 BI, Rowntree Company Archive, R/DF/P/3/2, 'Cocoa Manufacturers Ltd. Report for Year Ending September 30th, 1930', 9.
77 University of Birmingham, Cadbury Papers, no. 274, A. O. Iredale, 'Report on Visit to Nigeria, November–December 1924'. For analyses of the complex roles, experiences and beliefs of white women in the colonies see Hilary Callan and Shirley Ardener (eds), *The Incorporated Wife* (London: Croon Helm, 1984); Helen Callaway, *Gender, Culture and Empire: European Women in Colonial Nigeria* (Basingstoke: Macmillan Press, 1987). See also chapter four on women from Rowntree who worked in the empire.
78 BI, Rowntree Company Archive, CML/Misc 1, plan for Owo Bungalow, c.1950.
79 Anthony D. King, *The Bungalow: The Production of a Global Culture* (London: Routledge and Kegan Paul, 1984), 215.
80 Although, as King observes, building patterns also reflected trends in housing in Britain according to the class background of the colonial officials. *Ibid.*, 209.
81 *CWM*, August 1953, 11.
82 BI, Rowntree Company Archive, CML/F/3/8, Accounts ledger for October 1938–March 1941.
83 Southall, 'Cadbury on the Gold Coast', 249–50, 128.
84 R. Galletti, K. D .S. Baldwin, and I. O. Dina, *Nigerian Cocoa Farmers: An Economic Survey of Yoruba Cocoa Farming Families* (Oxford: Oxford University Press, 1956), 40.
85 *BWM*, April 1950, 97.
86 Galletti, Baldwin and Dina, *Nigerian Cocoa Farmers*, 220.
87 Miles, 'Rural protest in the Gold Coast', 155.
88 *Ibid.*, 158.
89 There had been earlier hold-ups but not on such a large scale. Nigerian farmers, however, do not appear to have taken part. See chapter three for a more in-depth analysis of the cocoa hold-ups.

90 David Meredith believes that the wartime arrangements were 'simply a continuation' of the pre-war buying 'pool'. Meredith, 'The Colonial Office, British business
interests and the reform of cocoa marketing in West Africa, 1937–1945', *Journal
of African History*, 29 (1988), 298.
91 Nigeria was not directly governed by the British from London, and the country
maintained its own government. However, the Colonial Officials stationed there
clearly exercised a great deal of power.
92 Meredith, 'The Colonial Office', 297.
93 *Ibid.*, 298.
94 J. Young (Purchasing Department), 'Cocoa – Food of the Gods', *CWM*, Spring 1960,
13.
95 See Ezekiel Ayodele Walker, 'Structural change, the oil boom and the cocoa economy of southwestern Nigeria, 1973–1980s', *Journal of Modern African Studies*,
38: 1 (2000), 77.
96 Walker argues that funds were misdirected. He also highlights the massive impact
of the oil industry. *Ibid.* See also chapter three.
97 Young, 'Cocoa – Food of the Gods', *CWM*, Spring 1960, 13.
98 Blitz, 'Impressions of Nigeria', *CWM*, Autumn 1953, 11.
99 Hall suggests a similar trend at Cadbury. Hall, 'Turning a blind eye', 45.
100 Knapp, *Cocoa and Chocolate*, 114.
101 BI, Rowntree Company Archive, R/DD/SA/27, 'The Romance of the Cocoa Bean',
August 1944, 2.
102 *Ibid.*
103 Knapp, *Cocoa and Chocolate*, 28–9.
104 *Ibid.*, 25.
105 *Ibid.*, 17.
106 Attempts to establish 'model' cocoa plantations run by white planters in West Africa
were expensive and unsuccessful. See Austin, 'Mode of production or mode of
cultivation', 154–75.
107 Knapp, *Cocoa and Chocolate*, 48. Knapp's description is echoed in the *CWM*,
where women are described gathering cocoa pods on the Rowntree estates: 'Deftly
lifting the baskets on to their heads, they trip through the trees, and tumble the
pods on to the heap.' *CWM*, March 1923, 172.
108 BI, Rowntree Company Archive, R/DD/SA/27, 'The Romance of the Cocoa Bean',
August 1944, 2.
109 Cadbury UK, 050/003163, photographs from Trinidad and West Africa; *CWM*, March
1923, 172. See chapter four for a more detailed analysis of photographs of cocoa
workers.
110 BI, Rowntree Company Archive, R/DF/P/20, Urquhart, 'Prospects of the Growing
of Cacao', 1951, 7. This report was published by and for Cadbury.
111 Blitz, 'Impressions of Nigeria', *CWM*, Autumn 1953, 10.
112 Paul Bareau, *Cocoa: A Crop with a Future* (Bournville: Cadbury Brothers, 1953),
10, 13.
113 NNA, CSO26, 36148/S.140, Captain Haig, 'Proposals for the Reorganisation of the
Nigerian Cocoa Industry by the Registrar of Cooperative Societies, 1944–45',
33–4.
114 The Cocoa Chocolate and Confectionery Alliance, 'Report of the Cocoa
Conference Held at Grosvenor House, London, W.1.' (London: 1957), 299.
115 BI, Rowntree Company Archive, R/DF/P/22, 'Report of Preparatory Meeting on Cocoa
Research 29th–30th January, 1964', 60.
116 NNA, CSO 26, 26298/S.10, 'Establishment of Young Farmers' Clubs in Schools',
1934, 1, 6.
117 See for example Chantal Coady, *Chocolate: The Food of the Gods* (London:
Pavilion Books, 1993).

CHAPTER THREE

'There is no operation involved with cocoa that I didn't do':[1] women's experiences of cocoa farming

> I went to the cocoa farm first on a day my parents were harvesting. They told me to break a cocoa pod and drink the juice. It was very sweet so I picked interest in going to cocoa farm. (Grace)[2]

Alice's assertion (in the title of this chapter) of her complete engagement with the tasks on the cocoa farm should be read in the context of studies, and general assertions, which would deny her place in the history of the industry. Studies of Nigerian cocoa production (at least, those written in English) almost invariably invoke the figure of the cocoa farmer as male. Official documents of the colonial period refer to cocoa farmers implicitly as men, seeing no need to even consider the question of women cocoa farmers. More recently, a variety of secondary literature has openly concluded that women did not farm cocoa in Nigeria. Women are either made invisible or their labour is devalued as 'just' harvesting and transport. This neglect of women's experiences in western-produced narratives, coupled with the direct involvement of the York-based Rowntree firm in the Nigerian cocoa industry, prompted me to conduct my own research into the experiences of Nigerian women.

The main body of this chapter therefore deals in some detail with the ways in which Nigerian women have been active agents in the cocoa industry and what this has meant to them. My analysis is based on fifteen interviews conducted with older women cocoa farmers. Most of these women were in their sixties, which places their earliest experiences of farming in the 1940s, although some of the older women would have been farming as children in the 1930s. Although it was not possible to determine whether cocoa produced by these women and their families had once been bought directly by Rowntree, the firm's buying agents had been active in the regions of Ibadan and Ondo in which they lived. Their experiences of farming may therefore help us to understand the lives of women who did indeed farm cocoa for use in Rowntree products. These testimonies will be considered alongside documents held in the Nigerian National Archives at the University of Ibadan and a critique of the secondary literature.

Whilst my research certainly does not constitute a representative survey of women in Nigeria, it will put women at the forefront of its analysis. Rather than reproducing the relational analyses of women's quantitative contributions to the farms in comparison with men's, I will study women as farmers in their own right. I discuss the ways in which the particular circumstances of cocoa farming in Nigeria, particularly the colonial context, have had an impact on Nigerian women. Moreover, I consider how they have actively carved out their own roles within the developing cash crop economy. Although the scope of my fieldwork was necessarily limited, I hope that it provides a way into a transnational analysis of women at different stages in the production of cocoa: handling the raw material in Nigeria and transforming this into Rowntree-branded confectionery in Britain. More broadly, I explore how an analysis of cocoa production demands recognition of the intersections between capitalism, patriarchy and colonialism, and the effects of such structures on women's lives.

Before the establishment of the West African industry, women in South and Central America, and in the Caribbean, were already involved in diverse ways in the production and sale of cocoa to the western market. Again, there has been relatively little research in this area, with the exception of some important recent publications by Caribbean Studies scholars. In the opening section of this chapter, I draw on these secondary sources to provide an overview of what is currently known about the lives of some of the earliest women cocoa farmers. The work of women in the British West Indies in particular will provide an important historical background as well as a comparative perspective to the work of women in Nigeria. Taking up the theme from chapter two, I want to challenge assumptions about the cocoa farmer, revealing the politics behind seemingly valueless evocations of this gendered figure.[3]

Women and cocoa production in the West Indies

From slavery to indentured labour

As indigenous Amerindians, as African slaves and as indentured Indian migrants, women's labour has been exploited in the interests of cocoa production in the Caribbean.[4] From the late fifteenth century, the introduction of cash crop farming to the region had a serious impact on the lives of the declining indigenous population, curtailing their shifting agricultural practices due to enforced demands on both land and labour. Indra Harry notes a gendered division of tasks in these early cocoa estates, whereby women were involved in the 'secondary' though clearly crucial tasks of harvesting.[5] By the late eighteenth century, however, cocoa was being produced by predominantly African slave labour.

Existing analyses of the slave production of cocoa provide little detailed insight into women's experiences. Harry can only suggest that 'most likely women worked alongside their male counterparts' on coffee and cocoa plantations.[6] Describing the slave population on the cocoa estates of Venezuela, William Gervase Clarence-Smith points out that 'women and children were valued for weeding and processing'. In Brazil, women, children and older slaves were apparently seen as particularly suited to the tasks of cocoa farming, with the result that elite planters bought more female than male slaves in the nineteenth century.[7] However, general research on the organisation of labour on slave plantations in the British West Indies has concluded that men and women were given tasks according to strength rather than sex, being treated solely as units of production. Under the slave system, women will have played a key part in cocoa farming.[8]

In response to fears over the impending emancipation of slave labour from the early nineteenth century, plantation owners brought over workers from India on fixed contracts to work the sugar, coffee and cocoa plantations. The practice of indenture continued until 1917, with the termination of all contracts in 1921. By 1901, there were 218 Indian women and 481 Indian men working on cocoa estates in Trinidad.[9] Rowntree themselves employed 100 'East Indian Coolies' (seventy-five men and twenty-five women) on their West Indian estates in 1904. However, a report in 1908 confirmed that their Vinery estate employed no indentured labourers but only those who were '"free" or time-expired'.[10] Reddock sees a shifting sexual division of labour in the Caribbean as both 'concurrent with and related to [the] ethnic division of labour' caused by the arrival of indentured labourers. According to her research, Indian workers predominated in the sugar industry and African workers were still in the majority in cocoa and coconut production. Unfortunately she does not elaborate as to how gender and race intersected in the division of tasks according to sex.[11] As mentioned in chapter two, official photographs of cocoa farming in the West Indies, for Rowntree and for Cadbury, show women engaged in the 'lighter' tasks of cocoa farming, such as removing and sorting cocoa beans from the pods. Indian women feature regularly in such images. This tells us more about the fascination with exotic 'coolie' women, however, than about the proportions of African and Indian women on the estates. Rowntree estates employed just twenty-five Indian women in 1904, compared to 178 'Negro' women.[12]

Tasks and conditions for women

Although scholars disagree over the causes and precise time-scale, most conclude that in the post-emancipation Caribbean there has been an increased demarcation of gender roles in agricultural production.[13] Phillips Lewis has found a stricter gender divide on the cocoa estates than on the sugar plantations, although this became less marked for those women able to command status in the industry as estate owners or cocoa dealers.[14] It would be impossible to reach any conclusions here as to how and why certain tasks became assigned as men's or women's work; indeed, there is evidence that in practice the division could become blurred. Nevertheless, it is useful to outline which tasks were broadly defined as men's and women's work on the cocoa estates of the twentieth century. Varied written accounts (supported by photographic evidence) suggest that women were employed to remove cocoa beans from the pods, spread out the beans to dry, and polish them. Meanwhile, male workers took care of the cocoa trees: clearing the forest and planting new trees, weeding and pruning. Men would also harvest and break the pods. Both men and women would 'dance' the cocoa, to remove excess pulp. Children – girls and boys – could be employed in tasks such as catching beetles and sifting cocoa.[15] It was common for whole families to be employed by the estate in this way, with basic living accommodation provided close to the site. In 1902, the *CWM* reported forty 'coolies' living in single room barracks on the Vinery estate in Jamaica, with a number of 'negroes' living either in the barracks or in cottages.[16]

As day labourers or as resident labourers on estates in Trinidad in the early twentieth century, women would be working full time from seven o'clock in the morning until five in the evening, with a lunch break from twelve until twelve-thirty. In addition, they had responsibility for producing and preparing food and providing other services such as healthcare for their families and neighbours. From evidence given to the West India Royal Commission in the late 1930s, Phillips Lewis records that women worked, on average, two and a half to three days a week on cocoa production. Other sources, as illustrated below, suggest that women could work between five and six days. These disparities may be due to seasonal fluctuations, with women working more hours during harvest time, but also to women choosing to spend more time producing their own crops for domestic and commercial use. For a day's work in 1920, women might receive thirty to thirty-five cents. Wages were essentially set according to gender and age, although most estates allocated pay with reference to the task completed. Men earned the most at fifty to sixty cents per day in 1920; children earned fifteen to thirty cents. Men employed on task work, rather than day rates, could increase their income still further. Deductions would then be made for rent, food rations and other amenities on the estates, at equal rates for men and women.[17]

A Wages Committee Report from 1920 offers a brief but fascinating insight into the lives of two individual women workers on the Henry estate: Princess Wallace and Kalapdayee. Both women were married and Princess Wallace had three children aged between six and fifteen. Reddock summarises the findings from the report:

> Princess Wallace ... did gathering, weeding, and general work and earned 30c a day; her husband earned 50c, her eldest son 30. Before January 1920 she earned 25c a day ...; she worked six days a week. She provided her own hoe and cutlass and used one of each per year. She also kept eight fowls, and was a member of a Friendly Society to which she paid 1s (25c) per month. ... Kalapdayee, was employed ... as a daily labourer. She gathered and broke cocoa and earned 30c daily, by day or task work. Her husband earned 60c a day. She worked five or six days a week depending on the availability of work and had to provide two cutlasses and one hoe each year. In addition she worked with her husband on a cocoa contract and grew vegetables. (Wages Committee Report, 1920: pp. xxxi–ii)[18]

Research on cocoa farming in the second half of the twentieth century found weeding and cutlassing on cocoa estates to be men's work.[19] Yet here we see two women engaged in these tasks, even providing their own cutlasses. The Herskovitses also described women weeding with cutlasses in their study, *Trinidad Village*: 'women bring out the young plants, weed them, pick and dry the pods, take out the beans from the pods and with hoe or cutlass cut away the weeds that choke the trees'.[20] Such primary sources are crucial in presenting women's significant roles in the post-slavery cocoa industry. There is clear evidence of a gendered division of tasks but also elements of cooperation and suggestions of the limitations of models that assign certain tools exclusively to male labourers.

Reddock notes that in the 1920 Wages Committee survey, the number of women listed as paid employees on plantations was substantially lower than that of men. This is partly linked to the decreasing numbers of women working in agriculture that Reddock observes during the period 1898–1931. However, similar to staff lists at the Rowntree factory in York, women often do not feature due to their position as seasonal labourers; local and familial connections to chocolate production allowed for complex patterns of labour. As Reddock comments, 'The practice of housing labourers on or near the estates facilitated the involvement of the entire family during crop time and the dismissal of women and children for the rest of the year during which they worked on their own fields.' Where men took on long-term contracts in cocoa production in the West Indies, women could also contribute their unpaid labour.[21]

Working on an estate became increasingly problematic for some men and women, who wished to distance themselves from such wage labour. Reddock suggests that this was achieved in a number of ways: 'First by moving off the estate land, then by withdrawing wives from direct wage-work in the fields or the factory, then withdrawing children from field labour.' Yet Reddock also notes that the estates, and waged work in factories, offered many women a degree of independence which they valued, although they aspired to a very different life for their own children.[22] African women continued to work on cocoa estates in the nineteenth and twentieth centuries. However, the number of African Caribbean women in formal agricultural employment declined during the twentieth century and large numbers migrated to the cities.[23]

After the Second World War, there were attempts to revive the West Indian cocoa industry through the Cocoa Rehabilitation Scheme, with some success. Women were still present on the estates in the 1950s, working predominantly on picking the cocoa beans. They were paid by the day, rather than on the volume picked, earning approximately '70–85 cents, whereas workers on task-rate earned an average of $1.50–$3.00 during a six- to seven-hour day'. As plantations regained their dominance in food production over peasant farms, women looked elsewhere for work, including as unpaid family labour on the cocoa estates.[24] According to Momsen, women increasingly came to see themselves as a 'reserve' labour force, employed at times of seasonal and longer-term shortages.[25]

Independent production on small farms

Although the history of cocoa in the Caribbean has tended to focus on plantation and estate agriculture controlled by European planters (in contrast to the success of the small holders of West Africa), cocoa was also produced on small farms and estates owned by former slaves and indentured labourers. By 1931, there were 41,656 acres of land devoted to smallholdings.[26] Caribbean historians have demonstrated the need to value fully women's labour in cocoa production in this context, rather than seeing it solely as 'helping out' male farmers.[27] Although women have, at times strategically, supported a gendered

division of labour, particularly with reference to the dangerous practice of crop-spraying, and have themselves hired male labourers where
necessary, there is evidence that in practice women would undertake
the same tasks as men.[28] In Guyana, for example, Olive Senior found
that, 'A male farmer expressed a common viewpoint when he said,
"when there is a push, the woman does work equal and straight with
me" . . . although the task itself would remain sex-stereotyped.'[29] This
pragmatic approach, as we shall see, was a feature of the narratives
of Nigerian women farmers.

Labour on the farms was not perceived by Caribbean women as
detached from their other duties in terms of childcare or housework.
As Barrow describes, 'Income generation is an essential component
of being a mother, grandmother, wife or daughter.'[30] Whereas for
many female chocolate workers in York, at least in the period after
marriage and children, women would narrate their 'decision' to return
to work, there appears to have been no such conscious choice for women
cocoa farmers. Even so, some women appear to have relished their work
rather more than others. Harry found that, 'To a large extent, women
farm out of necessity in Trinidad. Unlike Guyanese women . . . and
Vincentians . . . , few respondents had a great love for this occupation.'[31]
Indeed, this could be one reason why Harry found such a firm gendered division of labour in her research; women were refusing to be
drawn into tasks defined as 'men's work'. Certainly, Barrow notes a
remarkable degree of equality in relation to women's access to land
and resources but finds that gender differences arise from the different
place farming has in women's lives as a whole.[32]

Free African Caribbean and Indian women engaged in cocoa farming on their own account from an early stage, despite difficulties in
gaining access to and maintaining land. Phillips Lewis notes that women
were already owners of valuable estates in the period 1870–71, years
before laws were passed in Britain allowing married women to own
property. By 1905, women owned fifty-one of 635 cocoa estates in
Trinidad. Some of these had been inherited; others were purchased
using savings or were bought jointly with husbands (although single
women apparently outnumbered married/widowed women as pro-
prietors until the 1970s).[33] Drawing on oral testimonies, Shaheeda
Hosein has emphasised the significance of land ownership for Indian
women migrants and their daughters in Trinidad. Hosein's important
research demonstrates how land provided a way to independence and
to status for both men and women within the Indian community. One
interviewee recalled how her mother had bought cocoa lands in 1917
and had then continued to invest in both land and production:

My mother first buy seven acres of land in Sangre Grande. . . . That was cocoa land that she start to work for sheself. In the 1930s, . . . she start to rent 100 acres from the Mendez Estate, a cocoa estate in north Manzanilla. She eventually buy the 100 acres from the owners [. . .] she give plenty people work on the cocoa.[34]

Whilst this woman was clearly exceptional in the high standing she achieved in her community, Hosein offers a number of individual stories of women's success through acquiring land, often cocoa-producing land.

The cocoa industry was a significant presence in such women's lives, providing work, a home and, for some, independence and wealth. Research on small farmers in the Caribbean in the second half of the twentieth century suggests that cocoa has re-emerged as a significant crop for both men and women. In a survey from 1982, cocoa was the primary crop of just over 26 per cent of women farmers, and the second crop, again, of just over 26 per cent of women.[35] However, Phillips Lewis has found that there have been gender differences in patterns of land ownership and estate management, with women tending to sell off large, multiple estates, particularly where they are geographically scattered, and to consolidate holdings within a local area.[36]

It is clear that women have had crucial and often diverse roles in the cocoa-farming industry in the British West Indies. Shepherd emphasises the extent of women's involvement in Trinidadian production:

Women of several ethnic groups were involved in all sectors of the cocoa industry as labourers, contractors, own-account peasant farmers, large-scale farmers and employers and exploiters of labourers. They were produce dealers and intermediaries in the marketing process, sometimes filling more than one of these roles at the same time.[37]

As we shall see, connections can be made between women cocoa farmers in the West Indies and West Africa in terms of the extent and nature of their involvement in the trade. Barrow stresses that 'the Caribbean woman has much in common with her traditional African counterpart' in conceptualising 'income generation' as an integral part of her familial roles.[38] More detailed comparative research is needed to further explore these links and the ways in which cocoa production has been gendered in both regions. However, as Momsen points out in a critique of Ester Boserup, similarities between the experiences of African Caribbean and African women should not be read as the product of slave memories of the gendered organisation of labour in Africa. The experiences of slave labour on the plantations would have ruptured any such continuity. Indeed, the cocoa industry itself moved from the Caribbean to West Africa, undermining any attempt to create a linear narrative of 'memory'. According to Momsen, gender roles under a free labour system were defined in the specific local and historical context: based on family relationships and, to some extent, the nature of the product itself, and not according to African traditions.[39] The invocation by Barrow of a 'traditional African counterpart' is thus problematic both in creating a solely African ancestry for Caribbean women and in asserting a stable, homogenous, version of African women and their working lives.

Gender and perceptions of cocoa farming in West Africa

Academic discourses of gender and development

Western academic narratives of the transition to cash cropping in Nigeria have long tended to exclude women, citing men (whether African or European) as the main historical actors behind every innovation. Where scholars have paid attention to the gendering of work on cocoa farms, their conclusion is most often that women have been excluded from, or at best have opted out of, the key tasks. The debate then turns to whether colonial or indigenous patriarchy should be held to account. Ester Boserup, for example, perceives commercial agriculture to be a male domain, largely as a consequence of the gendered assumptions of the European colonialists.[40] This emphasis solely on western patriarchal ideologies in enforcing gendered roles has since been questioned. Benería and Sen argue that the increased dominance of commercial cropping over subsistence farming 'was a product not of European patriarchal culture, but of the process of capital accumulation. Thus, women's loss of status results from the interweaving of class relations and gender relations.'[41] Although this is clearly a more sophisticated analysis on one level, it still relegates women to the subsistence sector and locates a lack of status in the exclusion of women from the public domain of international trade.[42] Benería and Sen's notion of a 'loss of status' sets up a model in which women become disadvantaged in the modern, capitalist, rather than traditional world. The complexities of women's lives and of the tensions and intersections between the traditional and modern are therefore lost.[43] In this argument, women's role in commercial agriculture is solely in their continuing provision of food and childcare, indirectly allowing men more time to work on cash crops.

Guyer also shifts attention away from the interventions of the patriarchal colonialists in the organisation of agricultural labour. However, she concludes that farming had always been a predominantly male task for the Yoruba and that the gendered division of labour in cocoa farming reflected continuity rather than change. So, rather than viewing the availability of hired male labour amongst the Yoruba as 'compensating for the lack of female labour', she points to sources which 'mention that hired labour and female labour are not directly interchangeable'. Although she does at least recognise that women contribute their labour, she does not fully explain the ways in which they do so. Instead, she makes the general observation that 'women's indigenous obligation to supply harvest, processing, and transport labour was extended to include cocoa without change in definitions of the division of labour'. Guyer uses women's 'traditional' roles in the family to downplay their important part in the 'modern' cocoa industry.[44]

Whilst stressing continuity in women's obligations to provide certain kinds of labour on the farm, Guyer does recognise that women exercised some degree of agency. Migrant women, for example, were apparently 'more willing' to help their husbands in setting up a new farm than women living 'under settled conditions'. Her recognition of women's choices at this stage of farming is in contrast to her assertion of women's obligations to help in harvesting and it is unclear whether she believes women are excluded from the cocoa industry, or whether they are 'opting out' in pursuit of their own enterprises. She certainly suggests that women's ability to earn an independent income is helped by the sexual division of labour in cocoa farming, in which men do the majority of the work.[45] Although this makes an important point in suggesting how women may strategically support a division of labour by sex, Guyer continues to undervalue women's importance to cocoa farming.

Re-evaluating women's labour

In contrast to the majority of existing research on Nigeria, there has been a move over the last twenty years to re-assess Ghanaian women's labour in cocoa farming. Benjamin Asare, Gwendolyn Mikell, Christine Okali and Dorothy Vellenga, for instance, have all documented the situation of women in the cocoa industry in Ghana.[46] Working against the pervasive discourse of women as absent from cocoa farming, these academics provide unambiguous recognition of the important role women have had to play. As Mikell writes, 'Rural women, like their male counterparts, had been involved in the cocoa industry from its inception. Indeed, cocoa farming would not have been possible without the labor of wives and children.'[47] Likewise, Grier asserts that 'female labor played a central role in almost every aspect of cocoa production and sale'. She stresses:

From the very beginning, the labor of women and girls was critical to the production of cocoa. Studies of the organization of cocoa production in the 1930s and 1940s point to female labor as the main source of permanent labor. In the labor-intensive processes of establishing a cocoa farm (clearing the virgin forest, planting the cocoa seeds or seedlings, and intercropping with food crops), of weeding the farm, of harvesting, drying and fermenting the beans, and of conveying the dried beans to the nearest market center, the labor of women and girls predominated.[48]

Such bold and clear statements are vital in the context of confusion over, if not refusal to acknowledge, women's role in cocoa farming.

Ghana has always produced more cocoa than Nigeria, thus stimulating greater academic interest.[49] The matrilineal system in some areas also facilitated the independent ownership of farms by women and has therefore been an ideal starting point for challenging the relegation of women to 'temporary' tasks.[50] Yet many of the observations regarding Ghanaian women also apply to Nigerian women, as I demonstrate in the rest of this chapter. Unfortunately, finding written sources to support the thesis that women in Nigeria are active producers of cocoa is fraught, partly due to the unstable political environment there in recent years. The most comprehensive study of cocoa farming in the country remains that by Galletti, Baldwin and Dina.[51] Completed in the 1950s, it perpetuates many of the racist ideologies held at the time regarding the 'native' farmers. Nevertheless, the sheer extent of this study, and the fact that it has at least recognised the role of women in the cocoa economy of the Yoruba people, makes it indispensable, if to be used with caution.

Julian Clarke is one of the few more recent scholars to challenge the received wisdom of Nigerian cocoa farming as a male domain. He believes that women made an 'increasingly impressive contribution' to agriculture and in particular to the production of cash crops, although he goes on to observe that 'the most noticeable alteration in the position of women was a massive move into small and medium scale trading operations'. Clarke, in contrast to Guyer, questions assertions of continuity in the organisation of labour, claiming that 'cocoa production emerged within a new structure of production. . . . both as the result of the breakdown of the large households and as one of the primary conditions of the immense growth of production levels during the colonial period.' He sees Yoruba women becoming 'increasingly involved in the various labour processes' of cocoa production, 'at least partially because of the increasing unavailability of dependent male labour'.[52] I now turn to the narratives of individual cocoa-farming women to consider the impact of this involvement on themselves and their local communities.

[101]

Women on the cocoa farm: a complex picture

The interviewees

My oral history research in Nigeria was necessarily conducted under very different conditions from those governing my research with York-based women. In York I was able to draw on family and other local connections in finding interviewees but in Nigeria I was dependent on the assistance of local organisations to make contact with women in rural areas. Even more than usual, this became a collaborative project and I am indebted to two non-governmental organisations for setting up and helping to conduct the interviews. Five women were interviewed in the villages of Agbebo and Esioye near Ibadan with the help of male representatives from the Farmers Development Union (FADU); ten interviews were then organised and carried out in Bamikemo village in Ondo state through Enterprise for Development International (EfDI).[53] Both organisations were involved in providing loans to Nigerian farmers, as well as funding education projects, and two women mentioned their participation in FADU training schemes. My translator for the Bamikemo interviews, Wunmi, had previously been involved in EfDI research in this area and was known to some of the people in the village. As a young woman with family connections to the cocoa industry, she appeared to have a good rapport with women in the village. Such existing connections were invaluable to me in putting people at ease. However, they were also clearly structuring the interview process in subtle ways. The research usually conducted by these organisations has a clear development aim and my project was often presented in the same mould.

The necessity of a translator and constraints on the amount of time we could spend with each interviewee required me to construct a detailed questionnaire for use in the interviews, rather than relying on a more fluid approach. Topics included childhood, married life and childcare, as well as domestic and farming work. By using a broad range of questions I hoped to gain a rounded sense of women's lives, rather than simply their cocoa-farming activities. This was an attempt to replicate as far as possible the life history approach I adopted when interviewing women in York, though in a more structured, often frustratingly linear form.

Questions in an early draft of the questionnaire clearly revealed my Eurocentric assumptions about notions of children and family. For example, the question, 'Did you work for your parents as a child?' was seen as almost offensive by representatives of EfDI, as it was unthinkable that Nigerian children would not have worked for their parents. I thus changed my question to, 'What kind of work did you do for your parents?' However, I also had to assert the need to keep certain questions in, as my colleagues had their own preconceptions about women's role in cocoa farming which made them see certain questions as irrelevant. The questionnaire therefore underwent many changes: from consulting with people at EfDI, from my own experiences after the initial five interviews with FADU, from the alterations made by Wunmi and our subsequent compromises, and from my final additions after our first day's interviewing at Bamikemo.

The following findings are based predominantly on the ten interviews conducted in Bamikemo village in Ondo state. Ondo has long been the main cocoa-producing region in Nigeria, with a greater proportion of the population involved than elsewhere. Bamikemo is a large village of approximately 18,000 people, situated about eighty kilometres from the town of Akure. The women interviewed there were all of the Yoruba tribe, six of them were Christian and four were Muslim. They varied in ages from thirty to seventy, with the majority in their sixties, and one woman answered the questionnaire on behalf of her mother who was out on the cocoa farm.[54] Probably in response to my request to speak to women cocoa farmers, most of the women did indeed own farms. However, one woman worked solely on her husband's land. These interviews were more indepth than those recorded near Ibadan and were, with one exception, carried out by Wunmi and myself.[55] Although the interviews often took place in the presence of friends and family (usually children and other women), these were essentially one-to-one interviews rather than the family and group interviews conducted by FADU. It was only in the interview with the daughter of a female cocoa farmer that some of the younger men of the village took an active interest.

Before I look in detail at the practice of cocoa farming by women, I will explore more broadly some of the factors, such as age, marital status and geographical location, which may structure women's experiences. These were not always relevant for the women I spoke with but it is crucial to recognise potential differences between women and the different experiences individuals might have within the life cycle.

Regional difference

The sheer size of Nigeria, coupled with the number of different tribes and variety of cultures, means that generalisations are problematic.[56] Cocoa is farmed mainly in the south-west. As already discussed, my research focused on Bamikemo village in Ondo, although I also conducted interviews in two villages in Oyo state. It was certainly not difficult to find women involved in cocoa farming in these particular areas. However, my findings are not based on a random sample and should not be read as typical, though they will have relevance for some women in other cocoa-farming areas.

I did not conduct enough interviews in the Ibadan region to draw any conclusions about regional differences from Ondo state. Galletti, Baldwin and Dina's survey suggests some regional disparities, with women in Ondo spending more time on cocoa farming than those in Ibadan.[57] This is possibly due to the urban character of Ibadan, which may have encouraged greater involvement in trading. But it may also have been due to the researchers simply using different criteria to determine women's involvement. As Dixon-Mueller observes:

> whether women in farm families are defined as economically active or inactive depends in part on a necessarily arbitrary decision as to where the household ends and the farm begins, in spatial terms, or where housework ends and production begins, in economic terms.[58]

Still, even from Galletti, Baldwin and Dina's statistics, women appear to have been involved to some extent in every cocoa-producing area.

Statistics undoubtedly underestimate the role of women. Galletti, Baldwin and Dina state that women in Ondo spent only 6.3 per cent of their total working hours on the cocoa farm, whilst those in Ibadan spent the least percentage (0.4 per cent) of their time farming cocoa. The regional difference between the men in these areas is negligible (28.7 per cent and 28.2 per cent respectively). Whilst the percentage of women's time spent on farming cocoa is fairly low, it should be remembered that the survey found that women spent more hours working than men overall, 'mainly because they have to attend to the house as well as to their business in the markets and on the farms. Many . . . regularly exceed fifty hours in the week.'[59] However, there is not the same understanding for women as there is for men that there are 'difficulties . . . in allocating the labour time and cash expenses of farmers, who might in the course of a day work intermittently on cocoa and food farms'.[60] Despite the limitations of this study, there is at least a recognition that some women do engage independently in cocoa farming. In Ondo, for example, 'women . . . cultivate crops of their own and have cocoa farms of their own more often than in other areas'.[61] This is a welcome acknowledgement considering the conclusions of subsequent studies.

Generational difference

Women's involvement in cocoa farming varied not only according to local customs but also in relation to their age. Generational difference emerged as a very important factor in the interviews, with cocoa farms usually acquired later in life. Most women remembered their first experiences of cocoa farming to have taken place in childhood, and recalled learning how to farm cocoa through watching and working with their parents.[62] As Seliatu recalled, 'I found myself gathering the pods but was not quite happy because it could not be eaten. So I did not understand why we had to be working on them.'[63] The women also mentioned having taken their own children to the cocoa farms, although this seems to have been limited in recent years due to more children attending school. These findings suggest limitations in the thesis that women may have been less involved in cash crop farming due to childcare commitments.[64]

That the women interviewed in Bamikemo worked mostly on the farms of their parents as children again undermines the Eurocentric notion of a single male farmer as the sole breadwinner. Abigail A. also recalled working on another man's farm when she was around twenty years old and still living at home.[65] This was not for money but in exchange for labour, as this man's children would then come to work for her father: 'I went first to a cocoa farm as hired labour to help in gathering harvested cocoa. But I was not paid in cash. The children of the man came to work for my father.' These informal exchanges often go unrecorded in western versions of history, although several scholars have observed the importance of pawnship in cash crop economies, as discussed in the following section.

Older women, particularly widows who have inherited the farms of their husbands, are depicted, where they are represented at all, as more likely to have an independent and involved role in the industry. Certainly, the majority of the women I spoke to who were in their fifties and sixties (both widowed and married) had their own cocoa farms. They were still actively farming and supervising their farms and hired labourers, although, as Roberts notes, 'even older women will face restrictions in their access to the labour of others'.[66] Seliatu, the oldest woman interviewed at seventy years old, commented, 'In spite of my age I can still spray and harvest my crop. I do those things by myself.' Grace, in addition to managing her farm, also held the position of being chief of the market women in Bamikemo. So these older women were indeed occupying positions of increased status within cocoa farming and the community as a whole. Meanwhile, they continued to engage in childcare and other domestic responsibilities. Whilst many of them still had relatively young children of their own to take care of, they were also providing a carer role for their grandchildren. The continuation of these complex responsibilities into later life must be seen as a factor in limiting the time women are able to devote to their cocoa farms.

Pawnship

The practice of pawnship, or *iwofa*, in West Africa has been well researched by Gareth Austin, Judith Byfield and Toyin Falola. When someone needed a loan, perhaps to purchase cocoa trees, they would either work themselves for their creditor or, more likely, send a member of their family to work, instead of paying interest on the debt. Colonial authorities aimed to stamp out the custom, yet historians have observed how the feminisation of pawnship allowed it to become increasingly invisible, particularly to western eyes. As Toyin Falola observes, it was easy to conceal young girl pawns by presenting them as future wives.[67] If marriage took place, the loan became part of the bridewealth. Grier highlights how, in Ghana, female pawnship in many senses 'paid' for the cocoa industry, particularly after the economic crises of the 1930s: 'By the Depression . . . many cocoa producers had already pledged or mortgaged their farms . . . and were left with no way of securing additional capital other than by pawning a female relative.'[68] With Nigeria suffering from similar economic conditions, it is likely that pawnship would have been increasingly employed to secure capital. But if women could be exploited within the cocoa economy as pawns, they could also be positioned as exploiters of pawn labour. Byfield sees women not simply as 'victims' of pawnship but as using the system 'as both borrowers and creditors'.[69] As Grier comments, 'Women . . . could and did exploit the labor power of other women and of girls, men, and boys.'[70]

Labour conditions in cocoa farming have recently come under scrutiny following accusations of child slavery. In April 2001, a ship arriving at Benin was thought to be carrying child slaves from Nigeria. This brought the international spotlight onto the exploitation of child labour, resulting in a pact signed by several chocolate manufacturers, human rights groups and the Ivory Coast government to end 'chocolate slavery'.[71] Perhaps not since the São Tomé and Principe scandal of the early twentieth century has so much attention been devoted to the labour practices implicitly condoned by the western chocolate manufacturers.[72] Research published by the International Institute of Tropical Agriculture in August 2002 has revealed the extent to which children have continued to be integral to the chocolate industry. They found an increased use of children as family labour but also as salaried workers, though their survey did not find extensive evidence of slavery as such.[73] The practice of pawnship did differ significantly from slavery in particular ways, drawing on kinship obligations. Byfield explains, 'Pawns . . . were not aliens to their community. They retained their independence and political rights, while slaves lost both.' The practices may have intersected but they were not identical. Indeed, pawnship may have been an answer to economic uncertainties experienced within the colonial economy.[74] Researchers from the 2002 survey certainly suggest that the low prices paid for cocoa by manufacturers since the late 1980s have fuelled an increased use of child labour.[75]

Marital status

It is as wives that women have most often featured in histories of cocoa farming. Indeed, all of the interviewees for this study were or had been married.[76] Upon marriage, women's labour obligations shift to the farms of their husband. Most women, describing their contribution to their husband's farms, simply said that they worked there whenever they were needed. Farming for their husbands was regarded as a priority to come before any of their own enterprises. When asked how much time she spent working on her husband's farm, Grace responded, 'Anytime he calls on me to follow . . . No specific day or time.' As Roberts observes, the obligation of wives to provide such labour is 'considerable and . . . not reciprocal'. Wives are indeed exploited as a source of labour in such a situation but they also have a degree of agency and power within the relationship. As Roberts goes on to point out: 'wives do have material interests and claims upon such household/male enterprises including and exceeding those of personal consumption, notably the interests of their children'.[77] Alice, for example, responded to the question, 'How much do you earn from your cocoa farm?' with, 'No particular one [money] comes to me but my husband takes care of the family, especially the children.' Alice spoke of receiving money from her husband to buy food and occasionally clothing. Some women did then receive financial compensation for their labours on the farm.

A wife's labour could also be recognised by her husband helping her to establish her own profit-making enterprises. Alice did not have her own farm but she did engage in trading and used the money from this to support herself and her children. Her husband's contributions to family spending will thus have eased the drain on the money she earns independently and vice versa. So, whilst a wife's role as family labour is often theorised in terms of the lack of direct monetary rewards, women in Nigeria and Ghana were willing and able to demand due recompense for their work on the farms.[78] Court records in Ghana document instances of women demanding divorce where they felt that their labour on the farms was being exploited. Women could be given the land on which they had been working, either by their husband or by the courts. They might then work hard to ensure that their daughters inherited these farms, to guarantee their economic independence upon marriage.[79]

The persistence of polygyny in Nigeria is suggestive of an economic element to the practice.[80] Even women who identified as Christian were often part of a polygynous marriage. The advantages of polygyny to the husband in cocoa-farming areas are clear, as he then has several wives to provide labour on his farms. Alice told how all four wives would work on her husband's farm. Nevertheless, the practice of polygyny does complicate conjugal duties as different wives take on different responsibilities and a different status within the family. Thus Roberts has observed that senior wives have more time to devote to their own enterprises and consequently become increasingly financially independent as 'Junior wives may eventually substitute for the labor obligations of a senior wife to her husband'.[81] A junior wife does not have any obligation, however, to provide labour for the senior wife. The differing relationships between wives of the same husband can result in different ways of organising labour. Some women I interviewed reported very good relationships with other wives. They described how they would all work together to accomplish household tasks and childcare. Yet most women did not help each other on their own farms, probably more due to time constraints than to any antagonism. For some women, relationships with other wives have not been so easy. As Grace recalled, 'I was the second wife. I was [on] good terms with the first one but when the second one came a lot of misunderstandings arose in the house.'

Farm ownership

As became clear from the interviews, as well as providing labour as a result of familial obligations, women in Nigeria may be cocoa farmers in their own right. Farms were acquired in a variety of ways, indicating the complex networks at play in the industry. Several women had been given land to farm by their husbands. They sometimes planted cocoa on this land themselves, or it may have already had cocoa planted on it. Other women inherited land from their mothers or other family members and were either farming themselves or supervising. Indeed, the fact that the mothers of some of the women interviewed had had their own cocoa farms places the active and independent involvement of Nigerian women still further back in the chronology. Caroline – at thirty years old the youngest woman I spoke with in Bamikemo – had inherited land jointly with her brother. He was doing most of the farming and supervising but she was also taking a supervisory role. For some women it had been possible to purchase their own land. However, it was not clear in all cases whether this was purchase in the western capitalist sense or more in the nature of a lease. Abigail O. had been given land to farm by the king of the village.

Raji, meanwhile, described her farm as, 'On lease but I am not pay-ing anything on it. We give small tokens and other gifts to landlords yearly.' Indeed, such negotiations have been complicated over the years by the introduction of currency during the colonial era. Observers have since tended to interpret the practice of gift giving as identical to the practice of paying rent.[82]

Roberts has written of the difficulties faced by women in accessing labour and points to this as one explanation as to why women have not been more independently involved in the cash crop economy.[83] The women I interviewed were able to hire both male and female work-ers, but this seems to be on the decline due to the cost. Seliatu described hiring two men from the village and also women 'to harvest and trans-port produce to the house'. She paid them daily: 200 naira for the men and 140 naira for the women. Grace, meanwhile, responded to a question about whether she enjoyed working on the cocoa farm with, 'I don't really have the strength. I use hired labourers in most cases.' Of course, these women do face certain obstacles in finding labour. They usually have access to the labour of their children (although this is decreasing as more children attend school) but not to that of other immediate family members as their husbands certainly do. Women reported working side by side with the men and women they hired, though where possible, particularly as they got older, they preferred to take a supervisory role. With less structured interviews I would perhaps have been able to gain further insights into women's relation-ships with their hired labour. Certainly, for women in York, relations with fellow workers were key to their working experience and to their oral histories.

Working on the farm and beyond

Women's tasks
Despite claiming that women do not play a significant role on cocoa farms, several sources list particular tasks that are undertaken by women. These tasks are usually described in terms of 'light' work – as opposed to the 'heavy' jobs of planting, clearing and spraying – reflecting, and constructing, a gendered division of labour. Galletti, Baldwin and Dina's study concluded that, 'In no part of the cocoa-producing areas are they [women] expected to . . . cutlass cocoa farms. Their share in the farm labour is more in the harvesting of food crops, the breaking of cocoa . . . and the carrying of produce home from the farm.'[84] Guyer, writing in 1980, largely confirms this model, citing farm-ing in Yoruba societies as largely men's work with women making 'important contributions' but only at very specific points.[85]

So what exactly were the tasks considered to be 'women's work' on West African cocoa farms? According to the secondary literature, women were expected to help primarily in the harvesting of cocoa. This involved gathering the pods as they were cut down from the trees; breaking them open (although this is occasionally seen as men's work, possibly as it involves the use of a machete);[86] scooping out the beans from the pod; transporting the beans to be dried and fermented; and helping in the drying and fermenting processes (although this has emerged more from the oral interviews than from other evidence). These activities were certainly engaged in by the women interviewed for this project and they seem to have been performed by women in most cocoa-producing areas, as discussed earlier in this chapter. Such tasks are portrayed in most written accounts as peripheral to cocoa production, thus justifying the labelling of cocoa farming as a male occupation; yet they are vital stages in preparing the cocoa for sale. Cocoa that is not properly prepared will not fetch a good price on the market, if it is bought at all. Manufacturers, particularly RFC, wanted to encourage the production of high-quality cocoa in order to enhance the status of their own products. This was to be achieved, with the assistance of the colonial government, partly through education but also through price incentives and by simply refusing to buy cocoa that failed to meet their set criteria.[87]

Oral evidence suggests that women have been both willing and called upon to help at *all* stages of cocoa production. With regard to their own cocoa farms, they described performing the full range of tasks required. Indeed, most of the women I interviewed, many of them in their sixties, were still actively farming.[88] They described their work in planting, tending for and occasionally even spraying cocoa. Grace asserted, 'Cocoa farming operations are never restricted to men. Men and women can do the same task. It is only spraying that is difficult for women because of the weight of the pump tank.' Spraying was done by women but was considered 'heavy' work not suited to women because of their perceived inferior strength in comparison to men – a division reinforced by the design of the tanks. So although the women's narratives undermined any clear-cut gendering of tasks, sex specialisation did and does still exist at some level. Grace stated, 'I work with men and women. It depends on the type of work I have to do. Take for instance, women scoop better than men. Children are also better scoopers. Men spray and weed better.' As for women in the Caribbean, the discourse of gendered labour may thus be accepted and put into practice to a certain extent (particularly by female farm owners), even where it conflicts with individual experiences on the farm.[89]

Figure 6 Scene of cocoa preparation in Nigeria, undated. The man is breaking open the cocoa pods whilst the woman scoops out the beans.

In referring to the gender division of labour generally in Yoruba society, particularly in contrast to the Beti of Cameroon, Guyer has observed that, 'The sexual division of labour . . . seems less clearly embedded in an elaborated cultural logic of male and female differences and oppositions. Discussions of the division of labour by sex are phrased in terms of pragmatism.'[90] Certainly, the women of this study used such terms in describing their tasks. The fact that many of them were indeed doing 'heavy' work was justified by 'pragmatically' stating that the work needed to be done. Several women would have appreciated more help on the farm. Grace was particularly clear on this: 'Farming work is tedious for women. Women should be provided with money

[111]

so as to get them engaged in trading activity and enable them to hire labourers to work for them.' Rather than feeling excluded, women drew on the physical strain of cocoa farming to describe why they should not be expected to continue with this type of work into old age. The discourse of gendered tasks is actively employed by the women; they are not simply subjected to it as certain sources would suggest.

So, Nigerian women have indeed been active agents at all stages of cocoa farming. In trying to establish some sense of the specific tasks women have undertaken, however, I would not wish to suggest any homogenous experiences of production. Indeed women's experiences of labour in cocoa farming have been many and varied, as I have outlined in the previous section. Their individual role depends on their position within the family, community and the cocoa chain itself.

Working conditions

It was difficult to access, at least through the medium of question-naires, precise details about working conditions for women on the cocoa farms. The issue of time spent on cocoa farming was particularly problematic. There are two main harvesting seasons (March–May and August–December) but the farms also require tending between these times. Alice described: 'July–August we have more to do. But cocoa farming activities is always round the year.' Women were also working on other crops and on domestic work, as well as on trading activities. Grace said she worked on her cocoa farm, 'Anytime there is work to do . . . or when I didn't go for my trading activities or when I didn't follow my husband to his farm.' Most women simply said that they worked on the farms whenever there was work to be done. This obviously varied according to whether there were specific problems with the crop such as disease. However, it appears that women spent around six to eight hours daily on farm labour, with two to three days per week working on their own farms. More detailed research would be needed to be able to determine just what proportion of this time was devoted exclusively to cocoa, if indeed this was ever the case.[91] By contrast, although there were complicated overlaps and intersections between work, family and leisure time for York women, their working hours at the Rowntree factory were highly regulated and imposed by management.

Another striking characteristic of the Rowntree factory, as I demonstrate in chapter five, is that it was a highly gender-segregated environment. Although parents, children and siblings were all employed at the factory, they tended to be spatially separated by gender, age and status.[92] Adult women could gain positions of power in their departments as chargehands and overlookers but would have had very limited jurisdiction over male workers in the factory. There were no such institutionalised divisions on the cocoa farms. Nigerian women, when asked with whom they were working, often listed both men and women, whilst some said they worked solely with their male hired labourers. This raises interesting questions, which I am not able to answer here, on the effects of this upon women's experiences of farm labour. Does it work to preclude the strong women's friendship groups which seem to have been prevalent at the Rowntree factory? If so, does this result in a more direct experience of patriarchal control for women at work? Of course, the answers to these questions will be affected by the position of the woman concerned. For women owning their own farms, their relationship to their hired male labourers will be one of power, at least in certain contexts. The relationships between family members working on the same farm will be different again, although (as mentioned previously) I did not come across any instances of wives from the same family helping each other on their own farms. The experiences of Nigerian women thus complicate the gendering of the cocoa chain.

Women certainly conceptualised their life on the farms as hard. When asked about a memorable day, many of the interviewees described particularly bad weather, when they were beaten by rain. As well as the climate, women also had to contend with dangerous wildlife. Raji remembers, 'Stressful and tough experiences. Tree fall that nearly claim[ed] a life. Tse-tse fly and other unpleasant situations.' The environment thus posed its own problems. Moreover, the work on cocoa itself was narrated as difficult, particularly as the women got older. Although Grace initially denied that cocoa farming had affected her health, she then said, 'But gradually the effects are being accumulated. My body is not as strong as before. There is stress in farming activities.' Other women felt they had aged prematurely and had grown weaker. This tied in with their demands for better technology.

Despite extensive research into the science and technology of cocoa farming – partly funded by manufacturers – basic farming methods have remained much the same. In contrast to industrialised chocolate manufacture, there has been little mechanisation of farming techniques, partly related to the failure of attempts to farm cocoa more intensively.[93] Where there have been technological improvements, these have often failed to reach the producers. Walker sees this as partly due to the incompetence of bodies such as the Technical Committee on Producer Prices.[94] New chemicals have been introduced, however, in the form of pesticides and fertilisers. This has led to recent concerns about their harmful effects on the health of unprotected cocoa workers.

Notwithstanding the difficult conditions under which cocoa farming is often conducted, several women did say that they enjoyed the
work. This is often explained in terms of having to do it. Because there
are jobs which cannot be avoided in the production of cocoa, the women
have actively cultivated an interest and enjoyment in these tasks. Such
a construction of a positive working history was similarly apparent
in the narratives of York workers. Cocoa farming was also seen as
relatively lucrative and thus worth the effort. As Alice put it, she
enjoyed the farming, 'Because we earn our living from it.' Whilst women
in York mentioned the money they earned through the chocolate
industry, there was less of a direct link between this and enjoyment.
Many women at the factory colluded with a devaluation of the worth
of their own earnings as just 'a little bit to help'.[95]

Roles outside the farm

Women have been directly involved in the cocoa industry not just
through the practice of farming itself but also in intermediary roles such
as portering, trading and as buyers. As Grier observes for Ghanaian
women, 'Cocoa trading, even if only in small amounts for a larger
buyer, must have been another option for women seeking greater
autonomy, along with carrying goods.'[96] Prior to the widespread use
of lorries, women could be employed in headloading the cocoa, acting
as porters to take the cocoa to the traders. In interviews, women
described how they still have a role in transporting the cocoa to be dried
and fermented. Early western observers were surprised at the numbers
of women engaged in such heavy work. Grier quotes the Gold Coast
Medical Department in 1913 on women headloading: 'The carrying
was "in the hands of young adults, *principally girls*, who were carrying loads of cocoa evidently quite beyond their physical strength"'.[97]
In 1910, E. J. Organ reported for Cadbury that in Ghana he had seen:

> some 20 women, each with a woolly-headed pickaniny slung on her
> back . . . These women carry the bags of cocoa on their heads, running
> down to the beach, and returning for another box. They receive a brass
> tally for each bag, representing $1^1/_2$d, and there is one 'mammy' who
> can make as much as 3/-. The average, however, is $^1/_3$d and the work is
> very arduous.[98]

This quote is itself illustrative of racist and sexist discourses at
work, whereby indigenous women are constructed to emphasise their
strength but also their difference.[99] Referring to 'head carriage' in 1917,
the Governor of Ghana suggested the social and gender hierarchies of
the practice: '[It is] the first form of labour from which the natives
emancipate themselves . . . not only on account of its intrinsic severity,

but also because it is regarded as one of the lowest forms of labour to which men can be put.'[100]

Nigerian women sub-buyers, whose activities were less physically demanding and consequently less transgressive of gender norms, were more respectfully represented by Galletti, Baldwin and Dina, writing as they were in the postwar period, though there were still undertones of distrust:

> Women sub-buyers . . . are found more in the Akoko and Owo areas in the east of the main cocoa belt, where they have a good reputation for honesty and punctuality in delivery. In pre-war days they were said to have an evil reputation as money-lenders. But if they made improper gains then they seem to do so no longer.[101]

Although their numbers were probably small, these middlewomen and the more ubiquitous middlemen could be an important link between small producers and the manufacturer, selling cocoa to the buying agencies for a profit. A famous Ghanaian woman broker appears in the *Bournville Works Magazine*, alongside the Cadbury agent of the 1920s and 1930s, Mr T. E. Baker. She is described as 'the late Mary Reynolds, remarkable not only for her commercial genius, but also for her skill in preparing the complicated dishes – palm oil chop and ground nut chop'.[102] Such diversity of women's experiences in direct relation to the cocoa industry is too little represented. Because women were not always solely responsible for cocoa farms, their labour has continually been underplayed, if not ignored completely.

Boserup identifies African men as the primary growers of cash crops under European rule, with women as subsistence food farmers.[103] Whilst this model has been used to render women invisible as cocoa producers, it does make the important point that women's labour has facilitated the participation of men in lucrative cash crop industries. By taking care of children, for instance, women allow men to spend their time free of this responsibility. This argument has also been used to stress the productive value of 'domestic' labour in western cultures. Women in Bamikemo described performing domestic duties without any help from husbands, although there were suggestions that the ideologies which once excluded men from this type of work are changing. Abigail O., aged fifty, drew an implicit distinction between current and past practices: 'During our time it was a bad thing for husband to help in household works.' Caroline, aged thirty, said that her husband did help with small household chores. Certainly, some women said that there was no difference between the tasks they assigned to male and female children, though I was not able to determine whether this was also dependent on the age of the children

[115]

concerned. Children of both sexes were expected to take on responsibilities both within the house and on the farm.

As well as providing services in the home, many of the women interviewed conducted their own enterprises, particularly in trading. Food and other goods produced in the home were sold in the market place for a profit. One particularly interesting means of earning money – suggesting alternative methods, and meanings, of cocoa consumption – was the making and trading of soap from the husks of the cocoa pod.[104] Women also traded in goods which they purchased in the market place: several were selling branded soft drinks. Economic activities were varied, reinforcing the point that these women had no simple pattern of employment and would certainly defy any easy notion of 'separate spheres'.[105] Grace told me, 'I sew clothes before but now I only do trading, buying and selling farm products like yam, gari etc.' Seliatu traded in kola nuts and described how she had sold salt as a girl in 'a small trading set up for me by my parents as a child. I owned all the proceeds.' Women usually managed the money earned from their own enterprises themselves.

The separate accounts (or 'separate purse') kept by West African women and men has been interpreted as giving women in the Nigerian context more power than those in the west, where women's wages are more likely to be pooled (though in both cases this varies according to the individual and to local culture).[106] Roberts criticises the 'reification of this practice', observing that 'women's own-account enterprises are by no means autonomous of male headed households, but rather a condition of women's relationship to them and within them'.[107] Whether or not they were giving their money to their husbands, or providing for themselves, Nigerian women's earnings indirectly and directly eased the drain on profits from cocoa farming. For instance, the money earned from women's own-account enterprises is often used to care for their children. This liberates men to some extent from the need to provide money for food, clothing and even education for their families, allowing them more freedom to pursue cocoa farming and to use the profits to reinvest in their farms. This is not to imply that all women are entirely self-supporting. Husbands have an obligation to provide for their wives in particular ways. However, I do wish to highlight the complexities of the 'family' economy in cocoa-farming regions. Women must be recognised as key economic agents in the success of the cocoa industry, even whilst their direct role in cocoa farming goes unacknowledged and undervalued.

As Guyer observes, cocoa production was not just 'added in a mechanical way' to the usual tasks, and required a degree of restructuring. She concludes that subsistence food farming decreased, requiring cocoa-producing families to buy their food on the market. This provided an opportunity for women traders: 'the fact that the food supply was quickly commercialised was made possible by, and reinforced, the existing system of women's processing and marketing'.[108] Whilst this is undoubtedly true to a certain extent, I would not agree wholeheartedly with Guyer's conclusions on the 'increasing sex specialisation of rural occupations'. Women in Bamikemo appeared to be combining a number of different tasks and occupations. More convincing is Guyer's observation that cocoa 'opened up opportunities for occupational diversification among Yoruba women'.[109] We have already seen how women have taken on a wide variety of roles in the cocoa industry: as traders and buying agents, for example. With more time, it would have been interesting to try to establish how women defined themselves in terms of their occupation: whether as farmer, cocoa farmer, trader, mother or perhaps all of these and more.

Impact of cocoa on women and their communities

Having discussed women's active involvement in cocoa farming, it is important to consider the impact of this crop upon their lives and communities. In the following paragraphs I examine the various ways in which cocoa affected Nigeria and the Nigerian people: from the physical changes it demanded of the land, to the social and political consequences of cash crop farming in a British colony. I do not wish to offer a one-way reading of women and cocoa, in which the introduction of the new crop changed the lives of women. Rather, I emphasise the ways in which the cocoa industry developed through the interaction of different factors such as colonial involvement, indigenous farming practices and existing social systems. Women are not and never have been passive bystanders in the cocoa economy, and I demonstrate how they have responded actively to the practices and politics of cocoa production.

As discussed in chapter two, cocoa was not a crop indigenous to Nigeria. It thus had a physical impact on the country as areas of virgin forest were cleared to make way for cocoa farms.[110] In certain cases, villages sprang up purely as a result of the introduction of cocoa, thus creating a very particular type of social community/environment. Berry notes that 'by 1905 hundreds of people were moving into the sparsely populated forests south of Ibadan town'.[111] Bamikemo itself was founded on rubber, but soon moved into cocoa farming. Cocoa created migrants from within and from outside the cocoa-growing regions, as people moved to set up cocoa farms or to work as hired labour on existing farms. According to Berry, this was still prevalent in the 1970s.[112] These hired labourers, once they had learnt the techniques of cocoa farming, were often able to start their own farms. Although migrants are usually referred to as male, women and children also relocated as a result of the cocoa economy. Indeed, none of the women I spoke to had been born in Bamikemo and most moved there upon marriage, to join husbands already established as cocoa farmers.

Much has been written on the migrant cocoa communities of Ghana. Okali, for example, comments on the indeterminacy and transience of cocoa-farming communities there. She observes that many farmers and their families still do not consider their cocoa farms to be home: children are sent back to the towns to be educated and families are divided.[113] My own findings are more in line with Berry's observation of how Nigerian cocoa-farming families developed villages into large permanent settlements:

> Today many of these cocoa farming villages are quite large, and most of the inhabitants live there all year, paying only occasional visits to their home or other towns for family ceremonies, festivals or business purposes . . . In other words, Yoruba farmers have extended their 'traditional' urban type of settlement into the areas opened up for cocoa growing.[114]

What did become obvious was the complexity of spatial and living arrangements, which made the question, 'Where do you live?' a highly ambiguous one. I visited women in their homes in Bamikemo, which most women said to be fairly close to their farms (one to two kilometres away). In addition, most seemed to have some basic accommodation much closer to their farms, which served as shelter in bad weather or as sleeping quarters if they had had a very long day. Many women also spoke of having homes in an urban area such as Ondo, where they would go for weekends, or perhaps for celebrations.[115] Urban houses could be much larger than homes in Bamikemo village. Seliatu, for instance, described her house at Isandurin as having sixteen rooms, compared to three rooms in her house in Bamikemo.

For the majority of women interviewed, the money they earned themselves through cocoa and other enterprises had been used to pay for their children's education. This has had the effect of encouraging the children of cocoa producers to move to urban areas in search of better-paid employment. Most women I spoke with seemed to view this as a good thing and did not want their children to become farmers. Only a few hoped that their children would follow in their footsteps. Investing in property was another way in which women involved in cocoa farming could spend their income. Seliatu was the owner of her own real estate and she explicitly mentioned using profits from trade and farming to invest in housing. However, Nigerian women were also using the money earned from cocoa to make improvements to their homes, such as adding toilets or electricity. Despite confident assertions in the *CWM* in 1960 that cocoa had brought great social improvement to farming villages, farmers were clearly still struggling to establish certain basic facilities and to get access to adequate healthcare from their rural locations.[116] In the lucrative global chocolate industry, it is the producers of the most vital ingredient who have benefited least.

As discussed in chapter two, commentators from the colonial period were quick to criticise farmers in their use of cocoa profits, and mourned the lack of civilising power of the money earned. This kind of racist statement must be examined more closely. Clearly, profits for farmers have not always been good. One of the frequent responses to questions about the cocoa industry was to complain about low prices and particularly about the actions of local buying agents who were seen to be cheating the producers. Women described the problems they faced when trying to sell their cocoa, as a lack of education meant that they could never be sure that buying agents were giving them the correct price. When asked what she thought of these buying agents, Seliatu responded, 'I may not know if they are cheating me because I cannot read or write and I do not understand the scales.' Grace commented, 'At times they cheat me when it comes to using scales to measure cocoa, for I do not know how to read and write.' Some women told me that their husbands or families would help them at this stage, and the villagers used their own scales to weigh the cocoa to try to avoid being cheated. As owners of cocoa farms, the women I interviewed were acutely aware of issues surrounding the industry. They are active agents and take a keen interest in the politics of cocoa. Seliatu, when asked for her final thoughts after the interview, commented, '[The] welfare of farmers should be supported. Better access to inputs should be promoted.' However, where husbands or other men were present at interviews, they, rather than the women themselves, tended to answer questions concerning pricing and so on. Farmers in Bamikemo were selling mostly to the Tonikoko Farmers Union at the time of the interviews, which seemed to be offering the fairest deal.

Many women remembered long periods of poor cocoa prices. Seliatu recalled a particularly bad time 'long ago', when they had had to burn their cocoa. From the Second World War until the liberalisation of cocoa in 1986, prices were controlled by the cocoa marketing board. Government price-fixing is a complex issue in which the major chocolate manufacturers are implicated.[117] It was ostensibly intended to guarantee stable prices, using any profits for welfare schemes, but farmers complained of low prices and corruption within the board.[118]

There has also been the question of middlemen, and indeed middle-women – particularly before the advent of the cocoa marketing board – making profits at the expense of the cocoa producers. A high level of concern about middlemen and women, as displayed in government archives, has tended to mask the low prices being paid by chocolate manufacturers. For instance, the Report of the Cocoa Commission Committee, 1939, worried that farmers would fall prey to 'unscrupu-lous small middlemen'.[119] However, some sources do recognise the scapegoating of these figures. Captain Haig of the Registrar of Cooperative Societies, observed, 'Although the Yoruba middleman and middlewoman have earned for themselves a reputation for rapacity which extends beyond Nigeria (it is notorious on the Gold Coast), yet it would be wrong to assume that they are especially blameworthy.' He shifts the blame onto the European firms, stating:

> The case against the European firms so far as cocoa-buying is concerned, is not that they have exploited the producer, but that they have employed, consolidated and perpetuated a system which has made it pos-sible and indeed inevitable that the African buyer should exploit the African farmer.[120]

Unlike many European firms, Rowntree, Cadbury and Fry oversaw (at least in theory) the whole of the buying process: buying directly from producers rather than through independent middlemen and women.

(Re)connecting York and Nigeria

A chocolate conscience?[121]

The 'under-development' of cocoa-producing villages in Nigeria is in stark contrast to the prosperity of chocolate-manufacturing towns in the west.[122] In York, the confectionery industry, particularly the Rowntree firm, had an important impact on the local economy. As a relatively unindustrialised city, York benefited enormously from the profits made by the chocolate industry. Moreover, the Quaker fami-lies who founded these factories have played an important role in social welfare locally and nationally. The Rowntrees had an impact on the physical environment of York – through the building of New Earswick, the creation of parks and so on – whilst the Rowntree trusts continue to carry out welfare work today on both a local and a global scale. Yet, with the exception of relatively small donations, this same impulse towards philanthropy has not been felt in Nigeria.

RFC, like the Cadbury agency in Ghana, made many charitable dona-tions to local organisations. In 1925, for example, they donated a total of £6 10s, the majority of which went to the Lagos Cathedral Fund.[123]

From October to November 1938, the ledger records donations of £6 to the Agege African Mission and Church, £5 5s to the Ekite Medical Mission, and £3 3s to the World Wide Mission in Ibadan. Donations of between 5s to £1 5s were also made to local schools in 1939.[124] As Southall has observed of Cadbury, however, such donations tend to '[pale] into insignificance when compared with some of the other disbursements that the firm and the family were currently making in England'.[125] Southall thus highlights an important disparity: money earned from an industry dependent on colonial materials was used to support projects in Britain to a greater extent than in the developing regions of British West Africa. Moreover, this money could have been ploughed into the cocoa economy itself, guaranteeing a better deal for farmers and thereby allowing them to develop their own communities. Instead, Rowntree demonstrated their own ideological agenda in the choice of beneficiaries for their philanthropic donations.

Rowntree did eventually expand their welfare schemes to other countries in Africa, making some quite explicit connections between the people there and in York. In an article on the Joseph Rowntree Social Service Trust in the *CWM* from 1967, clear links are made between the apparently disparate events of the founding of the University of York and of a school in Botswana:

> Any day now you can see undergraduates going around the City [of York]. Imagine yourself thousands of miles away in a school of Botswana where two little Bamangwato girls are giggling happily over the mysteries of dressmaking. These young people in York and Serowe have something in common. The link is the Social Service Trust.[126]

The author both sets up and undermines the contrasts between these scenes. Later in the same article the author observes that, whilst Joseph Rowntree had stipulated that the trusts he established should concern themselves solely with Britain, 'Had J. R. been alive 50 years later he would have been one of the first to recognise Britain's responsibility for the welfare and education of people in former colonial territories. Indeed, the solution of these problems was now directly connected with this country.'[127] Despite this assertion of responsibility, I have not found any evidence of coherent welfare schemes in Nigeria along the lines of those in Botswana, only charitable donations in response to specific requests.

Records of the York Committee suggest that such requests caused tensions between a recognition of the relationships and responsibilities brought about through trade, and a reluctance to become further entangled in the cocoa-producing colonies as they gained independence.[128] In 1961, for example, the Committee decided against the purchase of a £3,000 organ for the University College at Ibadan: 'Although York had substantial interests in Nigeria, both in respect of cocoa beans and gum arabic, the Donations Sub-Committee felt that these interests did not justify the gift of an organ . . . After discussion, the Committee agreed to make a donation of £250.'[129] As discussed in chapter two, Rowntree did lay claim in the *CWM* to having had a positive influence on cocoa-farming communities but this was described in terms of the economic benefits of the cocoa chain and Rowntree's fair dealings with producers. Southall, in contrast, notes that Cadbury in Ghana placed increasing emphasis on 'indirect benevolence and public responsibility'.[130] Evidence of a tangible desire by Rowntree to actively promote economic development in Nigeria is in the photos of young, male Nigerians visiting York for training in order to become involved in the trading aspect of the chain. For instance, in 1967 the *CWM* recorded a visit by Mr Kunle Oyedipe (an Administrative Officer in the Nigerian Federal Ministry of Trade) to study the export function at the factory. These young men formed a connecting link between the farmers and the firm, ironically allowing Rowntree themselves to become more distanced from the producers.[131]

Chocolate politics

Women and men in the cocoa-farming areas have not allowed exploitation through low prices to go unchallenged, and several women described being part of a cooperative or taking part in local protests. Grace told me, 'We danced around the town in a peaceful demonstration.' She went on to say, 'But in most cases [the] government don't come to make things get improved. They are always silent on the issue.' As smallholders selling their crop to the larger firms, cocoa-farming families were able to maintain some degree of autonomy. Whilst they were essentially subject to the whim of the manufacturers/buying agents in the price they received for their cocoa crop, they did have the option (as a last resort) of withholding their product altogether. As discussed in chapter two, when the producers perceived the manufacturers to be forming a monopoly designed to reduce competition between them and keep prices down, a series of cocoa hold-ups followed (principally in 1938 and 1945). Yet archival evidence suggests that Nigeria did not participate in the main cocoa hold-ups, unlike Ghana, despite clear signs that they would.[132] I am not sure of the reasons for this, or even if the assertion is entirely true. The Nowell Report on the marketing of West African cocoa (published in 1938) suggested it was due to a lack of organisation amongst producers, and the lesser importance of cocoa as an export crop compared to Ghana.[133] However, perhaps the Nigerian colonial government had an

[122]

interest in downplaying the conflict over cocoa prices. Other protests were provoked by what was seen as unnecessary interference in cocoa-farming processes, such as the introduction of a new type of tree.

Typically, women have been excluded from histories of the cocoa hold-ups and other protests. Yet cocoa farming has clearly been a politicising force in women's lives. Two women, including Grace, remembered dancing around the village in peaceful protest at the poor cocoa prices; others recalled the building of a cocoa store so that cocoa could be kept for longer instead of having to be sold at the dictated price (for fear that otherwise the cocoa would simply be left to rot). There is a long history of political action by Nigerian women both in their own village communities and beyond, not just in relation to the cocoa industry. Perhaps most famously, the Igbo women of southeastern Nigeria protested against colonial rule in the Ogu Umunwaanyi (Women's War) of 1929. Singing and dancing were tactics used by these Igbo women, alongside more destructive actions.[134] The women interviewed in Bamikemo had contributed both time and money to protests against unfair treatment in the cocoa industry. Esther told me she 'contributed money so as to make the case in court'.

Since the 1970s oil boom, the situation for cocoa farmers has under-gone dramatic changes. The cocoa communities have been neglected, although there have been various unsuccessful schemes, funded by profits from oil, to revitalise the industry.[135] Women have undoubt-edly been affected economically. When asked for their memories of the colonial era, several women responded quite simply with 'cheaper prices'. Grace elaborated:

> [There were] no problem[s] then. We had food to eat, more than enough. Things were not expensive, life was quite easy. Though it is good to have independence, but we don't really have the feelings of independence. There is a great difference between the rich and the poor. Life is not convenient for me. For me, I prefer the time of the colonial masters.

This is not so much an endorsement of colonialism as a comment on its legacies for Nigeria. However, women have been active in pursuing an improved way of life for their communities. Ronke, one of the queens of Bamikemo, is a prominent member of the Country Women Association of Nigeria (COWAN) founded in 1982 – an organ-isation which works to give women access to loans, as well as being active in areas of community health.[136] The village of Bamikemo does now have a reasonable road, some electricity, a post office and a basic health centre. Raji thanks the women's society for this: 'When women['s] society was formed in the village, a lot of social amenities were brought in through their constant efforts.'

Asked for their final thoughts after the interview, many women were keen to stress to me the need for continued development in their village. I will end with just two women's comments: 'I quite appreciate your visit, but we really want to feel the impact by you conveying our problems to your people so they can see in anyway to assist cocoa and food crops farmers' (Grace); 'I am happy about your visit to this place. But make sure you relay our suffering situation to the people in the developed countries so that they can come in to help us. Farmers are really suffering' (Abigail A.). The women I met were highly aware of the connections that *should* be being made, urging me to recognise my responsibilities in both the cocoa chain and the research process.

Conclusion

Put simply, women in the former British colonies of the West Indies and West Africa (including Nigeria), have been, and continue to be, central to the global chocolate industry of which the Rowntree firm was once an influential part. More specifically, as Rowntree was buying cocoa directly from these regions, female producers and traders there have influenced the production of chocolate in York. In return, the fortunes of the York factory have reverberated within cocoa-farming regions. Women at these different sites of production need to be studied not only in their own right but also in relation to one another.

Whilst my own research in Nigeria has been limited, my findings indicate the need to write Nigerian women back into the cocoa chain in order to better recognise their stake in the future development of the industry. There needs to be an increased understanding of how the mechanisms of the chocolate industry, and the ideologies perpetuated from within it, have impacted upon the lives of Nigerian women in cocoa-farming regions. The profits made by chocolate manufacturers have certainly not been shared with cocoa producers. Yet the Rowntree firm, for one, was committed to at least a degree of profit sharing in England. I hope that by deconstructing the structures of power inherent in the cocoa chain I have suggested the need to recognise the connections between women's labour in York and Nigeria – without oversimplifying cultural and social differences – and to challenge the unequal distribution of wealth according to gender, race and colonial politics.

In writing my own version of the Rowntree history, I have had to come to terms with my location in the unequal relationship between York and Nigeria, and with the possibility that the nature of my research may only reproduce such inequalities.[137] Indeed, the very process of this research has in a strange way mirrored the production of chocolate from raw material to finished good. I was made uncomfortably aware of this when reading Daphne Patai's work:

> An individual telling her own story can be construed to be in possession of raw material, material without which the entrepreneurial researcher could not perform the labor of producing a text. In this situation, it is the researcher who owns or has access to the means of production that will transform the spoken words into commodities.[138]

Nigerian women have provided cocoa for the Rowntree factory and stories for a Rowntree history. As with cocoa, it is unlikely that the producers of this raw research material will be enabled to consume the finished product. These are important considerations but I do not believe that they should result in a 'retreat' from writing about 'other' women.[139] Rather, I agree with Julie Marcus that 'it is a matter of writing power back into our texts, of placing ourselves within those relations of power'.[140]

What was important to many of the women interviewed was that their story was communicated to people in the west. They wanted to feel the impact of being heard, rather than becoming an audience for their own histories. This is not to suggest that they were otherwise silent, waiting to be 'discovered' by western historians. As discussed in this chapter, the women I spoke with have set up successful women's organisations and cooperatives, for which they have gained international recognition, and they are taking control over the production and sale of their produce. They are organised and vocal, maintaining their own challenges to the postcolonial order that still exploits their labour.

Notes

1 Alice describing working for her parents. Alice was about sixty-six years old and lived in Bamikemo village, Ondo State. Quotations will be from questionnaires used in interviews. My interpreter in Bamikemo, Wunmi, wrote the answers in English and I will thus use her translations, with any additions by me in brackets. I have anonymised the interviewees for the purpose of this book by using only first names.

2 Grace was head of the market women in Bamikemo. She was around sixty-five years old.

3 The title of 'farmer', within a western discourse at least, brings with it implications of gender, age, status, power, ownership and individualism. Jane I. Guyer suggests that in studying gendered roles in African agriculture, 'one has to put aside the essentially European designation of "farming" as a single occupational category'. Guyer, 'Food, cocoa, and the division of labour by sex in two West African societies', *Comparative Studies in Society and History*, 22 (1980), 363. However, I refer in this chapter to 'women cocoa farmers' and 'cocoa-farming women' in an attempt to recognise their full involvement, even as this relies for its impact on a western understanding of farming. Similarly, in the Caribbean context, Harry emphasises that women need to be seen as 'women farmers' rather than as 'working

farmwives'. Indra S. Harry, 'Women in agriculture in Trinidad: an overview', in Janet H. Momsen (ed.), *Women and Change in the Caribbean: A Pan-Caribbean Perspective* (London: James Currey, 1993), 217.

4 On coercive labour practices in cocoa production in Brazil from the seventeenth to the nineteenth centuries, see Timothy Walker, 'Slave labor and chocolate in Brazil: the culture of cacao plantations in Amazonia and Bahia (17th–19th centuries)', *Food and Foodways*, 15 (2007), 75–106.

5 Harry, 'Women in agriculture', 206–7.

6 *Ibid.*, 207.

7 Clarence-Smith, *Cocoa and Chocolate*, 197; Walker, 'Slave labor and chocolate in Brazil', 93.

8 See Janet Henshall Momsen, 'Gender roles in Caribbean agricultural labour', in Malcolm Cross and Gad Heuman (eds), *Labour in the Caribbean: From Emancipation to Independence* (Basingstoke: Macmillan, 1988), 142, 154; Olive Senior, *Working Miracles: Women's Lives in the English-Speaking Caribbean* (London: James Currey, 1991), 106; Christine Barrow, 'Small farm food production and gender in Barbados', in Momsen (ed.), *Women and Change*, 183. Momsen noted in 1987 that only in the past fifty years had wages been differentiated by sex, and that age continued to be more important than gender in the assignment of tasks in Grenada until the 1930s. This questions the assumption that Victorian ideals about 'separate spheres' took hold in the Caribbean as a justification for unequal pay in the post-emancipation era. As Richard Phillips explains, the exchange of ideas between metropole and colony was never straightforward. Henshall Momsen, 'Gender roles', 154; Phillips, *Sex, Politics and Empire: A Postcolonial Geography* (Manchester: Manchester University Press, 2006), 221.

9 Kathleen Phillips Lewis, 'Women in the Trinidadian cocoa industry, 1870–1945', *Journal of Caribbean History*, 34 (2000), 29.

10 *CWM*, February 1904, 147; *CWM*, September 1908, 576.

11 Rhoda E. Reddock, *Women, Labour and Politics in Trinidad and Tobago: A History* (London: Zed Books, 1994), 71.

12 *CWM*, February 1904, 147. For examples of photographs, see *CWM*, February 1908, 481–2; Cadbury UK, 050/003163, Cadbury photographs from Trinidad and West Africa. Phillips Lewis does note that Africans and Indians worked together on the estates, sometimes leading to cultural conflict and misunderstandings. Phillips Lewis, 'Women in the Trinidadian cocoa industry', 42.

13 Verene A. Shepherd, *Women in Caribbean History: The British Colonised Territories* (Oxford: James Currey, 1999), 85–6; Reddock, *Women, Labour and Politics*, 47; Momsen, 'Gender roles', 154. Phillips Lewis has found an even greater gender divide on family-owned farms in the later decades of the twentieth century than at its start. Phillips Lewis, 'Women in the Trinidadian cocoa industry', 43.

14 Phillips Lewis, 'Women in the Trinidadian cocoa industry', 21; also Harry, 'Women in agriculture', 212.

15 Phillips Lewis, 'Women in the Trinidadian cocoa industry', 26–7; Reddock, *Women, Labour and Politics*, 74; Shepherd, *Women in Caribbean History*, 97–8; Harry, 'Women in agriculture', 212, 214.

16 *CWM*, May 1902, 29. See Phillips Lewis, 'Women in the Trinidadian cocoa industry', for an excellent analysis of living conditions on the estates.

17 Phillips Lewis, 'Women in the Trinidadian cocoa industry', 23–4, 27–8; Reddock, *Women, Labour and Politics*, 76.

18 Reddock, *Women, Labour and Politics*, 74.

19 See Momsen, 'Gender roles', 154.

20 Melville J. Herskovits and Frances S. Herskovits, *Trinidad Village* (1947), 46, as quoted in Reddock, *Women, Labour and Politics*, 74.

21 Reddock, *Women, Labour and Politics*, 76.

22 *Ibid.*, 77.

23 *Ibid.*, 72; Momsen, 'Gender roles', 151.

24 Reddock, *Women, Labour and Politics*, 194–5.

25 Momsen, 'Gender roles', 151.
26 Phillips Lewis, 'Women in the Trinidadian cocoa industry', 30.
27 Barrow, 'Small farm food production', 181. See also later in this chapter for a critique of male farming models in relation to Nigerian women farmers.
28 On the hiring of men for spraying, see Momsen, 'Gender roles', 154.
29 Senior, *Working Miracles*, 105.
30 Barrow, 'Small farm food production', 190.
31 Harry, 'Women in agriculture', 218.
32 Barrow, 'Small farm food production', 191.
33 Phillips Lewis, 'Women in the Trinidadian cocoa industry', 35–8.
34 Mrs. S. D., personal interview, Trinidad, 27 November 1997. Quoted in Shaheeda Hosein, 'A space of their own: Indian women and land ownership in Trinidad 1870–1945', *Caribbean Review of Gender Studies*, 1 (April 2007), 9.
35 John S. Brierly, 'A profile of Grenadian women small farmers', in Momsen (ed.), *Women and Change*, 200.
36 Phillips Lewis, 'Women in the Trinidadian cocoa industry', 37.
37 Shepherd, *Women in Caribbean History*, 97; also Phillips Lewis, 'Women in the Trinidadian cocoa industry', 21.
38 Barrow, 'Small farm food production', 190.
39 Momsen, 'Gender roles', 141–2, 147, 157.
40 Ester Boserup, *Women's Role in Economic Development* (New York: St. Martin's Press, 1970), 53–4.
41 Lourdes Benería and Gita Sen, 'Accumulation, reproduction and women's role in economic development: Boserup revisited', *Signs*, 7: 2 (1981), 288.
42 This tendency to theorise women's oppression solely in their exclusion from the so-called public sphere has been criticised by some feminist scholars who discuss the power inherent in the domestic sphere and women's agency in choosing this life. See Behar, *Translated Woman*, 300–1.
43 See Aihwa Ong, 'Colonialism and modernity: feminist re-presentations of women in non-western societies', *Inscriptions*, 3/4 (1988), 86.
44 Guyer, 'Food, cocoa, and the division of labour', 365, 364. The experiences of the women I interviewed reveal the limitations of such gendered arguments over hired labour by illustrating that women as well as men could be hired to work on cocoa, and that women farmers themselves employed hired workers.
45 *Ibid.*, 364, 372.
46 Benjamin Asare, 'Women in commercial agriculture: the cocoa economy of Southern Ghana', in James Valentine Udoh (ed.), *Women and Sustainable Development in Africa* (Westport: Praeger, 1995), 101–12; Gwendolyn Mikell, *Cocoa and Chaos in Ghana* (New York: Paragon House, 1989); Christine Okali, *Cocoa and Kinship in Ghana: The Matrilineal Akan of Ghana* (London: Kegan Paul, 1983); Dorothy Dee Vellenga, 'Matriliny, patriliny, and class formation among women cocoa farmers in two rural areas of Ghana', in Claire Robertson and Iris Berger (eds), *Women and Class in Africa* (New York: Africana Publishing Company, 1986), 62–77.
47 Mikell, *Cocoa and Chaos*, 101.
48 Beverly Grier, 'Pawns, porters, and petty traders: women in the transition to cash crop agriculture in colonial Ghana', in Toyin Falola and Paul E. Lovejoy (eds), *Pawnship in Africa: Debt Bondage in Historical Perspective* (Boulder: Westview Press, 1994), 173, 175.
49 A. G. Hopkins cites that, 'Between 1945 and 1960 . . . Nigeria produced between a fifth and a quarter of world tonnage, being second only to Ghana.' Hopkins, 'Innovation in a colonial context', 83. However, whereas Nigerian agriculture has been neglected with the development of the oil industry, Ghana has continued to be a major cocoa producer. Agricultural exports only accounted for 5 per cent of exports from Nigeria in the mid 1970s, compared to 85 per cent in 1960. Walker, 'Structural change, the oil boom and the cocoa economy', 72.
50 Dorothy Vellenga observes that matrilineal women are more likely to acquire farms through efforts in their own enterprises. However, she posits that this may be a

'forced independence' due to polygyny and the 'ambiguity of inheritance practices'. Women in matrilineal areas should not necessarily be defined as 'better off'. Vellenga, 'Matriliny, patriliny, and class formation', 76.

51 Galletti *et al.*, *Nigerian Cocoa Farmers*.

52 Julian Clarke, 'Households and the political economy of small-scale cash crop production in south-western Nigeria', *Africa*, 51: 4 (1981), 819–20.

53 My translators from FADU were Samuel Dele, Paul Adejunro and Tayo Sadare. Enterprise for Development International was originally TechnoServ but is now an entirely Nigerian organisation.

54 This was an interesting interview in that it demonstrated the transmission of histories of cocoa farming from generation to generation.

55 Two further EfDI representatives helped me enormously: Kayode Farinloye conducted one of the interviews whilst Tony Jonise helped to recruit women interviewees.

56 There are more than 250 ethnic groups in Nigeria. See Toyin Falola, *Culture and Customs of Nigeria* (Westport: Greenwood Press, 2001), 4.

57 Galletti *et al.*, *Nigerian Cocoa Farmers*, 294.

58 Ruth Dixon-Mueller, 'Women in agriculture: counting the labor force in developing countries', in Mary Margaret Fonow and Judith A. Cook (eds), *Beyond Methodology: Feminist Scholarship as Lived Research* (Bloomington: Indiana University Press, 1991), 229.

59 Galletti *et al.*, *Nigerian Cocoa Farmers*, 294.

60 *Ibid.*, 289.

61 *Ibid.*, 297.

62 Wunmi often translated this as 'indigenous knowledge'. This is interesting in that cocoa was an introduced crop, and therefore had originally required the development of new knowledges. It also defies the attempts of the Department of Agriculture and manufacturers to educate cocoa farmers themselves.

63 Seliatu was around seventy years old and lived in Bamikemo. She grew up in Isundirin, Osun State.

64 Roberts critiques the 'naturalism' model, which 'claims an association between the low intensity of labor in women's farming systems and the constraints of child-bearing and rearing.' Penelope A. Roberts, 'Rural women's access to labor in West Africa', in Sharon B. Stichter and Jane L. Parpart (eds), *Patriarchy and Class: African Women in the Home and the Workforce* (Boulder: Westview Press, 1988), 100.

65 Abigail A. was sixty-eight years old and lived in Bamikemo. She grew up in Ogbomoso.

66 Roberts, 'Rural women's access to labor', 106.

67 Toyin Falola, 'Pawnship in colonial southwestern Nigeria', in Toyin Falola and Paul E. Lovejoy (eds), *Pawnship in Africa: Debt Bondage in Historical Perspective* (Boulder: Westview Press, 1994), 255; See also Gareth Austin, 'Human pawning in Asante 1800–1950', in Falola and Lovejoy (eds), *Pawnship in Africa*, 119–59; Judith Byfield, 'Pawns and politics: the pawnship debate in western Nigeria', in Falola and Lovejoy (eds), *Pawnship in Africa*, 187–216.

68 Grier, 'Pawns, porters, and petty traders', 174.

69 Byfield, 'Pawns and politics', 206.

70 Grier, 'Pawns, porters, and petty traders', 169.

71 'Pact to end African "chocolate slavery"', BBC News, 2 May 2002, http://news.bbc.co.uk/2/hi/africa/1963617.stm (accessed 16 January 2008).

72 Satre also makes this connection: 'If Henry Nevinson were writing in the early twenty-first century, he would demand that the huge international chocolate conglomerates use some of their enormous resources to ensure that the cocoa farmers earn a decent price for their products and that the farmers never use slave laborers.' Satre, *Chocolate on Trial*, 222.

73 International Institute of Tropical Agriculture, Sustainable Tree Crop Program, 'Child labor in the cocoa sector of West Africa: a synthesis of findings in Cameroon, Côte

d'Ivoire, Ghana and Nigeria', August 2002, www.globalexchange.org/campaigns/
fairtrade/cocoa/IITACocoaResearch.pdf (accessed 16 January 2008).
74 Byfield, 'Pawns and politics', 187, 206.
75 International Institute of Tropical Agriculture, 'Child labor in the cocoa sector',
22.
76 This, coupled with a lack of any other sources, makes it difficult to consider the
position of women who did not marry. Marriage was certainly presented as almost
inevitable by the women themselves but the limitations of the questionnaire did
not allow for a more detailed conversation about this.
77 Roberts, 'Rural women's access to labor', 104–5. Asare similarly points to the
obligations of wives to assist on their husband's farms in Ghana, using this as
evidence of their involvement in commercial cocoa production. Asare, 'Women
in commercial agriculture', 103–4.
78 See Okali, *Cocoa and Kinship*, 146.
79 Mikell, *Cocoa and Chaos*, 103. Similar research could usefully be carried out in
relation to Nigeria.
80 Boserup stresses the economic aspect of polygyny but, as Falola points out, the
practice cannot be explained solely in these terms. In the north of Nigeria, for example, as in other strict Muslim cultures, wives may be seen as status symbols. Boserup,
Women's Role in Economic Development, 37; Falola, *Culture and Customs*, 125.
81 Roberts, 'Rural women's access to labor', 106.
82 Berry suggests that 'the traditional Yoruba system of rural land tenure has been
"commercialized", but not altogether overthrown, by the spread of cocoa cultivation'.
Berry, 'The concept of innovation', 89. See also Gareth Austin, 'The emergence of
capitalist relations in South Asante cocoa-farming, c.1916–33', *Journal of African
History*, 28 (1987), 262.
83 Roberts, 'Rural women's access to labor'.
84 Galletti *et al.*, *Nigerian Cocoa Farmers*, 202.
85 Guyer, 'Food, cocoa, and the division of labour', 364.
86 Boserup links the gendering of agricultural labour to the type of technology used,
though she stresses that this is not immutable. So, whilst new equipment often
requires less physical strength to operate, men have monopolised its use. Boserup,
Women's Role in Economic Development, 53.
87 The quality of cocoa is a topic of frequent discussion in official records. See NNA,
AR5/PB6, Annual Reports of the Cocoa Marketing Board, 1947–53.
88 This may well be due to the absence of a new generation of cocoa farmers in the
light of increased opportunities for education and alternative employment. Walker
suggests that the expanding civil service was a particularly attractive employer in
post-independence Nigeria. Walker, 'Structural change, the oil boom and the cocoa
economy', 82.
89 This discontinuity between 'common sense' ideas about appropriate work for men
and women and actual experiences of work can be seen earlier in this chapter with
reference to the West Indies but also in the narratives of York factory workers (see
chapter five).
90 Guyer, 'Food, cocoa, and the division of labour', 362.
91 Women farmers may carry their children on their backs while working, for example, combining childcare with cocoa production.
92 Family structured worker experiences at the Rowntree factory in a number of
different ways, as explored in chapter five.
93 See Clarence-Smith, *Cocoa and Chocolate*, 164.
94 Walker, 'Structural change, the oil boom and the cocoa economy', 84.
95 See chapter five.
96 Grier, 'Pawns, porters, and petty traders', 177.
97 *Ibid.*, 175.
98 Organ, quoted in Southall, 'Cadbury on the Gold Coast', 127 (archive reference:
Cadbury UK, 186/219).

99 In the nineteenth century, the work of working-class white women was sometimes perceived in terms of racial degeneration. McClintock uses mining women as a strong example of this: 'Women's work . . . became the measure for the position of miners in the hierarchy of the British "race," and marked them as lagging behind in the nether regions of racial degradation.' The treatment of women was used as a measure for 'civilisation'. McClintock, *Imperial Leather*, 116.

100 Southall, 'Cadbury on the Gold Coast', 124.

101 Galletti *et al.*, *Nigerian Cocoa Farmers*, 41–2.

102 'Tribute to a "Coaster"', *BWM*, October 1955, 327.

103 Boserup, *Women's Role in Economic Development*, 53.

104 This was mentioned by women in both the Ondo and Oyo regions. The practice challenges the valuing of cocoa by western capitalism as solely a 'raw material' for chocolate. Some women in Trinidad registered for licences to sell their own 'stick-cocoa' and chocolate. Phillips Lewis, 'Women in the Trinidadian cocoa industry', 41.

105 I would also question the validity of separating the domains of domestic and paid work for women in York. Paid and unpaid work may intersect in a variety of ways in women's experiences and in their interpretations of these experiences.

106 Carl Chinn concludes that the working women of the 'urban poor' in England had control over their own wages and the family finances. This may well have been true in some cases but Chinn may overstate the case in his desire to emphasise the 'heroism of these women'. Carl Chinn, *They Worked All Their Lives: Women of the Urban Poor in England, 1880–1939* (Manchester: Manchester University Press, 1988), 101.

107 Roberts believes the 'separate purse' has been used to explain women's ability to run their own enterprises, without a consideration of other factors which might constrain such activity. Roberts, 'Rural women's access to labor', 103–4.

108 Guyer, 'Food, cocoa, and the division of labour', 368.

109 *Ibid.*, 369.

110 Clarence-Smith, *Cocoa and Chocolate*; William Gervase Clarence-Smith and Francois Ruf, 'Cocoa pioneer fronts: the historical determinants', in W. G. Clarence-Smith (ed.), *Cocoa Pioneer Fronts since 1800: The Role of Smallholders, Planters and Merchants* (Basingstoke: Macmillan Press, 1996), 1–22.

111 See Sara S. Berry, 'Christianity and the rise of cocoa-growing in Ibadan and Ondo', *Journal of the Historical Society of Nigeria*, 4: 3 (1968), 450. See also Sara S. Berry, *Cocoa, Custom and Socio-Economic Change in Rural Western Nigeria* (Oxford: Clarendon Press, 1975), 57–8.

112 Berry, 'The concept of innovation', 86.

113 Okali refers to Dominase in Ghana as a 'camp'. Okali, *Cocoa and Kinship*, 31.

114 Berry, 'The concept of innovation', 88. For more on migrant farmers in Nigeria see Berry, *Cocoa, Custom and Socio-Economic Change*.

115 Unfortunately it was not always clear to whom these houses actually belonged.

116 Young, 'Cocoa – Food of the Gods', *CWM*, Spring 1960, 13. See also chapter two.

117 See Meredith, 'The Colonial Office'. See also chapter two.

118 *Cocoa Express* (Nigeria), June–July 2002. See also Walker, 'Structural change, the oil boom and the cocoa economy'.

119 NNA, CSO 26, 36517 Volume I, 'Report of the Cocoa Commission Committee, 1939', 51.

120 NNA, CSO 26, 36148/S.140, Haig, 'Proposals for the Reorganisation of the Nigerian Cocoa Industry by the Registrar of Cooperative Societies 1944–45', 5.

121 See Gillian Wagner, *Chocolate Conscience*. Whilst Wagner correctly emphasises the good intentions of the Quaker companies in her title, I hope, by adding a question mark, to suggest the ambiguities and ambivalences inherent in the welfare projects of the Rowntree firm when placed in the historical context of colonialism.

122 Karl Maier points out the irony of referring to Nigeria as a 'developing' nation when the Nigerian 'people are far worse off now than they were thirty years ago'. Karl Maier, *This House Has Fallen: Nigeria in Crisis* (London: Penguin, 2000), xx.

123 BI, Rowntree Company Archive, CML/F/3/2, Accounts Ledger for 1926.
124 BI, Rowntree Company Archive, CML/F/3/8, Accounts Ledger for 1938–1941.
125 Southall, 'Cadbury on the Gold Coast', 180.
126 *CWM*, Christmas 1967, 8.
127 *CWM*, Christmas 1967, 10.
128 The York Board had been established in 1931 to oversee the York side of the Rowntree business. The Committee made decisions on matters from advertising policy to recruitment. See Judith Burg, *A Guide to the Rowntree and Mackintosh Company Archives, 1862–1969* (York: University of York, 1997), vii, 25–6.
129 BI, Rowntree Archive, R/BY/1/2, York Committee Minutes, June 1960–June 1962, Chairman's Business, 23 August 1960 and Chairman's Business, 4 July 1961.
130 Southall, 'Cadbury on the Gold Coast', 175.
131 *CWM*, Christmas 1967, 11. See chapter four for more on Nigerian visitors to the York factory.
132 NNA, CSO 26/2, 12723, Volume XIV, see the Annual Report for Oyo Province (1937), 23.
133 NNA, CSO 26, 34883, Volume I, 'Report of the Commission on the Marketing of West African Cocoa: Press Communique', *Nigeria Gazette Extraordinary*, 25 October 1938.
134 See Misty L. Bastian, '"Vultures of the marketplace": southeastern Nigerian women and discourses of the *Ogu Umunwaanyi* (Women's War) of 1929', in Jean Allman *et al.* (eds), *Women in African Colonial Histories* (Bloomington: Indiana University Press, 2002), 260–81. More recently, women took on a major oil firm, Chevron Nigeria, and demanded a share of the profits. They held male workers hostage on the oil terminal in southern Delta state, threatening to take off their clothes if they tried to leave (a traditional way of shaming men). See '"Deal reached" in Nigeria oil protest', BBC News, 16 July 2002, http://news.bbc.co.uk/1/hi/world/africa/2129281.stm (accessed 7 July 2004).
135 Walker, 'Structural change, the oil boom and the cocoa economy', 71–87.
136 'Enabling rural women', Leaflet produced by COWAN, n.d.
137 On the dangerous overlap between 'representation' and 'colonisation', see Antoinette Burton, *Burdens of History* (Chapel Hill: University of North Carolina Press, 1994), 212.
138 Daphne Patai, 'U.S. academics and third world women: is ethical research possible?' in Gluck and Patai (eds), *Women's Words*, 146. Ruth Behar has also conceived of texts as commodities, seeing both as produced by the labours of people differently located. She is not so explicit about the exploitative processes of production, however, focusing more on the polyglot nature of texts. Behar, *Translated Woman*, 17.
139 Alcoff critiques the 'retreat response', observing that it is too often a desire to avoid criticism, thereby bolstering the power of the author. Linda Alcoff, 'The problem of speaking for others', *Cultural Critique*, 17 (1991), 17.
140 Julie Marcus, 'Racism, terror and the production of Australian auto/biographies', in Judith Okely and Helen Callaway (eds), *Anthropology and Autobiography* (London: Routledge, 1992), 106.

CHAPTER FOUR

Minstrels, missionaries and the Minster: race, imperialism and the historic city

Today, tourists flock to 'historic York'. They visit the Minster and the Shambles; they walk along the ancient city walls.[1] York makes a healthy profit from its past: selling itself as a Viking and a Roman city, a medieval city, a beautiful city steeped in a very particular construction of history. Moreover, it is presented by the tourism sector as the gateway to the Yorkshire Dales, a quintessentially 'English' rural landscape, the home of 'Yorkshiremen' and plain-speaking Yorkshire hospitality.[2] York thus may seem an unlikely subject for a study of British imperialism. Yet the city boasted two important industries from the nineteenth century in railways and chocolate manufacture, both with significant ties to empire.[3] As we have seen, confectionery production was only made possible by materials and labour sourced from the colonies. Tourists see little of this imperial heritage, though they might pass the former Terry's chocolate factory while sitting on an open-top tour bus, or enjoy a Kit Kat in the café at the Jorvik Viking Centre.[4] Unlike port cities such as Liverpool and Bristol, York has not yet made explicit its historic ties to empire. The significance of imperialism for the people and places involved in chocolate manufacture demands further interrogation.

Concern with the impact of imperialism on the domestic as well as the colonial sphere, the 'centripetal' rather than 'centrifugal' effects of imperialism, has been a significant trend in historical research over the last twenty-five years. Critics including John MacKenzie, Mary Louise Pratt, Catherine Hall and Sonya Rose have studied the ways in which imperialism did not simply work in outward directions from the metropole. As Pratt describes, 'Borders and all, the entity called Europe was constructed from the outside in as much as from the inside out.'[5] The work of Hall and MacKenzie is particularly relevant for my own study in that they have broadened their analysis of the 'metropole' to include more than just London. They both discuss imperialism as present in smaller, provincial towns, although they focus on the larger cities of Birmingham and Glasgow respectively. Hall, in *Civilising Subjects*, offers an analysis of Birmingham, which brilliantly tackles the complexities of imperial identities in the self-proclaimed 'midland metropolis'.[6]

York was certainly not an 'imperial city' in the same ways as Birmingham, Liverpool or Glasgow. It was more likely to be perceived in the nineteenth and twentieth centuries, at least by non-residents, as a provincial capital of little national or international importance. Yet, whilst York could certainly be conceived of as 'peripheral' within England, it was also presented locally as a 'second city' in its own right. I hope to illuminate how such identities were situated in the context of imperialism and in relation to the chocolate industry in particular. For if we are really going to understand how empire was experienced within Britain, we need to extend our analyses beyond London. How did people in the peripheries of the nation, who had perhaps never been to the capital or beyond perceived local boundaries, come to understand imperialism and their place in the imperial order?[7]

Rowntree & Co. maintained strong material and sentimental connections with the city of York, even as the firm expanded both nationally and internationally. Their in-house journal, advertising and other officially produced materials offered ways of reading the city.[8] The firm thus provides a way into thinking about how York has been located, constructed and represented in relation to imperialism. This chapter draws on company sources to explore the complex interrelatedness of 'home' and 'empire' for Rowntree and for York.[9] I examine the role played by the firm in influencing understandings of race, empire and the city, as well as in providing a space for employees effectively to act out 'local' and 'imperial' consciousness.

I begin this chapter with the ways in which Rowntree constructed their relationship to York and the versions of the city they represented and created. I then consider how Rowntree represented the rest of the world, and their own place in the British empire. Finally, I suggest how the factory was a site of implicitly imperial pastimes and the spatial embodiment of imperial ideologies. Workers were involved in making global, often imperial connections at an economic, social and cultural level not only through the chocolates they produced but through migration and missionary work, and through the performance and spectatorship of race in factory minstrel shows. The Rowntree firm and their employees were not detached from the British empire but were living and working within and through it in specific ways. White workers' understandings of their connections to empire, however undeveloped, were shaped both by local conditions and narratives, and by the discourses of their employer, as well as by media such as the BBC and cinema.[10]

The firm, the city and the nation

City of our dreams: imagining York

Rowntree adopted a variety of local images and narratives. York had special meaning as the site of the first Rowntree factory and as the home of the majority of its workers over generations. The city thus featured heavily in the workers' magazine, *CWM*, and in company publicity in terms of both product marketing and general promotion of the Rowntree name. It was 'historic', 'ancient' York that tended to dominate. An early piece in the *CWM* from October 1902 lamented the destruction of one of the city's oldest houses: 'In an ancient city like York, the streets, the houses, the churches, chapels, and hospitals are pages in the story of the sixty generations who have dwelt here within historic times.' Nevertheless, the author of this piece accepted that 'that "which decayeth and waxeth old is ready to vanish away"'.[11] The article concluded by looking forward to the future of the city, indeed the future of the nation: 'Should we not aspire to build with such regard to use, beauty, and honest workmanship, that the men of five centuries hence may part as regretfully from the structures of Edward VII.'s time, as we do from those of the Tudor sovereigns?' *CWM* was never simply a factory journal; it was a space for local histories and for debates about local and national futures. This reflected the broad interests and roles of Rowntree management in local and national politics, as well as their commitment to engaging and educating their workforce in subjects beyond the factory. Moreover, tapping into local pride was a way of transposing local loyalties into company loyalty, bypassing the potentially more contentious arena of the shopfloor.[12]

That Rowntree allowed their workers – and their wives – to attend the final rehearsal of the York Pageant of 1909 suggests the importance they attached to the knowledge of local histories and the fostering of local pride. The intended significance of the event was spelled out in the magazine: 'One of the results of the late Pageant . . . is that we are all reminded of how important a place our city was in the past.'[13] Workers watched the history of York in procession, through the Romans, the Vikings and the Normans. They could then read about it, and view photographs of the key players, in *CWM*. The long history of York, prior to industrialisation and modern empire-building, was strongly emphasised. This was not an unblemished past, as the author recalled, 'The grim scene of the persecuted Jews, self-dying to save their honour' at Clifford's Tower. Yet York people are barely held accountable; instead it is 'the Lion-hearted King' who is blamed for failing to watch over his subjects.[14] From this pre-industrial history, Rowntree factory workers resident in the city were to construct local identities: 'It has given us as citizens a character, the more honourable part to sustain and, if possible, exceed; the less honourable, to put behind us.'[15] It is 'the past' which defines York and its people; a past which is being constantly (re)defined both within the company and within the city.

Rowntree narratives concentrate on the former significance of York as a political, religious, economic and cultural centre, implicitly and at times explicitly confirming perceptions of the city as a 'provincial' backwater town in the present. An article by J. B. Morrell from 1953, entitled 'The Streets and Buildings within York City Walls', empha-sised once again the 'long history' of the city, dating back to the Roman occupation: 'we have the remains of the Roman fortifications and many articles used in the daily life of the Roman British citizens'.[16] As a Roman 'colonia' York had been part of an empire – the very empire that would become such an important trope for Victorian imperialism. As we shall see, the significance of the city as a Roman fort fed into notions of York as the 'second city of the realm'.[17] However, the emphasis on York's Roman history also located the city in a pre-industrial past and worked to negate any involvement with the economics of British imperialism from the late nineteenth century. As in the 1902 piece, Morrell emphasises York's 'luxurious' architectural heritage: 'Old York within the walls is a Georgian town, it is full of classical porches and fine dwelling houses.' Again, there is no social or economic context given to the architecture of the city, no sense of the origins of the wealth behind such grand buildings. Moreover, it is the lack of industrial development, of being, as Morrell puts it, 'by-passed' by the industrial revolution, which has preserved the 'historic' landscape of the city.[18]

Histories of racial and imperial violence haunt the proud local tales of the *CWM*. In the 1902 piece on the 'Vanishing House', for example, the author observes, but does not explain, 'rows of grotesque negro heads' along the cornices. Focusing particularly on the late seventeenth-century history of the house, the author notes, 'It is a curious coincidence that the three favourite beverages of tea, coffee, and cocoa were all introduced into England at the period of which we are speaking.' This 'coincidence' leaves little room for histories of exploitation in procuring such beverages; the luxury drinks were simply imported 'from the Continent, as soon as any demand arose for them'.[19]

Twenty-one years later, an article on the Merchant Adventurer's Hall relishes in the fantasy of ghosts from York's mercantile past. Sitting in the Hall, the author imagines himself as 'a York boy in the thriving, bustling days when ours was the greatest trading city in the North of England, second only to London in wealth and importance'. He overhears 'swarthy sailors' relating 'Terrible stories of the sufferings of Christian sailors captured by the Moors and Turks . . . ; of the horrible living death of the galley slaves'. These gruesome and exotic tales are safely contained in the distant past. From the late sixteenth century, according to this particular narrative, York would have no share in England's imperial adventures, the river Ouse being unable to carry the 'ships of greater burden': 'then, alas! the prosperity of York was swiftly ebbing, and merchants and ship captains were shut out from the glory and glamour of the new world'. The tone of the piece is ultimately ambiguous, as the author appears to mourn the 'sad, sad story' of York's fall from glory yet clearly enjoys this 'quiet, sleepy' city.[20] There is no mention of the significance of the railway industry in York, with its grand station, or indeed of the chocolate industry itself, either of which could have offered an alternative narrative of modern prosperity.

The local focus of the works' magazine continued into the 1950s and 1960s, with an increasingly nostalgic tinge made possible by post-war prosperity. Discussions of how to cope with diseases, poverty and economic depression were replaced by musings on 'Institutions of York', such as the York Regatta and the Art Gallery.[21] Such pieces evoked a sense of community and belonging through persistent references to 'our City'. In autumn 1966, the Yorkshire Museum was the focus of attention, an institution with an 'appeal more peculiar to the citizens of York' than to tourists. Here, Rowntree workers would be able to 'feel and see . . . the greatness of York's past' and would learn to understand 'the importance of preserving these aspects of our city which reflect its antiquity and make it such an evocative experience to live here'.[22] Such articles drew readers' attention to the rich, and tangible, history of the city, which in itself conferred national significance: 'There is no town in England where the extent and development of architecture can be shown so well as in York.'[23] That the value of York's buildings was not always self-evident, however, that 'Historic York' needed to be worked at, is apparent from Morrell's comment on the Assembly Rooms, built in 1736: 'York did not realise until it was restored and redecorated for the Festival of 1951 what a wonderful building it possessed.' Again, the author places the city within a national framework of meaning, as making an important contribution to the Festival of Britain.[24] The history of York is thus retold in very specific ways, emphasising the beauty of the city's architecture as a local and national treasure, yet divorcing this from any taint of economic activity. Industry, including chocolate manufacture, conveniently takes place beyond the city walls: 'The new factories [are] . . . well placed on the outskirts of the city.'[25] Any tensions between modern industry and the historic town were thereby resolved.

Whilst the particular urban space of York was an almost constant preoccupation of the *CWM*, the magazine also reflected and promoted regional Yorkshire identity. This ranged from editorials rendered in Yorkshire dialect to idealised photographs of Yorkshire scenery. The back cover of the magazine from summer 1953, for example, depicts the York Mansion House, under the heading 'Beautiful Yorkshire'. The photograph was accompanied by a description of how the Mansion House had been a site for providing 'hospitality to many very distinguished visitors from all over the world'. As we shall see in more detail later, international visitors were significant in suggesting York's important place in national and global (formerly imperial) economic networks. Yet the overall tone of such images of 'Beautiful Yorkshire', which were frequently used as covers to the *CWM* throughout the 1950s, was of an inward-looking local pride.[26] For instance, on the back cover of the Christmas edition of 1953 was a picture of an isolated cottage in Swaledale, accompanied by lines from Emily Brontë:

> There is a spot, 'mid barren hills,
> Where winter howls . . .
> . . .
> But what on earth is half so dear –
> So longed for – as the hearth of home?[27]

The warmth and comfort of home (as protected domestic space) within a winter landscape is powerfully evoked here. The Yorkshire countryside, though harsh, is also 'home'.

Such visual and literary representations served to fix York and Yorkshire in time, representing 'historical' buildings and an 'unchanging' (with the exception of the four seasons), quintessentially English rural countryside. Rowntree, then, were complicit in representing and creating a York divorced from more 'modern' political and economic concerns such as colonialism and decolonisation. In their vision, particularly in the postwar period, York is a beautiful city, untarnished (thanks in part to the Quaker industrialists and philanthropists) by vast industrial developments, poverty or the taint of racism. This could be a useful marketing tool, as I will demonstrate in the following section. However, Rowntree could also create more complex and contradictory versions of the city.

The relationship of Rowntree to York was framed in tones of benevolence, cooperation and moral duty: 'Over the years there has naturally developed a very close connection between the company and the city and we have always been conscious of our responsibility towards the maintenance of community life and prosperity.'[28] Key Rowntree figures, such as Benjamin Seebohm Rowntree and J. B. Morrell, took an active interest in local issues and often performed civic or political roles. Seebohm Rowntree's renowned surveys of the extent of poverty within York were celebrated within the work's magazine.[29] An extract from Morrell's *The City of Our Dreams*, meanwhile, detailing his vision of York's future, was printed in the *CWM* of summer 1939 for the consumption of Rowntree employees (though we cannot be sure whether, or how, they were to read it).[30] If workers flicked past such serious items in the *CWM*, there is no doubt that they experienced the Rowntree legacy in other ways. The firm had a significant impact on the physical and social environment of York, creating spaces such as parks and swimming baths. In such a way was the firm and the city intertwined for both Rowntree workers and York residents, as well as for visitors. As one retired female employee explained to me, 'Rowntrees is York, or was York.'[31] Cocoa farmers and other producers do not register in these narratives of the local firm.

'I'm Plain Mr York of York, Yorks': marketing the city
In 1926, the Rowntree firm created the character 'Mr York' as part of an advertising campaign for their Plain York chocolate bars. This portly white gentleman, in top hat and bow tie, drew on ideas about a certain kind of Yorkshire/English masculinity: plain-speaking yet ever the gentleman, polite and chivalrous.[32] According to Fitzgerald, Mr York's 'portly simplicity' was intended to evoke the chief characteristic of the chocolate, 'its plainness'.[33] Plain chocolate was what we would now more commonly call 'dark' chocolate. As noted in chapter one, advertising for products such as Dairy Box and Cadbury's Dairy Milk emphasised the addition of milk (the goodness of the 'English' countryside), implicitly purifying the colonial product of cocoa. In the Mr York campaigns, however, it is the very 'plainness' of the chocolate which is made coterminous with a manly Englishness and Yorkshireness. Though the chocolate is seemingly closer to its colonial raw material, then, it can still harbour very English meanings.[34] Mr York's name, and that of his namesake chocolate, symbolises the close connections the Rowntree firm chose to stress between themselves and the English city of their origin. Indeed, whenever the character introduces himself, he repeats the location of York, as the

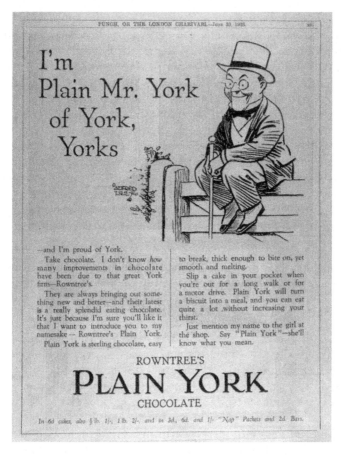

Figure 7 Mr York, the local white patriarch, in 1926.

brand name of the chocolate, three times. The existence of Mr York is revealing of the use of 'York', as both a physical and imagined location, in marketing campaigns.[35]

Prior to the 1930s and the invention of new Rowntree brands, images of York served an important purpose in selling a range of products. The Minster, a symbol of the north as well as of York itself, appeared frequently on packaging and other promotional materials, as did other signifiers of York and Yorkshire.[36] Advertising and packaging for Plain York featured a York coat of arms, clearly presenting the product within a framework of civic loyalties. Consumers were buying both the chocolate and the pleasing image of 'Ancient York'. For York residents, this presented opportunities for the expression of local affection and pride; for others, the chocolate offered the possibility of historical tourism.[37] More broadly, images of York offered connotations of longevity and tradition to Rowntree products, as well as associations of a distinctly 'English' heritage (although the bar walls which featured so strongly were remnants of Norman conquest).

In representing the city in its graduate recruitment literature of the 1950s, however, Rowntree directly challenged perceptions of York as a 'medieval backwater', drawing instead on the language of evolution, civilisation and national as well as regional identity: 'The southerner often has the idea that tundra begins at the Trent and that Yorkshire has barely recovered from the Ice Age. We are, though we say it ourselves, a fairly civilised people, cultured and outwardly average, normal Britons.' The firm hoped to attract talented graduates through aggrandising the Yorkshire location:

> Ever since the Romans came people have enjoyed living here: whether your interest be in the arts, or in darts, in shunting or in hunting, there is ample opportunity in the district. If you are bored, a fast train will take you to London . . . but it is not often needed.[38]

Again, acceptable colonisation by the Roman empire is voiced, as are the benefits of the railway industry. York is even placed on a par with London, the modern, if no longer imperial, metropolis.

Whilst Rowntree associated themselves strongly with the city of York, despite locating their factory just outside the city itself, Cadbury rarely capitalised on any connection with the city of Birmingham. As a crowded city of heavy industry, Birmingham did not lend itself in the same way to chocolate box packaging or advertising. It was useful only to emphasise Cadbury's central location in England and the closeness of the factory to a centre of industry and commerce. Disassociating themselves from their urban heritage, Cadbury stressed their rural location in Bournville. This was not an unchanging pastoral idyll, however, but a modern, clean and efficient space for work and play. In representing this space to workers through the factory magazine, Cadbury nevertheless took care to construct a history for Bournville which gave it legitimacy and a sense of a meaningful, shared past for residents and employees. The first edition of the *Bournville Works Magazine* (*BWM*), from November 1902, included a paper on 'The Historical Associations of Bournville and District', complete with a reference to the 'old Roman road'.[39] As for Rowntree, local spaces were important to Cadbury; these locations were quintessentially 'English' spaces, divorced from colonial relations in the present, though made possible by distant empires of the past.

The second city: royal connections

John MacKenzie has written of Glasgow as 'Second City of the Empire', competing for this title with cities such as Liverpool and Birmingham.[40] Yet York also laid claim to the title of 'second city' – not in such an explicitly imperial frame but still being placed as second in the nation to London. Though Hutchinson and Palliser feel that this 'proud title' had become 'an empty historical survival', it clearly still held meaning for local people as late as the 1950s.[41] In a speech broadcast as part of a radio show covering coronation celebrations in the north of England in 1953, Councillor J. Shannon, Sheriff of York, introduced himself, 'As the Queen's representative in the second city of the Kingdom'. He stressed York's loyalty to the monarchy: 'as unquenchable and steadfast as it was in the reign of Elizabeth the First and before'.[42] York's claim to the status of the kingdom's second capital was legitimised through reference to its long history of being 'capital of the north', once the headquarters of the monarchy in the north of England. I will now examine the ways in which Rowntree adopted images and rhetorics of the monarchy in presenting itself as an intrinsically patriotic enterprise, and the extent to which the firm engaged with the position of the royal family as figureheads of the British empire.

In 1899, Rowntree, along with Cadbury and Fry, sent out a substantial shipment of chocolate, on the orders of Queen Victoria, to soldiers in the Boer War. The chocolate (intended as a New Year gift) was packed in special tins bearing a stately picture of the Queen, and the words, 'South Africa. 1900.' British chocolate functioned here as both the fuel for imperial armies and the bearer of imperial symbolism.[43] Fittingly, it was Rowntree's 'Queen' brand of chocolate, made with the finest 'tropical' ingredients, which was chosen for the gift.[44] For supplying 40,000 tins of chocolate, Rowntree received the prestigious Royal Warrant. However, the provision of chocolate rations for soldiers conflicted with the pacifist stance of the Quakers. Bradley notes that the situation caused a crisis of conscience for Cadbury management. Similarly, Wagner details how Rowntree rejected the idea of sending out Queen's Gift Tins to retailers following the receipt of the warrant 'because it would be "pandering to some degree to the present war fever"'. The value of the warrant was, however, too great to abstain from the scheme altogether.[45]

Chocolate bearing commemorative images of the monarchy was not simply sent 'out' to the empire, it was also distributed in a domestic context. To celebrate the occasion of a royal coronation, and to demonstrate the patriotic fervour of the firm, Rowntree workers and local children received gifts of Rowntree chocolates packaged in images of royalty. Ordinary consumers, meanwhile, could save tokens from cocoa packaging to receive special coronation tins. Cadbury adopted a similar approach, with a number of special coronation products for consumption by both workers and the general public at home and overseas. In 1953, the *Bournville Works Magazine* reported that, 'Both Cadbury and Fry Coronation boxes have been much in demand in British territories overseas, notably in East and West Africa, the West Indies, Malaya, Hong Kong, Malta and Ceylon.'[46] Royal associations could also be physically inscribed on the company premises through dedicating new buildings and features to the monarch.[47] In 1902, for example, a new cricket pavilion had been unveiled at Rowntree in honour of the coronation. The firms thus played a role in fuelling and reflecting popular feeling towards the royal family, which was deeply entwined with patriotic sentiments.

John MacKenzie argues that from Queen Victoria's declaration of herself as Empress of India until the coronation of Queen Elizabeth II, the monarchy became the 'gorgeously opulent centrepiece' of the

Figure 8 Women at the York factory packing tins commemorating the coronation of Edward VII, 1902. The women are surrounded by, and are working directly with, patriotic objects and images celebrating the imperial monarch.

[142]

theatre of imperialism.[48] Rowntree management certainly made explicit connections for their employees between the royal family and the empire. At the planting of a White Bean tree to mark the Silver Jubilee in 1935, Benjamin Seebohm Rowntree evoked shared understandings of an imperial monarchy: 'No words of mine are necessary to emphasise the service which our King and Queen have rendered to the Empire.' He continued, 'The Throne is in itself an institution that makes for Imperial stability.'[49] Whether or not there was conscious, overt engagement by the majority of Rowntree workers with the politics of imperialism, the pride in receiving chocolate tins embellished with images of beloved kings and queens cannot be divorced from the position of the monarchy as the rulers of a vast empire. Chocolate was used to mark royal, imperial occasions, encouraging connections to be made between the firm and royalty, the firm and the nation, and the firm and empire. Rowntree products, and by implication those producing these products, could achieve greater importance and significance by such associations. As MacKenzie observes, 'imperial patriotism was . . . profitable'.[50] Cadbury clearly thought so: to commemorate the Silver Jubilee they created the 'Empire' box, which 'depicted in full colour the flags of the chief countries of the Empire'.[51]

Imperial patriotism was not reserved for special occasions, and the British chocolate manufacturers, at least until the early twentieth century, readily adopted royal themes in their packaging and advertising.[52] Chocolate tins, boxes and wrappers, emblazoned with symbols of the monarchy, were tangible, collectable souvenirs of an imperial royal family, the aesthetic figureheads of colonial industry. Both Rowntree and Cadbury created assortment brands under royal titles. Cadbury laid claim to producing the first assortment named after a reigning monarch with their 'King Edward' assortment, replaced in 1910 by the 'King George'. In the late nineteenth and early twentieth centuries, Rowntree assortments included 'Queen Mary', 'King George' and 'Prince of Wales'. There were also more explicit references to empires past and present with, for example, Rowntree's 'Emperor' chocolates. With the intervention of George Harris in the 1930s, Rowntree shifted their attention to the Black Magic and Dairy Box brands but Cadbury continued to use royal associations to market assortments such as 'Princess Elizabeth'.

With the nation still struggling to recover from the Second World War, having lost India, and with violent colonial rebellions in Malaya and Kenya, the coronation of Elizabeth II in 1953 was a moment to reassert the significance of Britain on the world stage. Although the rhetoric of empire was increasingly problematic, Britain could still be presented as a global power buoyed up by the combined strength

Figure 9 Workers leaving the York factory during coronation week. Front cover of *Cocoa Works Magazine*, Summer 1953.

of the Commonwealth.[53] The Rowntree company drew on these narratives of renewed national and international promise. The summer 1953 edition of the *CWM* had on its cover a photo of workers leaving the factory during coronation week. Above their heads a banner proclaimed, 'Long Live the Queen', whilst Union flags lined the path. Inside, a photo of Big Ben, a metonym for the capital city and the country as a whole, was entitled, 'This England'. Extracts from Shakespeare emphasised England's isolation as, 'This precious stone set in the silver sea,/ Which serves it in the office of a wall', but juxtaposed this with the prestigious place of the English in the world: 'Renowned for their deeds as far from home,/ For Christian service and true chivalry'.[54] The opposite page offered 'Some Reflections' which similarly harmonised national and international concerns and inter-Commonwealth divisions through the device of the monarchy:

Amidst the clamorous manifestations of loyalty on Coronation Day there emerged a unity which transcended such differences as exist among the members of the British Commonwealth. There was too a heartfelt desire that this family of nations over which the Queen reigns should be more glorious and more united than ever before.[55]

Historians are now challenging the orthodoxy that there was a lack of interest in empire after the First World War.[56] Certainly here, in the *CWM* of 1953, is a strong narrative of future imperial glory for Britain, if in the revised frame of the Commonwealth. Rowntree optimism for the future glory of this 'family of nations' patched over the deepening cracks in the old empire. Stuart Ward astutely interprets such faith in the Commonwealth as an 'anaesthetic' for the pain of decolonisation.[57]

The emphasis of the article then shifts from the family of nations to the renewed primacy and reputation of British manufacturing in the 'new Elizabethan age': 'We have it in us to out-distance any nation in the world in quality of work, output and staying power.' Rowntree urged their employees to renewed efforts in the name of the glory of the nation:

> Let us . . . dedicate ourselves to the task of making this new Elizabethan age one which will go down in history as being the age when the people of Britain re-discovered 'the will to work' and produced goods commanding world-wide respect and admiration.[58]

The international reputation of the firm was frequently stressed to workers through various mediums, including the training programme for new starters, but here it is given a much broader, implicitly imperial, patriotic context. Yet again, the labours of the colonies are subsumed under the industry of Britain.

Loyalty to the royal family was enacted locally as befitting the city's long history of royal associations. Rowntree bought into and exploited local royalist feelings, as demonstrated through the firm's participation in the coronation celebrations. Affection for the royal family, and the imperial patriotism they signified, was also a useful marketing tool for Rowntree products on a national and international scale. Royal connections were thus a key way in which York and the Rowntree firm were willingly implicated in the imperialist project. So how did Rowntree explicitly represent their place in the empire and in the world more generally? How did they construct and mediate relationships between their workers and the world 'outside' the factory, the city and the 'nation'?

Rowntree and the (imperial) world

Reading and representing empire

Whilst Rowntree were keen to construct themselves as a local company, thereby negating in many ways the critical importance of colonialism to their success, they also actively promoted their international significance. New workers at the factory were to be imbued with a sense of themselves as workers in an international arena, and those responsible for training staff in the 1930s were instructed to:

> point out to the girls how, even in their little way, they are important cogs in the huge wheel that is Rowntrees, and that carelessness or incompetence on their part may have a disastrous effect on the reputation of the firm – not only in England but in foreign lands.[59]

Ideally, women workers were to adopt a global outlook and to have some sense of the international destinations of their products. A display in a factory corridor in 1955, entitled 'Round the World with Rowntrees', graphically illustrated the global reach of Rowntree exports through linking confectionery packaging to various points on a map of the world.[60]

Women were also to be made aware of the origins of the cocoa and other materials they were working with. In a radio broadcast about life at the factory, Madge Munro, a young worker in the 1930s, described how 'newcomers ... attend lantern lectures and see the history of a chocolate from start to finish, hear just in what parts of the world our cocoa beans are grown, where we get our gum from, and what we use it for'.[61] Cultivating an interest in the work of the factory was a key aim in worker education at Rowntree; it is difficult to judge just how successful this scheme was. In oral history interviews, women often have only hazy memories of this time at the firm, possibly because it was not seen as relevant or useful in their daily working lives. However, when asked about where the cocoa was coming from, some women did mention Africa (though this may have been prompted by having already discussed my research in Nigeria) and one had memories of displays at the factory on the production of cocoa.[62]

The *CWM* was a key medium for the transmission of official Rowntree narratives on the origins of 'raw materials' used at the firm. From its first publication in 1902, as discussed in previous chapters, there were regular articles on the farming of products such as cocoa and gum. These were usually penned by a Rowntree official, following a trip to monitor processes at the source of production. Whilst there were very few images in the *CWM* in these early years, such articles were invariably accompanied by at least one photograph of foreign locations and peoples. As Pratt suggests, 'the imperial metropolis tends to understand itself as determining the periphery' and yet the metropolis 'habitually binds itself to the ways in which the periphery determines the metropolis – beginning, perhaps, with the latter's obsessive need to present and re-present its peripheries and its others continually to itself'.[63] The need to represent cocoa producers, and others, in the in-house magazine is indicative of the ways in which the producers of so-called raw materials, seemingly fixed at the start of the cocoa chain, were making their influence felt at the 'heart' of chocolate production in York. Indeed, at times, Rowntree narratives embraced the inter-relationship of workers in a truly global industry: 'the sand of an African desert is found in the Gum Store room; . . . the rose leaves on the chocolates packed by Miss Leake's girls were plucked last summer by a dark-eyed French maiden of old Provence'.[64] This 1912 series of articles, entitled, 'From the Five Continents to the Cocoa Works', established Rowntree in York as the centre of not merely an imperial, but a global industry: 'If the sun never sets on the British Empire, we may with even greater justice claim that it never sets on Rowntrees' employees.'[65]

Despite this impulse to make connections between Rowntree workers across the globe, racial, imperial and gender hierarchies were maintained. Tales of exotic workers and of traces of exotic locations finding their way into the York factory were intended for the titillation of white workers. Rowntree agents travelling overseas brought home stories of adventure and contact with strange peoples to be retold in the factory journal. The very first edition of the *CWM* contained the story of Mr J. Wilhelm Rowntree's narrow escape from an explosion on the Royal Mail Steamer, 'Para', on his way to the firm's plantations in the West Indies. Arriving safely, Mr Rowntree was relieved 'to hear the witless chatter of the negro boatmen'.[66] Such early encounters involve very little direct interaction, and there are certainly no reports of conversation with non-white workers.

Twenty-three years later, another Rowntree representative was being rowed ashore, but this time in the more threatening space of the 'Dark Continent'. A. V. Iredale, arriving in Accra on the Gold Coast, was transfixed by the 'ten lusty Kroo boys like beautiful bronze statues' who rowed his boat. Yet his desire is edged with fear, and he evokes, only half-jokingly, shared cultural stereotypes of 'cannibals' for his readers: 'Surf boats . . . look very much like the pictures we see of savage war canoes. However, I managed to avoid being the *piece de resistance* at a cannibal feast.'[67] Seebohm Rowntree also took a trip in 1925, reporting on his South African visit in the December issue of the *CWM*. The article, entitled 'B. S. R. Among the Blacks', recounts Seebohm Rowntree actually interacting with the people of the Transkei. B. S. R., however, places African people outside of the social and economic categories he would adopt in York. Accordingly, 'There is no poverty' amongst the 'natives'. The concept of poverty simply does not apply here; instead Rowntree focuses on the laziness and low expectations of the people of the Transkei: 'Very little work is done, for the standard of life is very low.' Like Wilhelm Rowntree, he draws on a stereotype of happy, uncivilised natives, frequently emphasising their lack of clothing and failure to conform to western cultural standards: 'Altogether the people seem a happy lot. They have no artistic ability, though the women often wear bead necklaces.'[68] The native 'other' is defined, for the benefit of readers back home in York, as contented yet as socially, culturally and morally inferior.

As well as stories, agents travelling in the empire brought home exotic artefacts to be placed on display for the entertainment and education of both visitors to the factory and the workers themselves. The *CWM* of December 1923 displayed photos of items collected by Mr S. H. Davies in the West Indies, under the heading, 'From the Land Where the Cocoa Grows'. The collection, held in the visitors' rooms of the dining block, included the jaws of a shark and a baby alligator.[69] Cadbury engaged in similar displays at their Bournville Works Museum. An article from only the second issue of the *BWM* depicts a 'swarthy' South African 'Witch Doctor', wearing his 'magical' belt: 'On the front of the belt you will notice the word Cadbury, which Nkentenknite says he copied from an empty box which he picked up on the other side of the Zambesi river.' The author treats the belt with amusement as a potential advertising tool: 'it may possibly be arranged to encircle with it some stalwart member of the official staff ("Export" by preference, because of their intimate connection with outlandish affairs), and to turn him loose with all its benevolent possibilities, upon the long-suffering British public'.[70]

Displays of objects and photographs within the factory, and on the pages of the works' magazine, indicate an anthropological urge to categorise colonial peoples within company discourse. Early editions of the *CWM* carry 'Scenes from Jamaica' in which photographs of the 'coolies' and the 'negroes' are juxtaposed. The intention is explicit: 'The third illustration shows some of the Jamaican negroes on the estate, and if the printer does his work well the great difference in features between these and the coolies will be easily seen.'[71] As mentioned in chapter two, Indian women of the West Indian cocoa plantations appear frequently in photographs, usually wearing beautiful necklaces and bangles. They are rarely depicted at work, but appear to have adopted a pose for the camera (though sometimes they are carrying baskets of cocoa pods). Whilst these women are treated as exotic beauties with 'picturesque' names, black Africans and black West Indians (particularly men) could arouse more complex responses of derision and condescension, mixed with fear and desire.

For A. V. Iredale, as illustrated above, African men were a source of fascination, fear and disgust. On his way to set up West African buying stations in 1925, he met a former king of Ashanti and he recounts for the *CWM* a tale of 400 human sacrifices apparently made at his 'enstoolment': 'which I just mention to illustrate how very few years, even now, West Africa is removed from savagery'. He must have a photograph of the king and takes 'one against his wish, which I am asking the editor to reproduce'.[72] The editor complied and the reader becomes complicit in voyeuristically observing King Prempeh, now a Christian and dressed in a western suit, from a safe distance. The *CWM* was a space where workers could view photographs of colonial workers and other exotic natives juxtaposed with photographs of white co-workers from the York factory. In the postwar period, as we shall see later in this chapter, the safety of distance collapsed and workers could come into contact with former colonial peoples in the physical space of the factory itself.

Representing the countries producing key ingredients was a constant preoccupation throughout the history of the *CWM*. As the firm expanded, associated companies were formed to manufacture Rowntree chocolates and confectionery. These companies operated in Scotland and Ireland, and in the dominions of Canada, Australia and South Africa. Although most had been founded in the 1920s or 1930s, it was not until the 1950s that they were considered to be of interest to *CWM* readers. The summer 1953 edition of the *CWM* introduced a series of articles: 'The Rowntree Associated Companies in Australia, Canada, Eire and South Africa are all engaged in the manufacture of chocolate confectionery, most of them reproducing York's staple lines. It is believed that the activities of these Companies will be of interest to readers.'[73] York maintained its status as the heart of the Rowntree enterprise, the centre of expansion, with associated companies mainly 'reproducing' York products.

The tone of these articles reflects a common theme at the time of the Rowntree 'family' with York at the head. In his Christmas message of 1953, the chairman remembered, 'not only those working in York but those other members of the family in numerous other places at home and abroad'.[74] The distinctions between home and abroad are maintained but transcended by the Rowntree 'family'. This fits with the broader contemporary discourse of the familial Commonwealth.

The metaphor of 'family', whilst suggesting connection and even intimacy, also suggests the power relations between different family members. The 'family' metaphor could thus be used to legitimise and effectively disguise what had been essentially imperial relationships. As Hall and Rose argue, 'the homely terms of family helped to make empire ordinary and a part of everyday life'.[75]

As well as articles directly related to the manufacture of Rowntree products, the *CWM* featured more general pieces which may have contributed to understandings of empire and colonialism. In very early editions of the journal, these could include fictional narratives that engaged explicitly with imaginings of empire. For instance, in April 1902, a piece was printed for children entitled, 'An Ostrich Story'. It is the tale of two young children, Toby and Lil, in South Africa with their parents: 'a whole new country, where there were . . . snakes and baboons, and locusts'. The children wander off and encounter a two-year-old 'kaffir' boy: 'He was very brown, and he was naked except for a little red shirt; quite a new kind of baby Toby and Lil thought.' The story evokes an exotic landscape, a 'fairy-land' for the children but full of dangers in the eyes of the adults. It draws on the assumed innocence of children and their ability to make friends across boundaries of race: 'children, like kittens, can make friends with-out speech'. In the end, the story reinforces the privileged perspective of white people, as it is only they who are allowed to speak. The two-year-old boy's language is 'all "clicks"' and he is led along by the 'two sturdy little people in white smocks'. Fortunately, the children escape being attacked by an angry ostrich and thus emerge unharmed from their adventure in this exotic world.[76] The Rowntree company thus offered a number of texts to their workers which represented, in various ways, empire and the firm's relationship to empire, as well as situating the York factory in relation to the international context more generally. The ways in which Rowntree workers negotiated with the meanings of these texts is more difficult to assess.

Go-betweens and intermediaries

It was not only male representatives of the Rowntree and Cadbury firms who travelled to the empire. Female employees sometimes gave up their positions at the factory to seek work and a more fulfilling life in the colonies and dominions. Their letters home, as reprinted in the *CWM* and *BWM*, offer a fascinating insight into how indivi-dual workers made sense of themselves 'out' in the empire, and how they interpreted their experiences for friends back home. In the late nineteenth and early twentieth centuries former chocolate workers from York and Birmingham took up positions as missionaries or accompanied their husbands to new roles in the colonies and reported back to their former colleagues. Mrs Alice Tabuteau, an apparently popular ex-Rowntree employee, wrote frequently to the *CWM* in the early twentieth century, describing her experiences in South Africa. She lived there with her husband, who had a senior position on the railways, and mentions acting occasionally as a midwife for the 'natives'. Two of her letters from the Transkei appeared on the front pages of the *CWM* in 1904, suggesting that they would have at least been glanced at by readers.[77]

Mrs Tabuteau's perspective is full of ambivalences, both challenging and reinforcing racist ideologies: 'The whites are mostly horrid, but I love the blacks; they are splendid in many ways, especially, as up here, they are not allowed to be served with drink, and therefore are not so demoralised as the Cape blacks.'[78] Distaste for the company of the Dutch whites suggests important distinctions within the category of whiteness and lingering resentments from the Boer War. Distinctions are also made amongst black people. Her patronising affection for 'the blacks' is reserved for those who remain sober. In the same year, Cadbury workers were also reading of the African adventures of former colleagues – Miss Winter and Miss Hadley – thanks to letters passed along by friends to the *BWM*. Miss Hadley describes the Africans she meets in terms of the chocolates produced by her friends at the factory: 'If it were possible for you to slightly blacklead a chocolate crème you would get exactly their colour.'[79] Race is translated into the visual language of the domestic and industrial labour performed by women, transforming the exotic into part of the everyday for Cadbury workers.

As illustrated by the letters from Mrs Tabuteau, ex-York workers provided links between the factory in York and the colonies and dominions. Though she is clearly happy away from 'congested' English towns, Mrs Tabuteau still ties herself to York: 'how different were my feelings when I saw the station – a mere shanty compared to our lovely York station'.[80] Extracts from letters of former employees who had emigrated, in which they remember their York colleagues, are scattered throughout the *CWM*. The extent of emigration to Australia prompted Rowntree to include a map of the dominion in the *CWM* of December 1909: 'So many of our friends have left York to seek their fortunes in Australia that it may be of interest to our readers to see the accompanying illustration, which . . . will help us to understand the immense size of our great colony'. Interest in the empire is structured by personal connections, rather than by a commitment to empire of itself. The implication of the illustration is that many workers would have little sense of where their friends were heading.

The author thus explains, 'our friends who have emigrated are at least assured of plenty of "elbow room"'. That the map was reproduced from the Reckitt's company magazine (a manufacturer of household goods in Hull) suggests that it was not only York residents who were believed to be ignorant with regard to the dominions.[81] An Australian visitor to the Bournville factory in the 1920s certainly found local people wanting in their awareness of the British empire: 'the people in the Midlands . . . in those days seemed to have a limited outlook on world affairs. Their knowledge of the colonies was in many cases deplorable.' By contrast, London was 'the Mecca of all people of the Commonwealth' and Londoners were 'generous and helpful'.[82]

If people outside of London had a 'limited outlook' on the world in the interwar period, this was about to be seriously challenged. The Second World War carried men and women from York to the far reaches of the empire and beyond. Their letters home, as paraphrased by the journal editors, occasionally provided York readers with ways to connect the distant experiences of their friends and family with their own lives at the factory: 'Having worked in the Melangeur department at York [Stoker Hunter] finds this helps him to endure the terrific heat.' The war also created opportunities for ordinary York workers to meet fellow Rowntree employees at associated companies in the colonies and dominions. Stoker Hunter 'visited a Rowntree factory in the southern hemisphere and found everyone pleased to see him when he made himself known'. In the same edition of the journal, servicemen and women from Rowntree, who were sent copies of the *CWM*, received an invitation from the manager of the Nigerian company: 'the staff of his company will be only too pleased to help . . . any employees of the Cocoa and Chocolate Works during their stay in that part of the Empire'.[83] Chocolate industry networks within the 'people's empire' were thus exploited and cemented during the war.[84] In the 1950s, letters from men on National Service continued to offer readers a personal connection to imperial and post-imperial politics.

With the possible exception of wartime, voices of white women and men in the colonies and dominions had to make themselves heard amidst more local concerns. A page from the magazine in 1953, for instance, includes an article on the 'Annual Outing of the Central Work's Council', which begins, 'Ilkley Moor seemed an appropriate choice for a Yorkshireman's outing.' Directly below this is a shorter piece, written by an anonymous woman, entitled, 'A Tribute From Burma'. In it, she describes waiting for 'the "runner" sailing up the Irrawaddy with our indented stores, with its usual 24 Kit Kat'. She engages directly with the romantic portrayals of 'the East', quietly subverting them: 'Let me whisper it, the exotic fruits and sweets of the East are not so glamorous as the novelists would have us believe, and the usual staple foods are odd to English palates.' She thanks Kit Kat, 'as an exile . . . for preserving for us such an example at [sic] the fine standards of living "at home"'. Kit Kat is a truly 'English' food in this instance, harbouring associations of 'home' for those exiled 'abroad'.[85] Letters and accounts from York women and men who have emigrated, as well as visits by them to their 'home' town, signify the literal presence of the dominions and colonies in York. Emigrants define York and England in relation to their new homes, then make these (re)definitions and representations available to those still living in the city.[86]

If York workers abroad provided one means of making connections with empire, visitors to the factory provided another. The factory itself was a space in which literal connections could be made, serving as a nexus of colonial relations in the context of chocolate production. From the 1950s, representations of visitors in the *CWM* were grouped together under the heading, 'They Came To See Us', reinforcing the dichotomy 'us' and 'them', whilst placing the motive for the visit with the visitors and the Rowntree firm as the attraction. This regular feature would usually include one or two pages in the journal devoted to photographs and descriptions of the visitors.[87]

As British West Africa gained increased control over its cocoa industry in the postwar period, African representatives were keen to visit confectionery-manufacturing sites in Britain. In 1953, for example, 'Some colour was provided at the Cocoa Works . . . by the visit of Mr. Obisesan who came clothed in his traditional Nigerian dress.'[88] Over ten years later, in 1967, 'Two visitors . . . who attracted considerable attention were Mr. and Mrs. Olaosebekin Idowu who toured York and the Cocoa Works clad in very impressive Nigerian national costume.'[89] Such captions are revealing: visitors from the colonies and former colonies are depicted as particularly 'visible' and often 'colourful', especially when dressed in non-western clothes. There is an interest and fascination in the visitors but with the effect of making them objects of exotic display. The selection of photographs, and the ways in which they frame their subjects, is telling. For instance, the arrangement of mixed group photographs of white York staff and 'coloured' visitors is indicative of racialised hierarchies, with white staff (usually men) most visible in the foreground of the picture. However, group photographs do become less formal over the years, reflecting the ideal of more mutual exchange.[90]

Clearly many African visitors to the factory were male representatives of the cocoa industry. However, there is evidence that African women did visit the factory, often as wives or daughters. A *CWM* article from autumn 1937 details the visit of the Alake of Abeokuta and his family: 'The girls in the factory were particularly attracted by the Alake's daughter.' Importantly, this piece suggests the possibility of contact between the visitors and the women on the shopfloor: 'In two departments the girls were so enthusiastic that they left their work to crowd around the party. They then proceeded to show what English community singing can be.' The 'girls' certainly seem to have made an impression on the Nigerian chief: 'the Alake spoke of his interest in seeing the various processes the cocoa underwent after leaving Nigeria, and the number of people, mostly girls, engaged in the work, and the cheerful manner in which the work was done'.[91] Whether the chief relayed quite such a positive story back to the Nigerian people is impossible to ascertain. Jeffrey Green, discussing African visitors to Edwardian Britain, suggests that these 'imperial visitors' often 'saw more than their supposed masters had intended'.[92]

An independent, postcolonial female visitor was Mrs C. E. Williams, Head of the Home Economics Division in the Western Nigerian Ministry of Agriculture, in 1968. She was an intermediary on her own terms, rather than in relation to her husband's position. As the *CWM* described, 'Mrs. Williams is particularly interested in popularising the use of bread made with cocoa in schools and in attempting to educate local people in Western Nigeria in the various ways in which cocoa can be used.'[93] The accompanying photograph shows her standing with two male members of Rowntree staff, suggesting the official nature of her visit and its direction by male factory management. Her role within the chocolate industry is a gendered one in its relation to food preparation yet it also gives her power, both in educating local people in Nigeria and in travelling to Britain and Europe. Her work reclaims cocoa consumption for producers, challenging the inevitability of the cocoa chain. Even if Rowntree workers on the shopfloor did not regularly meet such visitors, their presence and the manifestation of this in the journal could still suggest ways of thinking about the status of the factory and their position as Rowntree employees in relation to former colonial subjects.

There were, then, tangible manifestations of empire within the very walls of the factory in the form of textual representations and displays of material objects, but also in the shape of real people. Indeed, the factory building served as a space where connections could be made between coloniser and colonised, farmer and manufacturer. The Cadbury factory similarly played host to representatives of producers in an increasingly mutual exchange.[94] Such interactions are suggestive of the chocolate factory as an imperial space but also, to a certain extent, as a contested space, where the connections forged by the cocoa chain could be explored. This is particularly significant in reassessing the history of the York factory and its workers, for it suggests that even in this city of antiquity the people of the modern British empire were making their presence felt. But what of the less obvious ways in which imperialism was part of the everyday lives of Rowntree workers?

'All-British Chocolate': living the empire at home

The factory in a garden

Moving the Rowntree factory from Tanner's Moat to the outskirts of York in the early twentieth century was part of a conscious decision by Joseph Rowntree to create a healthier working environment, a 'garden factory'. Cadbury had already moved their works from the crowded, polluted city of Birmingham to the rural Bournville site. Of course, for both firms the relocation offered practical benefits in terms of room to expand and improved transport links. As food manufacturers, they could also trade on the benefits of this 'cleaner' environment, as Cadbury did routinely in their advertising campaigns (see chapter one). However, both firms emphasised the benefits of the 'garden factory' to their workers, particularly their female workers.

The concern of the Quaker chocolate manufacturers was not just with working conditions, but with urban living conditions more generally. Both Rowntree and Cadbury built villages close to their factories. Rowntree in particular were inspired by Ebenezer Howard and the 'garden city' movement in the design and planning of New Earswick.[95] Joseph intended this village to be a model of 'wholesome living conditions', where ordinary people (not just employees) could live in decent, affordable accommodation away from overcrowded, unhealthy urban areas.[96] Each house was to have a garden, with trees already planted, and the living rooms were built to benefit from maximum sunlight. Such architectural practices reflected assumptions, informed by ideologies of race, class and gender, about appropriate ways of living.[97] Gardens and buildings were not neutral spaces; they contributed to a discourse of civilisation, harbouring meanings of order and a particular version of 'Englishness', creating a pastoral idyll in contrast to industrialised urban areas. As Rebecca Preston comments of the nineteenth century, 'Love of gardening was seen as evidence of a highly civilised, economically buoyant and patriotic society.'[98] It is important then to look, if somewhat briefly, at the use of spaces such as gardens by the Rowntree firm and by the workers themselves.

The practice of gardening, as Preston observes, could be an explicitly imperial pastime in which 'exotic' plants were brought to British soil, renamed and domesticated. Nevertheless, she sees a return to the 'English' country garden in the twentieth century, by which time many tropical plants had become part of this 'English' countryside. It is this type of garden which formed the majority of the factory grounds and the gardens of New Earswick. Workers could spend their lunch breaks surrounded by a construction of pastoral English civilisation. Rowntree, however, also pursued explicitly tropical agriculture within their York grounds well into the twentieth century. In the firm's tropical greenhouse, established in the early 1920s, attempts were made to cultivate plants such as cocoa and banana trees, ostensibly for the education of visitors and for research purposes. This resulted in the 'First All-British Chocolate', presented to Princess Elizabeth in 1932.[99] As Preston comments, 'the introduction of foreign plant material on to British soil, and more precisely British domestic soil, was the ultimate horticultural expression of patriotic endeavour'.[100] So, whilst the seeds for such an enterprise came from the colonies, their contribution was conveniently forgotten in celebrating the first cocoa to be grown on British domestic soil. The tropical greenhouse also produced 'curiosities' such as a walking stick made from a cocoa tree – in this case allowing cocoa to become a prop for white British mobility.[101]

Images of workers relaxing in the factory gardens were frequently employed in the *CWM* and the *BWM*. Female workers in particular were photographed enjoying their lunch hour in the grounds during the summer. The grounds could also be the venue for entertainment such as brass band concerts. If gardens were important spaces at the York factory, they were represented as equally important in the South African branch of the firm. Indeed, without captions to the photographs, it would be difficult to tell the difference between workers using the gardens in South Africa and York. A photograph from 1935, for instance, depicts white women workers, in white uniforms, relaxing beside a lily pond at the South African factory.[102] Black African workers were excluded from this rural, civilised idyll. Through images of gardens, closeness with workers in associated companies is emphasised and an exotic landscape is tamed. Difference from workers in associated companies of the white dominions was usually assimilated into sameness in the end. A description of Christmas in Australia from 1953 works in this way, referring to 'English cousins' and emphasising that 'underlying the differences there are many close ties of kinship and culture, which these differences will never change'.[103] Gardening was part of this 'English' culture, a 'civilising' practice in which the gardener could bring order to untamed spaces.

Civilised pursuits

As well as facilitating official representations of the colonies in the context of chocolate manufacture, the company journal also functioned as an outlet for representations of empire and imperialist sentiment by the workers themselves. From the 1930s, *CWM* readers were encouraged on a regular basis to contribute articles and photographs relating to their lives outside the factory. Of course, not all workers would, or could, respond, given the limitations many faced of time, resources and enthusiasm. The series on 'My Hobby' of the 1950s and 1960s is dominated by pieces from male workers, often those of some status in the company. The hobbies of many of these men engaged directly with the empire or drew upon an imperialist mentality of exploration, acquisition, display and naming. One example is the article on stamp collecting by Mr T. Croft of the purchasing department:

> To anyone interested in adventure and voyages of discovery there are numerous stories told in stamps. . . . There are many stamps showing scenes from the discoveries of Captain Cook. New Zealand issued a stamp in 1935 of the landing of Captain Cook at Poverty Bay.[104]

Like the white explorers immortalised in the stamps, Mr Croft 'discovers' New Zealand. Stamp collecting, elevated in the title of the piece through its Greek-derived name of 'philately', allows for the incorporation of images of foreign lands and people into an activity conducted in the home and community. Organising stamps into albums imposed order on the exotic and allowed the conspicuous display of imperial exploration. The tales of discovery encapsulated in these stamps could create and reaffirm aspects of white British imperial identity.[105]

In the twentieth century, with few areas of the globe untouched by western exploration, extreme environments such as the Antarctic and Mount Everest became important sites of discovery and conquest. In 1910, Robert Scott visited Bootham School in York to give a lecture at which several Rowntree employees were present. As a result, a collection was established at the Cocoa Works, with the intention of funding a Rowntree sledge:

> It is thought that many of the readers of 'The C.W.M.' would like to have some part in helping forward this expedition, and subscriptions are invited towards purchasing a sledge to present to Captain Scott. A small plate would be attached to the sledge to commemorate the fact that it had been presented by employees at the Cocoa Works.[106]

A total of £5 12s 6d was raised, and Scott wrote to the workers thanking them for their 'patriotic support'.[107] York men and women could, then, become enthused by the conquest of foreign lands and were prepared to invest financially in what they saw as patriotic endeavours. They also made material contributions to expeditions, providing supplies of chocolate through their labours in the York factory. A photograph for the spring 1952 edition of the *CWM* portrayed Mr Edward Drinkel, an ordinary worker, packing a box labelled 'British Himalayan Expedition, 1952' and apparently wondering, 'where will this be unwrapped?'[108] A full house was later recorded at the Joseph Rowntree Theatre in December 1952 for a presentation by the leader of this expedition, Mr Eric Shipton, under the title 'Attempts to Climb Everest'.[109] Rowntree workers could have taken patriotic pride for their part in supporting such distant expeditions when they subsequently heard the news of the conquest of Mount Everest, revealed on the occasion of Queen Elizabeth II's coronation.[110] As Webster points out, however, the multi-national composition of the expedition team was exploited in the construction of a truly 'Commonwealth' victory.[111]

Some workers became explorers themselves through engaging in hobbies such as hiking and pot-holing. As Preston observes, 'By the non-agricultural classes rural landscapes in Britain were considered in similar fashion to uncharted territories abroad'.[112] Articles and photographs in the *CWM* by the Moor and Fell Club, formed in the 1930s, demonstrate this fascination with the uncharted territories of rural Yorkshire, drawing on similar discourses to those used for imperial exploration and discovery. Instead of the 'Dark Continent', these white male workers journeyed to the 'Bowels of the Earth'.[113] Over thirty years later, with the British losing their grip on colonial possessions, the language of imperial exploration was much more explicit. Describing his hobby of 'skin diving', P. Rodgers positioned himself as finishing the mission of the great male explorers: 'Those intrepid men Columbus, Livingstone, Scott and legions of others did a wonderful job of exploring this planet of ours. However, they only conquered one fifth of it; the remaining four-fifths is under water, so it looks as though we are going to be very busy for a long time finishing the job.'[114] The language of possession and conquest is striking; Britain may have lost its empire on the surface but Rodgers is hopeful of staking a claim to the land under the sea. These articles provide strident male narratives of exploration and conquest.

It is much more difficult to trace women's voices in the magazine. They are recorded in features such as 'People at Work', where employees are interviewed on the shopfloor about their jobs and their lives outside work. Here we can gain some brief insight into women's leisure activities. In 1962, Miss M. A. Dealtry, of Cream Manufacturing, who was working in the supervisory role of Teacher to new workers, was described as enjoying 'horse racing, as well as holidays abroad, particularly if she can travel by air'. Miss Dealtry enjoys the freedom to travel but in the bounded sense of taking a holiday. There is no indication of the regular commitment to 'exploration' as evident in the 'My Hobby' articles.

Physical activities such as hiking and sport were formally endorsed through the continuation school curriculum and social clubs at both Rowntree and Cadbury. For male workers, playing cricket for the company team would have been one way of participating in a particular version of white, English masculinity. Sporting ethics of 'fair play' were infused with imperial connotations. As Mike Cronin and Richard Holt describe: 'The world of cricket was often presented as a microcosm of England itself – and more widely of the British Empire – . . . English sportsmen . . . would look after the natives for their own good.'[115] Cricket could connect people across the empire, as illustrated by a Rowntree photograph from 1910 of black boys playing together in the West Indies. Captioned, 'Cricket Where the Cocoa Grows', the photo shows the game being observed from a distance by a white man. The text suggests comparisons with the Rowntree youth team, though the fact that several of the boys are wearing little, if any clothes, suggests that the comparisons were intended to be comic: 'This is not a snapshot of Rowntree's Juniors although the wicket keeper on the right looks suspiciously like Denis Shaw.'[116]

Women workers at both Rowntree and Cadbury were also able to join a works' cricket club and did so at least until the late 1930s. Playing cricket allowed women a degree of access to such discourses of English 'fairness' and to the world of 'manly games' envisaged by Joseph Rowntree at the opening of the cricket pavilion in 1902.[117] On the whole, however, physical exercise for female workers was conceived less in terms of an aggressive sporting ethic and more as safeguarding the biological and spiritual well-being of English womanhood. Photographs from 1936 depict Rowntree girls engaged in leisure pursuits which link them with both an idealised pastoral 'golden age' (a group of girls sitting by a lake, 'Piping at Eventide'), and the civilised poise of earlier imperial civilisations (girls dressed in white togas performing 'A Greek Dance').[118] Girls received none of the motivational mottos which appeared on the 'Boys' Pages' of the CWM in the 1930s, urging them to 'Play the Game'. The imperial masculinity of Kipling's 'If –' poem was tellingly subverted in 1933 for consumption by female office workers:

> If you can laugh without guffawing shrilly;
> If you can speak in accents soft and low . . .
> If you regard the manicuring process
> As something which from public view is banned . . .
> You, my dear, are worth your weight in gold.[119]

In the workplaces of the metropole, white women were needed to safeguard the values of respectable, civilised English femininity.

Rowntree and Cadbury encouraged physical activities as creating healthier, more productive workers, who would thereby benefit the nation as a whole. They also wanted to develop the mental capacities of their workforce. Reading was an activity explicitly encouraged by the firms through their works library.[120] In 1910, the front page article of the *CWM* was entitled, 'What Shall I Read?' There was an attempt to steer young readers away from 'unduly exaggerated' stories, particularly those being bought by boys at the Cocoa Works, towards more appropriate books held in the library. The author, F. J. Weetman, believed young readers had a 'natural curiosity to know something of life beyond their immediate surroundings, and natural desire to read of heroic deeds and adventures, . . . the ferocious attacks of a savage race in some far-off land'. *Treasure Island* was recommended as catering to these desires but in a more realistic way: 'the adventures are reasonable and the characters portrayed in harmony with the life and character of many of the old sea salts, the direct descendants of the adventurers who plundered the treasure ships of Spain, the buccaneers of the reign of Queen Elizabeth, the founders of many a British colony abroad'.[121] This was a version of British colonial history which could be endorsed by the firm.

It is informative to study references to the library catalogue. According to the March 1902 edition of *CWM*, books recently acquired included *Journal of a West Indian Proprietor* and *The War in South Africa*. By 1962, new additions included 'many light romances', westerns and local history; there were no obviously empire-related titles on the list.[122] Unfortunately it has not been possible to monitor how often particular books were taken out, or by whom, and how, if at all, they were read. The librarian did comment in 1902 that books 'not often asked for' included *The Potter's Thumb*, 'A story of English life in India.'[123] Perhaps the Rowntree readership was not so interested in imperial love stories; or perhaps the librarian felt that explicitly revealing the Indian setting of the book would attract more readers. Just over fifty years later, the librarian's recommendations catered to the imperialist adventurer spirit. For instance, *People of the Deer* is the story of 'experiences amongst the strange people of the Artic Canadian North' and is recommended 'for every reader who loves adventure and who is fascinated by strange customs and ancient peoples'.[124] There is a suggestion of anthropological enquiry here in the study of 'ancient peoples' – made 'ancient' and 'strange' only by the arrival of westerners. Clearly, assumptions are being made of the attraction of the exotic. In the library catalogue, however, exotic tales, along with travel books and descriptions of mountain conquests, are juxtaposed with more quintessentially 'English' stories of life on a Devon farm and in English villages. Stories of empire and adventure sit side by side with more 'domestic' narratives, seemingly unproblematically for either librarian or readers.

Everyday hobbies of Rowntree workers may be seen as evidence of an engagement, even if not always consciously identified, with an imperial mindset and the imperialist cultures which had long pervaded so many aspects of life in Britain. From stamp-collecting, to hiking, to reading, Rowntree workers in York pursued hobbies which made sense and were understood in the context of empire, imperialism and contemporary understandings of race. The in-house magazine served as a forum for sharing and encouraging imperialist pastimes: passions of collecting, categorising and exploring. However, these activities are gendered; women are rarely depicted taking part. We must look to other sources to uncover women's involvement in imperialist projects within York.

'Rowntree wrappers help missionaries': women making connections

Finding evidence of the ways in which working-class women were conscious of empire is difficult. There has been some important work on white women and imperialism but most of it is in relation to white women 'out' in the empire. As a result, the focus tends to be on middle- and upper-class women who could travel to the colonies as, for example, missionaries, missionary's wives or the wives of colonial officers.[125] Where the involvement of white women 'at home' in Britain has been studied, this is mostly with regard to the nineteenth and early twentieth centuries. Clare Midgley, for example, has high-lighted women's organising and support of anti-slavery campaigns through strategies such as petitioning, subscriptions and boycotting. Importantly, she does consider the involvement of working-class women in such activities, though this is mostly limited to one sec-tion in her book. Antoinette Burton, meanwhile, studies the 'armchair imperial feminists' of the Ladies' National Association who, though most had never been to India, campaigned for the repeal of the Contagious Diseases Act there. Both Midgley and Burton raise some important questions about the effect of gender, race and class on the dynamics of imperialism in a seemingly 'domestic' context.[126] I now want to consider how white, working-class women in York may have experienced imperialism in particular ways. Although these women left little substantial evidence of their practical, intellectual and emotional engagements with empire, there are still traces of the ways in which the Rowntree factory provided a space in York for at least some of them to make connections with the wider British world.

Women workers at the Rowntree factory, particularly through the departments they worked for, were often involved in charitable activities. Such practices were in keeping with the ethos of the Rowntree firm and were thus well represented in the *CWM*. However, as the charitable activities of the firm have been interpreted in official histories as industrial 'paternalism', with connotations of a strict but benevolent father figure, women's role has tended to be ignored. Early editions of the *CWM* are useful in detailing the large sums of money donated collectively by women employees to the Cocoa Works' charitable funds.[127] In 1922, for example, a record total of £1,087 12s 10d was collected, with £125 12s 8d from the Cream Packers (predominantly women). It is difficult to tell in some cases exactly where the money raised was going but frequent beneficiaries were local hospitals, pensioners and children's homes. There was certainly a local focus to much of the activities; again, entirely compatible with the original aims of the charitable trusts founded by Joseph Rowntree himself.[128]

Despite the prominent role of Rowntree women in *local* fundraising, there is evidence that female workers did indeed donate money to institutions with a national and sometimes an imperial remit. The Dr Barnardo's charity, for example, worked with disadvantaged children in Britain but sent some of these children out to the dominions to an apparently better life. In 1923, the factory hosted a talk on 'Barnardo Boys and Girls in Australia'. Almost ten years later, the *CWM* of April 1932 recorded a donation to Dr Barnardo's as part of the 'Charitable Institutions Collections' and included an article on Barnardo's Homes.[129] At least some Rowntree workers would also have been involved in raising money for charitable activity outside the factory, perhaps through their local church or church organisations. Accounts books for the Clifton Association of the Church Missionary Society (meeting between 1879 and 1913) record members' donations in 1908 towards a 'zenana mission'.[130] Women could become still more directly involved in missionary activity through membership of the York women's branch of the Church Missionary Society, or the Mothers' Union, though from the available sources it has been impossible to tease out whether working-class women from the factory were active in either organisation.[131] Within the factory, women workers at Rowntree had access to reports of missionary work. As illustrated in this chapter, early editions of *CWM* contained letters from women stationed on missions overseas. Sixty years on, the *CWM* for Christmas 1964 mentions a missionary film to be shown at the factory by the Christian Fellowship Society. Local contact with missionaries is one way in which York women may have learnt about empire and 'other' women.[132]

An interesting, postwar demonstration of how the spheres of work, local community and religion could intersect for Rowntree women appears in the *CWM* of spring 1968. A photograph of two children in costumes made entirely of confectionery packaging is captioned, 'Rowntree Wrappers Help Missionaries'. The costumes were made by Miss Janet Mawer of the Gum Experimental Section of Product Development for the Southlands Junior Missionary Association Christmas Fair. Here, a Rowntree worker – although the description of her department suggests she was involved in research rather than on the shopfloor – has clearly employed the imagery of the firm, embodied in its wrappers, to raise money within her local community for missionary activity. She has done this in a gendered way through the sewing of the costumes. As Valentine Cunningham observes regarding mission funding, albeit in relation to an earlier period, 'support came from England in the form that ordinary chapel-going and generally property-less (because married) British women could contribute it – in womanly stuff'.[133] This woman's act then has been reappropriated by the firm through its representation in Rowntree-produced media. Although the photo dates from an essentially postcolonial era, it demonstrates that some women in York could be mobilised in support of causes beyond their local communities, even as their actions took place within a distinctly local framework.

Women in York did engage with missionary work, through subsidising and supporting the activities of missionaries overseas and, sometimes, by becoming missionaries themselves.[134] They did this as workers, as mothers, as community members and as churchgoers. Their activities were often highly gendered, drawing on feminised skills such as sewing and hosting parties. However, these activities offered women ways to engage in projects which could be empowering. In imperialist missionary discourse, white women occupied a privileged position. Still, class continued to structure their experiences. Factory workers at Rowntree, particularly those who were full time, are less likely to have had the time to engage fully in societies such as the Mothers' Union. They may instead have found themselves the objects of the Union's concern to inculcate working-class women with the values of 'decent' family life and cleanliness in the home.[135] In this way, female Rowntree workers could have been both active agents of imperialism and the subjects of a domestic 'mission'.[136]

Staging and performing race at the factory

In a photograph from the spring 1951 edition of *CWM*, women and men from the planning department appear in blackface makeup as a 'Nigger Minstrel Troupe'.[137] Pages earlier, readers had been encouraged to think about 'Britain's Place in the World' as the Cocoa Works played host to visitors from India: 'The white man is going to be pushed out of Asia which is no longer his territory.'[138] Although essentially an American import, minstrel performances in Britain must be placed in the context of British imperialism. In this edition of the *CWM* we can gain some sense of how 'whiteness' and 'blackness' were being defined for consumption by York chocolate workers in an era of decolonisation. Whilst the 'white man' was being pushed out of Asia, white men and women could still try to control the 'black man' through the power of representation.

This was not the first instance of a minstrel performance by factory workers. Mr Henry Buckle, who had joined the firm in 1884 after a stint in the 1st Royal Dragoons, was interviewed as a pensioner in 1921. He recalled being a member of a 'Nigger troupe' with 'properties' provided by J. W. Rowntree. However, it appears that his troupe had long been disbanded by the early 1920s.[139] Minstrel shows (re)gained in popularity at Rowntree throughout the 1950s and 1960s, with annual performances by 'the minstrels and their maids'. To understand the appeal of minstrelsy to these York workers and their audiences, and the various ways in which 'race' and 'ethnicity' were performed at the factory, it is necessary to consider the broader history of minstrel shows in Britain.

The minstrel show is generally agreed to have its origins in nineteenth-century America.[140] Eric Lott asserts that minstrelsy was dependent on the 'material relations of slavery', even as it 'obscured these relations by pretending that slavery was amusing, right, and natural'.[141] Despite Britain's prominent role in the slave trade, slaves themselves did not constitute a substantial presence within the nation. John Blair, in a useful cross-cultural analysis, suggests some important distinctions between the appeal of the shows in America and England:

> While at home England preached the 'white man's burden' during its African expansion, the American population around mid-century was still over fifteen percent black. . . . The English . . . could imagine themselves as having it both ways, feeling superior to the Americans as contributing merely a half-way stage between Africa and civilization.[142]

It is in this context that minstrelsy, as Michael Pickering comments, 'quickly established a reputation for moral and cultural respectability' in Victorian Britain.[143] This reputation would survive well into the second half of the twentieth century.

Britain has prided itself over its 'enlightened' treatment of black people in the context of both slavery and colonialism. As Sonya Rose argues, the Second World War 'provided many Britons with a way to enhance their own sense of national pride by contrasting white American racist practices with what they believed to be British racial tolerance'.[144] This 'tolerance' was founded on a perceived absence of black people actually living permanently in Britain and on an imperial construction of British 'whiteness' as a benevolent civilising force. However, whilst Pickering may justifiably comment that, on the whole, white British audiences for minstrel shows in the nineteenth and early twentieth centuries lacked a sense of black people 'within the homeland as a social threat', by the time of the arrival of the Empire Windrush in 1948 this was beginning to change.[145]

Although York was not a primary destination for migrant workers, white locals were still exposed, partly through the national media, to reports of racial tensions and to racist discourse stirring up fears of black domination. Moreover, whether or not they had direct experience of meeting black people in York, white Rowntree workers were part of an industry in which the labour of black people in British colonies was crucial. This places factory minstrel shows in a specific context. At the time of the postwar shows, as reported in the *CWM*, many of the British colonies from where Rowntree bought cocoa were on the brink of independence. Elsewhere in the empire, violent struggles for freedom were under way. Rowntree workers themselves, conscripted to National Service, were stationed in Kenya and Malaya in the 1950s, fighting to hold on to colonial power. Minstrelsy, like the infantilised characters of Little Coco and Honeybunch, offered a way of clinging on to the power of representation and interpretation, and of dissipating, through humour, anxieties about the end of empire and the return of the colonised to the metropole.

It was in the 1930s that the BBC, bastion of respectable broadcasting, took up the minstrel genre with a radio version, the *Kentucky Minstrels*.[146] In the early 1950s, the minstrels made the move to television and in 1957 the extremely successful 'Black and White Minstrel Show' was launched. The programme survived until 1978, reaching audiences of almost seventeen million.[147] Given the success of the minstrel show format on BBC radio and television, it is unsurprising that white Rowntree workers were keen to engage in their own minstrel performances. In the early 1960s, the television show was given some of the credit for recent sell-out performances by the Youth Club: 'The B.B.C.'s "Black and White Minstrel Show", top television programme in Europe, sparked off the most popular theatrical production the Youth Club has ever introduced.' As Pickering points out, such amateur performances were themselves important in disseminating the minstrel show tradition.[148] The Rowntree performers even took their show overseas in 1962, with a trip to Munster in Germany to entertain both locals and British troops.

The BBC television show had an influence on Rowntree performers, who came to adopt the visual formula of male minstrels in blackface with the female maids providing the 'white' element. Romantic sequences between minstrels and maids offered an aestheticised and safe performance of inter-racial relationships, distancing them through fantasised settings. Behind the sanitised courtship rituals of the serenade, which drew on popular songs, was a tradition that placed black men as the sexual predators of white women.[149] Lott's theory of 'cross-racial desire' helps to make sense of such on-stage scenes, emphasising the complex coupling of fascination and fear which made minstrels so popular with audiences.[150] In postwar Britain, inter-racial relationships had taken on new significance. Aside from the increasing migration from former colonies, as discussed above, the presence of black servicemen during the Second World War had resulted in romantic and sexual encounters between black men and white women, and in a generation of so-called 'brown babies'.[151] The minstrel shows would have had added resonance in this context.

The Rowntree Players emulated the fast-paced format of the television minstrel shows, packed with musical routines. The vibrancy and 'high spirits' of the television programme were cited as key to its success.[152] The local press in York, commenting on a Rowntree show, similarly emphasised the 'sheer joie de vivre, colour and vitality' of the performance.[153] Attempts by the BBC and the press to account for the contemporary popularity of minstrel shows rarely tackle the element of race in any way, preferring to focus on the techniques of performance: the BBC, for instance, called it 'a triumph of stage management'.[154] This concern with the form and structure of the minstrel shows is suggestive of the 'high performance style' Blair identifies.[155] Pickering astutely observes that 'British minstrelsy contributed to the development and establishment of a racist and imperialist ideology all the more effectively because of embodying it within a theatrically vibrant medium of entertainment.'[156] In the literature surrounding British minstrel performances produced at the time, there are frequent references to the 'colourfulness' of the shows, references that invoke a trope of palatable racial discourse also present in the captions to images of 'coloured' visitors to the Cocoa Works.

Minstrelsy was not just about the performance of white notions of African American or African 'blackness'; a key element which appeared in both the television and Rowntree shows was the performance of 'Red Indian' sequences.[157] Photographs depict the stylised costumes worn by performers, with an emphasis on bright colours and feather headdresses, while in the background are totem poles and drums. Rowntree workers 'played Indian' at other times too, in plays such as *Annie Get Your Gun*. Philip J. Deloria and Patricia Penn Hilden have analysed this phenomenon in the US context, engaging with the history of the dispossession of Native Americans in the establishment of white America. From the twentieth century, Deloria suggests that Indian play was also used 'to encounter the authentic amidst the anxiety of urban industrial and postindustrial life'.[158] People in Britain did not have the same relation to Native Americans, or to any 'aboriginal' peoples within Britain itself.[159] Yet the fascination of 'authenticity' in the midst of an industrial society is an explanation which could equally hold true in the British context. Certainly, people in Britain were engaging, through literature and the cinema as well as popular songs, with representations of 'Red Indians'. In part this must be related to the Americanisation of British culture, but more detailed work needs to be done to understand the different ways in which British audiences might have made sense of such material.[160]

In the context of the British minstrel shows of the mid- to late twentieth century, playing Indian appears to have been just one of a variety of ways in which performers were playing with and indeed destabilising racial categories and identities. Blackface performers for the BBC donned Mexican hats, for example, or became high-ranking officers in the Navy. It would be easy to criticise minstrel shows at the Rowntree factory as racist expressions of white working-class people in York. However, they clearly demonstrate a tangled intermingling of fascination with the exotic other, identity play and masquerade. As Deloria argues, wearing a disguise can offer both a 'sense of personal liberation' in taking on a completely different identity and an affirmation 'of a *real* "me" underneath'.[161] Racial performance may have been liberating and unsettling whilst re-affirming the 'whiteness' of the performer. Lott describes these contradictory impulses as 'minstrelsy's mixed erotic economy of celebration and exploitation, . . . "love and theft" '.[162] Rowntree minstrel shows could be a way of dealing with racialised desires and fears present even in this 'white' city. As much as they might choose to emphasise a regional identity – indeed in order to reaffirm this identity – Yorkshire folk could also play around with alternatives from a range of possibilities made available to them partly through Britain's past imperial power.

The factory was not only an outlet for racial masquerade by white performers; it also provided a stage for non-white visiting artists. At a long-service party for workers in 1966, for example, 'The Pan Yue Jen Duo, a talented Chinese couple, held the theatre in suspense with diabolo spinning and feats of balancing.'[163] Blair and Pickering have written of the ways in which such performances of ethnicity, even by those who may lay 'authentic' claim to this ethnicity, were shaped by the desires and expectations of white audiences. Pickering cites the example of black actors actually wearing the blackface makeup of minstrelsy. However, they each acknowledge the agency of such performers. Deloria highlights the influence of 'real' Indians on 'Indian play', 'often attempting to nudge notions of Indianness in directions they found useful'.[164] The very existence of such entertainment at Rowntree provides clues as to the ways in which white, and non-white, people in York were constructing and refiguring race and ethnicity. It also highlights the role of the firm in providing a space for the performance and spectatorship of race and empire. Although it has not been possible to trace responses of workers themselves to such performances, the following chapter studies the meanings women attached to their working environment more broadly, and their individual experiences of factory space.

Conclusion

York, as a geographical and imagined location, was formed partly through relations of imperialism. From its early history as a significant settlement of the Romans, it continued to engage in overseas trade, becoming a space in the eighteenth century for the rich to spend and consume the fruits of empire. The dominance of the railway industry from the nineteenth century established the city as a key point on a national and imperial network. Moreover, the sale and later the large-scale manufacture of chocolate in York was the result of imperial 'discoveries' and the labour of the colonies. York, the walled city, has thus been anything but bounded; imperialism created and later permeated the ancient city walls.

York's place within the nation and the British empire has at times been acknowledged and embraced for the purpose of maintaining the city's image of political, royal and economic status. Rowntree certainly used such discourses. At other times it has apparently been more profitable to fix York in time, to create a seemingly static version of the medieval city. Such a strategy effectively places York outside the concerns of industry and imperialism. It becomes a metonym for 'Old England', emblematic of a past and a nation seemingly untainted by outside influences of culture or people. This version of York has been central to its successful rebirth as a tourist destination from the 1970s, generating capital even in its denial of industry. Yet it is also important to regional identity. Rowntree have certainly employed images of York as 'history' – as implicitly detached from the colonial project of chocolate manufacture – in communicating to their workforce as well as in advertising their products. Industrial Birmingham could never fulfil this role for Cadbury and it was the rural, yet modern, village of Bournville with which the firm came to associate most strongly.

York as an imagined location can contain multiple meanings simultaneously. Rowntree exploited and explored this multiplicity, juxtaposing explicitly imperial stories and images with apparently highly 'localised', 'English' images of historic, beautiful York. The Rowntree company was represented as international but with York as its heart; York was thus constructed as the centre from which everything travels outwards. But, as this chapter has demonstrated, there were centripetal as well as centrifugal forces at work. People and products moved backwards and forwards across the apparent boundaries of 'home' and 'empire' in ways that challenged the outward influence of imperialism and the linear progress of the cocoa chain from farmer to consumer. The factory itself became a nexus for these intermediaries and go-betweens, a site for colonial visitors and for visiting York citizens now resident in the dominions.

The responses of York women to these complex, multidirectional forces of imperialism are difficult to assess, particularly for white working-class women. Nevertheless, evidence of activities both within and outside the Rowntree factory does show women engaging actively and imaginatively with the implications of empire and racial discourse. For instance, some women contributed money, time and creativity to support missionary work, though they themselves may never have had direct contact with people from the empire. Female Rowntree workers also took part in the racial performance and spectatorship of factory minstrel shows. Such 'entertainment' could embody both racialised fears and desires. The element of disguise suggests the continual process of identity construction, with gender and race identities both undermined and yet reinforced in particular ways within the factory context.

A key aspect of studies of the 'empire at home' has been the belated recognition of the long history of people from the empire living within Britain. Official versions of York throughout the twentieth century, in tourist literature, factory-produced media and the local press, have underplayed, if not denied outright, the presence of racial minorities in the city. As we shall see in the following chapter, this masks the histories of migrants, particularly women, who have made York their home and Rowntree their place of work.

Notes

1 The Minster is the medieval church that dominates the city. The Shambles is a small medieval street, once the site of butchers' shops but now a famous tourist attraction.

2 As Edward Royle observes, 'The existence of Yorkshire . . . is more frequently asserted than demonstrated or explained. Yet if Yorkshire folk feel a reality . . . that feeling can become a historical "fact" as much as any river or mountain range.' Edward Royle, 'Introduction: regions and identities', in Edward Royle (ed.), *Issues of Regional Identity: In Honour of John Marshall* (Manchester: Manchester University Press, 1998), 6. In the same collection, see also David Neave, 'The identity of the East Riding of Yorkshire', 184–7.

3 York became a key point in the developing rail network of the nineteenth century. The opening of a new station in 1877, at the time proclaimed to be 'The Largest Railway Station in the World', suggests confidence in York as a worldwide force in the railway industry, and was a symbol of imperial grandeur. Joanna de Groot notes the imperial associations of railways 'at home' in Britain, sustained through the naming of railway locomotives 'after dominions, colonies and other imperial references'. Patrick Nuttgens, *York: The Continuing City* (York: Maxiprint, 2nd edn, 1989), 95; de Groot, 'Metropolitan desires and colonial connections', 177. The city is now home to the National Railway Museum, which celebrates the international but not explicitly the imperial dimension to the British rail industry.

4 During the early 2000s, the café was sponsored by Nestlé Rowntree and included wall-mounted displays about chocolate. The consumption of Kit Kat as 'locally produced' chocolate (dependent on the labour of people in York but also, less visibly, in cocoa-producing countries such as Nigeria) could be undertaken by visitors to York/Jorvik, as refreshment after their journey to the Viking city. Histories of modern imperialism do not feature.

5 Mary Louise Pratt, *Imperial Eyes: Travel Writing and Transculturation* (London: Routledge, 1992), 6. In 1984, John M. MacKenzie highlighted how, 'Imperial history and the imperial idea have been examined almost entirely in a centrifugal manner.' Just over twenty years on, however, Catherine Hall and Sonya Rose observe that questions over the effects of empire on the metropole have a long history 'and have been formulated and answered variously according both to the historical moment and the political predilections of those involved'. MacKenzie, *Propaganda and Empire*, 2; Hall and Rose, 'Introduction: being at home with the Empire', in Catherine Hall and Sonya O. Rose (eds), *At Home with the Empire*, 1.

6 Catherine Hall, *Civilising Subjects: Metropole and Colony in the English Imagination, 1830–1867* (Cambridge: Polity Press, 2002), 11; John M. MacKenzie, ' "The Second City of the Empire": Glasgow – imperial municipality', in Felix Driver and David Gilbert (eds), *Imperial Cities: Landscape, Display and Identity* (Manchester: Manchester University Press, 1999).

7 Ted Royle argues for the 'rise of provincialism' in nineteenth-century England, as 'a challenge to the dominance of London'. However, Royle also suggests that 'involvement in the economy of the Empire subordinated any sense of regional identity to participation in the imperial nation-state as a whole'. I would argue that Yorkshire identity was very much present even before the weakening of empire. I want to consider instead the extent to which York/Yorkshire identities were formed in relation to imperialism. Royle, 'Introduction: regions and identities', 9.

8 Mary Ann Caws suggests that we come to know a city through 'reading', through 'the imagination of that city-ness'. Mary Ann Caws, 'Introduction: "the city on

our mind"', in Mary Ann Caws (ed.), *City Images: Perspectives from Literature, Philosophy, and Film* (Reading: Gordon and Breach, 1991), 1.

9 As Antoinette Burton observes, invoking 'home' and 'empire' is problematic: 'Even the naming of Britain as an imperial space . . . potentially works to naturalize the distinctions between "home" and "empire".' I do not wish to reify 'York' as an otherwise stable location on which empire simply made a mark, but to see it as being constantly reinterpreted and reinvented. Antoinette Burton, 'Who needs the nation? Interrogating "British" history', in Hall (ed.), *Cultures of Empire*, 141.

10 Bernard Porter questions whether imperialism ever really 'caught on' amongst workers of the Victorian and Edwardian era. Although he allows for 'a general feeling of support' for the empire, he concludes it 'was nonetheless not very *important* to them'. I have adopted a much broader definition of imperialism than Porter; if Rowntree workers did not engage in 'thoughtful or joined-up imperialism' involving an element of domination, this is not to say that empire and its assumptions about race, class and gender were of no relevance in their lives. Rather, it is revealing of the particular dynamics of chocolate production and of their lives in York. Porter's work is, however, relevant in documenting some of the uneven ways in which imperialism could operate in Britain. Bernard Porter, *The Absent-Minded Imperialists: Empire, Society and Culture in Britain* (Oxford: Oxford University Press, 2004), 226, 199. On the significance of the media, see Webster, *Englishness and Empire*.

11 *CWM*, October 1902, 91.

12 David Nye argues that General Electric's *Works News* 'displaced attention' from work 'to points of agreement, such as America, or to neutral arenas, such as sports'. David Nye, *Image Worlds: Corporate Identities at General Electric* (Cambridge, Mass.: MIT Press, 1985), 91. Images and stories of York do function as a 'point of agreement' in the *CWM*; the subject of work, meanwhile, is largely avoided in these early issues. This is in keeping with the editor's initial conception of the magazine as an extension of the work of the Social Department (D. S. Crichton in *CWM*, March 1902, 2). The only workers who feature in early photographs are those on the cocoa plantations of the West Indies, thus providing a distant, exoticised image of labour. However, in later issues the subject of work and work politics is not entirely avoided, with references, for example, to the development of a Suggestion Box scheme and the proceedings of Works Councils. *CWM* is more complex than General Electric's *Works News* in addressing audiences from shopfloor workers, to office staff, to lower levels of management.

13 *CWM*, August 1909, 739.

14 *CWM*, August 1909, 737. Hundreds of Jews died at Clifford's Tower. Hutchinson and Palliser declare this 'the worst anti-Jewish pogrom in English history'. John Hutchinson and D. M. Palliser, *York: Bartholomew City Guides* (Edinburgh: John Bartholomew & Son, 1980), 28.

15 *CWM*, August 1909, 735.

16 *CWM*, Summer 1953, 13.

17 Hutchinson and Palliser, *York*, 41.

18 *CWM*, Summer 1953, 13.

19 *CWM*, October 1902, 90.

20 *CWM*, March 1923, 184–5.

21 *CWM*, Summer 1956, 24–5 and Spring 1960, 26–7.

22 *CWM*, Autumn 1966, 12–13.

23 J. B. Morrell, 'The Streets and Buildings within York City Walls', *CWM*, Summer 1953, 12.

24 *Ibid.*, 13. On the importance of diverse local events to the festival, see Becky E. Conekin, *'The Autobiography of a Nation': The 1951 Festival of Britain* (Manchester: Manchester University Press, 2003), especially chapter six.

25 J. B. Morrell, 'The Streets and Buildings within York City Walls', *CWM*, Summer 1953, 13.

26 Perhaps in response to the continuing expansion of Rowntree factories throughout the country, and the subsequent diversity of *CWM* readers, 'Beautiful Yorkshire'

[171]

was largely replaced by 'Beautiful Britain' on magazine covers from the 1960s. Even so, this was a predominantly rural Britain, devoid of modern industry.

27 'Beautiful Yorkshire', *CWM*, Christmas 1953, back cover.
28 'Sweet Reason: being an introduction to careers with Rowntrees' (c.1959). On loan from the Castle Museum, York.
29 Benjamin Seebohm Rowntree, *Poverty: A Study of Town Life* (London: Macmillan, 1901); Benjamin Seebohm Rowntree, *Poverty and Progress: A Second Social Survey of York* (London: Longmans, Green, 1941).
30 John Bowes Morrell, *The City of Our Dreams* (London: Fountain Press, 1940). This had been written mostly in 1935. See Hutchinson and Palliser, *York*, 85.
31 Jean, interviewed in 2000.
32 In the early twentieth century, top hats were still considered to be the appropriate attire for businessmen, particularly travellers (salesmen). For a discussion of the development of men's clothing in business, see Christopher Breward, 'Sartorial spectacle: clothing and masculine identities in the imperial city, 1860–1914', in Driver and Gilbert (eds), *Imperial Cities*.
33 Fitzgerald, *Rowntree*, 162.
34 Mr York did feature in milk chocolate advertising when, at a later date, Rowntree introduced their milk chocolate version of the 'York' brand. Fitzgerald, *Rowntree*, 168.
35 Benedict Anderson defined nations as 'imagined communities'. Subsequent writers such as Ted Royle have identified the existence of 'imagined' locations within the nation, such as regions and towns. Anderson, *Imagined Communities*; Royle, 'Introduction'.
36 David Neave comments, 'Probably for no other county is this sense of a separate identity promoted so extensively.' David Neave, 'The identity of the East Riding', 184.
37 The railway companies also presented York as a desirable tourist destination, rich in history. J. B. Priestley noted railway advertising with the slogan, 'Visit ancient York.' J. B. Priestley, *English Journey* (London: William Heinemann, 1934), 397.
38 'Sweet Reason'.
39 *BWM*, November 1902, 2.
40 MacKenzie, ' "The Second City of the Empire" '.
41 Hutchinson and Palliser, *York*, 41.
42 *Yorkshire Evening Press* (*YEP*), 4 June 1953, 3.
43 York was an important military post and there are still army barracks in the city. J. B. Priestley's account from the 1930s suggests that this was another means by which York residents could articulate imperial pride, though by this point the grandeur of imperial campaigns was a nostalgic memory: 'His talk was all of the vanished military glories of the city, of the time when soldiers *were* soldiers, real thirsty Kipling characters, and not mild lads who preferred a cup of tea to an evening of this landlord's beer.' Priestley, *English Journey*, 349.
44 Correspondence regarding Queen's Tins, Rowntree Archive, R/B4/2, BI.
45 Bradley, *Enlightened Entrepreneurs*, 134; Wagner, *Chocolate Conscience*, 108.
46 *BWM*, June 1953, 179.
47 *CWM*, October 1902, 86.
48 MacKenzie, *Propaganda and Empire*, 5.
49 *CWM*, July 1935, 5.
50 MacKenzie, *Propaganda and Empire*, 3.
51 *BWM*, June 1953, 179.
52 Chocolate was not the only product to rely on royal endorsements and associations. See Robert Opie, *Rule Britannia: Trading on the British Image* (Harmondsworth: Penguin, 1985).
53 On imperial politics at the time of the coronation, see Webster, *Englishness and Empire*, 92.
54 *CWM*, Summer 1953, 2.
55 *CWM*, Summer 1953, 3.

56 See Ward (ed.), *British Culture and the End of Empire*; also, Webster, *Englishness and Empire*.
57 Ward (ed.), *British Culture and the End of Empire*, 13–14.
58 *CWM*, Summer 1953, 3.
59 BI, Rowntree Company Archive, R/DP/PC/24, report by F. E. Sanderson of the Psychological Department at Rowntree, 'Some Observations on the Training of Juniors', c.1938.
60 BI, Rowntree Company Archive, 'Rowntree Photographs: Social, Welfare, Recreational', photograph no. 4446.
61 *CWM*, Christmas 1932, 845.
62 Unrecorded conversation with Lily, May 2002.
63 Pratt, *Imperial Eyes*, 6.
64 *CWM*, March 1912, 1255–6.
65 *CWM*, February 1912, 1234.
66 *CWM*, March 1902, 3.
67 *CWM*, April 1925, 93.
68 *CWM*, December 1925, 162–3.
69 *CWM*, December 1923, 244.
70 *BWM*, December 1903, 43.
71 *CWM*, February 1908, 481.
72 *CWM*, April 1925, 92.
73 *CWM*, Summer 1953, 14.
74 *CWM*, Christmas 1953, 2.
75 Hall and Rose, 'Introduction', 27. The discourse of 'family' was used in multiple ways by both the firm and its workers (see chapter five). However, as David Nye has observed of General Electric's *Works News*, the *CWM* showed remarkably little interest in the family groups who worked at Rowntree, with the exception of families newly formed through the workplace in terms of marriages and births. As Nye remarks, 'The biological family has been entirely effaced and replaced by a pseudo-community of the corporation'. Nye, *Image Worlds*, 85.
76 *CWM*, April 1902, 19. The Rowntree story bears comparison with missionary propaganda in the way in which children are presented. Nicholas Thomas examines a mission postcard from 1908 depicting a white girl holding hands with two black male children. As in the Rowntree case, there is apparently no danger in the association of white and black children; they are innocent beings with the potential to be converted. Nicholas Thomas, 'Colonial conversions: difference, hierarchy, and history in early twentieth-century evangelical propaganda', in Hall (ed.), *Cultures of Empire*, 305–7. See also Jeffrey Richards (ed.), *Imperialism and Juvenile Literature* (Manchester: Manchester University Press, 1989).
77 Mrs Tabuteau had already left Rowntree by the time of the first *CWM*. Her memories of speaking to 'my girls' from the dining room platform suggests she had been a supervisor of some kind. *CWM*, February 1904, 137.
78 *CWM*, February 1904, 137.
79 *BWM*, May 1904, 239–40.
80 *CWM*, January 1904, 125.
81 *CWM*, December 1909, 796.
82 Cadbury UK, 360/001932, 'Reminiscences by T. A. C. as a Cadbury Trainee', 14, 29 March 1961.
83 *CWM*, Easter 1942, 6–7, 2.
84 Webster adopts the phrase 'people's empire' to conceptualise wartime narratives of people across the empire pulling together against a common enemy. Webster, *Englishness and Empire*, 7 and chapter two.
85 *CWM*, Autumn 1953, 22. See also chapter one on the marketing of Kit Kat as a 'national habit'.
86 By showing the ways in which emigrants are taking white British values overseas, such articles undermine the dichotomy of 'home' and 'abroad' to a certain extent. As Kathleen Paul comments in relation to postwar emigration to the dominions,

this was reassuring: 'Populating the empire with "British stock" would ensure that even as dominions asserted their political autonomy, their cultural and economic links would still tie them to Britain.' Kathleen Paul, *Whitewashing Britain: Race and Citizenship in the Postwar Era* (Ithaca: Cornell University Press, 1997), 29.

87 The feature did not focus exclusively on visitors from overseas. It also covered visits by famous personalities and important figures in industry.

88 Obisesan was one of the directors of the Cocoa Marketing Board. *CWM*, Summer 1953, 15.

89 *CWM*, Autumn 1967, 30.

90 Nicholas Thomas has studied photographs from missions in a similar way, observing how the arrangement of missionaries and indigenous people express the hierarchies of a family group, with the white 'parents' often sitting in the centre, surrounded by their black 'children'. Thomas, 'Colonial conversions', 306.

91 *CWM*, Autumn 1937, 6.

92 Jeffrey Green, *Black Edwardians: Black People in Britain 1901–1914* (London: Frank Cass, 1998), 15. Though for a much earlier period, Philip Morgan highlights the important role of intermediaries: 'as people who went back and forth, interpreted, translated, exchanged, and explained'. Philip D. Morgan, 'Encounters between British and "indigenous" peoples, c.1500–c.1800', in Martin Daunton and Rick Halpern (eds), *Empire and Others: British Encounters with Indigenous Peoples, 1600–1850* (Philadelphia: University of Pennsylvania Press, 1999), 53.

93 *CWM*, Autumn 1968, 26.

94 See, for example, 'Visitors from Africa', *BWM*, July 1950, 200.

95 Ebenezer Howard set up the Garden City Association in 1899 as a reaction against migration from rural areas to overcrowded industrial cities. See Stephen V. Ward (ed.), *The Garden City: Past, Present and Future* (London: E. & F. N. Spon, 1992). Work on New Earswick began in 1902; Cadbury had been building homes on land near to the factory since the 1890s.

96 See Joseph Rowntree's speech of 1907, quoted in *One Man's Vision: The Story of the Joseph Rowntree Village Trust* (London: George Allen & Unwin, 1954), 35. Also Mervyn Miller, *Raymond Unwin: Garden Cities and Town Planning* (Leicester: Leicester University Press, 1992).

97 Aalen notes the connections between town planning, eugenics and concepts of social hygiene. Frederick H. A. Aalen, 'English origins', in Ward (ed.), *The Garden City*, 38.

98 Rebecca Preston, 'The scenery of the torrid zone: imagined travels and the culture of exotics in nineteenth-century British gardens', in Driver and Gilbert (eds), *Imperial Cities*, 196.

99 *CWM*, Christmas 1932, 876–7.

100 Preston, 'The scenery of the torrid zone', 194.

101 *CWM*, April 1935, 11.

102 *CWM*, October 1935, 12.

103 *CWM*, Christmas 1953, 13. Despite the discourse of a Commonwealth family, it was white people in the dominions and white settler countries who were defined as blood relatives, whereas black people in the colonies were 'friends'. See also Paul, *Whitewashing Britain*, 26; Hall and Rose, 'Introduction', 27.

104 *CWM*, Autumn 1953, 14–15.

105 The collector Robert Opie suggests that the very practice of collecting could be experienced as an imperialist project: 'you would go out and traipse into Africa, where no white man had gone before'. John Elsner and Roger Cardinal, ' "Unless you do these crazy things . . .": an interview with Robert Opie', in John Elsner and Roger Cardinal (eds), *The Cultures of Collecting* (London: Reaktion Books, 1994), 31. On the colonial politics of collecting and exhibiting material culture, see Chris Gosden and Chantal Knowles, *Collecting Colonialism: Material Culture and Colonial Change* (Oxford: Berg, 2001), 6; Annie E. Coombes, *Reinventing Africa: Museums, Material Culture and the Popular Imagination* (New Haven: Yale University Press, 1994), 6.

106 *CWM*, February 1910, 833.

107 *CWM*, May 1910, 879.
108 *CWM*, Spring 1952, 23.
109 *CWM*, Spring 1953, 10. Other outlets for popular representations of empire within the context of factory life were the showing of films at lunchtimes and departmental theatre trips after work.
110 See Peter H. Hansen, 'Coronation Everest: the empire and Commonwealth in the second Elizabethan age', in Ward (ed.), *British Culture and the End of Empire*, 57–72.
111 Webster, *Englishness and Empire*, 94.
112 Preston, 'The scenery of the torrid zone', 202.
113 *CWM*, Easter 1934, 974.
114 *CWM*, Summer 1962, 27.
115 Mike Cronin and Richard Holt, 'The imperial game in crisis: English cricket and decolonisation', in Ward (ed.), *British Culture and the End of Empire*, 112, 118; also J. A. Mangan, *The Games Ethic and Imperialism: Aspects of the Diffusion of an Ideal* (Middlesex: Viking, 1986).
116 *CWM*, September 1910, 927.
117 The front cover of the *CWM*, July 1937, shows young women workers playing cricket. On the opening of the pavilion, see the *CWM*, October 1902, 86.
118 *CWM*, July 1936, 12–13.
119 *CWM*, July 1933, 912.
120 In establishing the library, Joseph Rowntree deducted a penny from each worker's wages. See Wagner, *Chocolate Conscience*, 65.
121 *CWM*, May 1910, 863–5.
122 *CWM*, March 1902, 11 and Summer 1962, 21. On the merging of the empire and western genres in film, and the displacement of imperial by western adventures, see Webster, *Englishness and Empire*, 16, 142–3.
123 *CWM*, April 1902, 16.
124 'Further Suggestions from the J. R. Librarian', *CWM*, Autumn 1953, 27.
125 Barbara N. Ramusack, 'Cultural missionaries, maternal imperialists, feminist allies: British women activists in India, 1865–1945', *Women's Studies International Forum*, 13: 4 (1990); Callan and Ardener (eds), *The Incorporated Wife*; Callaway, *Gender, Culture and Empire*.
126 Midgley, *Women Against Slavery*; Antoinette Burton, 'The white woman's burden: British feminists and the Indian woman, 1865–1915', *Women's Studies International Forum*, 13: 4 (1990), 299.
127 We might usefully conceptualise women's charitable activities as 'maternalism', though such terminology erases class differences between women at Rowntree. In this sense, Ramusack's concept of 'maternal imperialism' may be useful. Ramusack, 'Cultural missionaries, maternal imperialists, feminist allies'.
128 As discussed in chapter three, Joseph Rowntree specified that money from the Rowntree trusts should be used for projects within Britain.
129 *CWM*, March 1923, 189; *CWM*, April 1932, 789, 780. On the work of Doctor Barnardo as collapsing the distance between 'home' and 'empire', see Seth Koven, *Slumming: Sexual and Social Politics in Victorian London* (Princeton: Princeton University Press, 2004), 124–5.
130 BI, Parish Records, PR.Y/PJC.15, Clifton Association of the Church Missionary Society, Accounts Book (1879–1913). The reference to a zenana mission suggests a missionary project run by women rather than men.
131 Formed in 1876, the Mothers' Union was essentially a middle-class organisation. The wording of their charter between 1896 and 1926 was explicit in its imperial vision, referring to the responsibilities of mothers in raising the 'future fathers and mothers of Empire'. Surviving journals, distributed to York members in the late 1930s and early 1940s, illustrate the existence of an overseas fund to pay for Mothers' Union workers in the colonies and the dominions. Olive Parker, *For the Family's Sake: A History of the Mothers' Union 1876–1976* (Folkestone: Bailey Brothers and Swinfen, 1975), 31. Journals available under Parish Records, PR.EAS.151, at the Borthwick Institute, York.

132 *CWM*, Christmas 1964, 7. Susan Thorne asserts the key 'authoritative' role of missionaries in bringing the empire home to Victorian Britain. Although Thorne believes that by the second half of the twentieth century the influence of missionaries within Britain 'had waned beyond all recognition', the York case provides glimpses into their continuing influence. Susan Thorne, 'Religion and empire at home', in Hall and Rose (eds), *At Home with the Empire*, 164–5.

133 Valentine Cunningham, ' "God and nature intended you for a missionary's wife": Mary Hill, Jane Eyre and other missionary women in the 1840s', in Fiona Bowie, Deborah Kirkwood, and Shirley Ardener (eds), *Women and Missions: Past and Present. Anthropological and Historical Perceptions* (Oxford: Berg, 1993), 93.

134 Women members of the Young People's Mission, for example, could become missionaries. Betty Sanderson was accepted for missionary training in 1958 and was later sent out to the Ivory Coast. Van Wilson, *Number 26: The History of 26 St. Saviourgate, York* (n.p.: Voyager Publications, 1999), 49.

135 Olive Parker feels that this approach was declining: 'As . . . differences between the classes grew blurred, there was less practical advice on home-making, diet and physical care and an increased insistence on the need for spiritual training.' Parker, *For the Family's Sake*, 33. However, Parker surely downplays the significance of class identity.

136 Interconnecting discourses of race and class constructed some white Britons as the target of civilising missions within the metropole. General William Booth had drawn direct parallels between the 'pygmies' of Africa and the poor of London. General Booth, *In Darkest England and the Way Out* (London: International Headquarters of the Salvation Army, 1890), 11. On the associations between 'darkest Africa' and 'darkest England' and the postwar shift to a united 'white' race in reaction to colonial migration, see Wendy Webster, *Imagining Home: Gender, 'Race' and National Identity, 1945–64* (London: UCL Press, 1998), 61–5.

137 *CWM*, Spring 1951, 22. Women had not usually been physically present in the Victorian minstrel show. However, as a BBC photograph confirms, women had appeared in blackface makeup in 1954, when the radio minstrels made the move to television. British Broadcasting Corporation, *The Black and White Minstrel Show* (London: British Broadcasting Corporation, c.1962). In later years, only men would appear on the television in blackface, with the women performing as white 'maids'.

138 *CWM*, Spring 1951, 11.

139 BI, Rowntree Company Archive, R/B4/THA/9, 'Reminiscences of R. & Co Pensioners by G. W. R. Wright', c.1921, 5; *CWM*, December 1921, 30.

140 There is a substantial literature on American minstrelsy. See for example: Robert C. Toll, *Blacking Up: The Minstrel Show in Nineteenth-Century America* (New York: Oxford University Press, 1974); Eric Lott, *Love and Theft: Blackface Minstrelsy and the American Working Class* (Oxford: Oxford University Press, 1995). By contrast, the minstrel show in Britain has been too little explored. Michael Pickering has now gone some way to addressing this gap: Pickering, 'Mock blacks and racial mockery: the "nigger" minstrel and British imperialism', in J. S. Bratton et al. (eds), *Acts of Supremacy: The British Empire and the Stage, 1790–1930* (Manchester: Manchester University Press, 1991), 179–236; Pickering, 'Race, gender and broadcast comedy: the case of the BBC's *Kentucky Minstrels*', *European Journal of Communication*, 9: 3 (1994), 311–33; Pickering, *Blackface Minstrelsy in Britain* (Aldershot: Ashgate, 2008). In June 2004, BBC4 broadcast a television documentary re-evaluating 'The Black and White Minstrel Show'.

141 Lott, *Love and Theft*, 3.

142 John Blair, 'Blackface minstrels in cross-cultural perspective', *American Studies International*, 28: 2 (1990), 60.

143 Pickering, 'Mock blacks and racial mockery', 181.

144 Sonya O. Rose, 'Sex, citizenship, and the nation in World War II Britain', in Hall (ed.), *Cultures of Empire*, 252.

145 Pickering, 'Mock blacks and racial mockery', 211. The Empire Windrush ship brought just under 500 Jamaican migrants to Britain. On the long history of black people in Britain, see Peter Fryer, *Staying Power: The History of Black People in Britain* (London: Pluto Press, 1984).

146 Pickering, 'Race, gender and broadcast comedy', 312.

147 BBC4, 'Black and White Minstrel Show – revisited', 6 June 2004.

148 Michael Pickering, 'Mock blacks and racial mockery', 181–2.

149 As Deborah Gray White comments, 'Black men . . . were thought to have such insatiable sexual appetites that they had to go beyond the boundaries of their race to get satisfaction.' White, *Ar'n't I A Woman?* 38.

150 Lott, *Love and Theft*, 6.

151 Hazel Carby, 'Brown babies: the birth of Britain as a racialized state, 1942–1948' (paper presented at American Research Seminar, Leeds University, UK, March 2007).

152 British Broadcasting Corporation, *The Black and White Minstrel Show*, 2.

153 *YEP*, 24 June 1969.

154 British Broadcasting Corporation, *The Black and White Minstrel Show*, 2.

155 Blair, 'Blackface minstrels in cross-cultural perspective', 60.

156 Pickering, 'Race, gender and broadcast comedy', 313.

157 Toll has identified this as an element of nineteenth-century minstrel shows. Toll, *Blacking Up*, 164–8.

158 Philip J. Deloria, *Playing Indian* (New Haven: Yale University Press, 1998), 7; Patricia Penn Hilden, *When Nickels Were Indians: An Urban, Mixed-Blood Story* (Washington: Smithsonian Institution Press, 1995).

159 This is not to imply that Britain itself was unaffected by histories of colonisation and immigration.

160 The popularity of American culture intensified after the Second World War. Yet, as Webster points out, the relationship with America was complex and could be fraught with anxieties. Webster, *Englishness and Empire*, 82.

161 Deloria, *Playing Indian*, 7.

162 Lott, *Love and Theft*, 6.

163 *CWM*, Christmas 1966, 20.

164 Pickering, 'Race, gender and broadcast comedy', 316; Blair, 'Blackface minstrels in cross-cultural perspective', 60; Deloria, *Playing Indian*, 8.

CHAPTER FIVE

'I think I was the only Chinese girl working there': race and gender in the chocolate factory

The white hands of the . . . chocolate makers are helped by other unseen hands some thousands of miles away, black and brown hands, toiling in plantations . . . (H. A. Gwynne in the *Standard*, 1908)[1]

We all wear white linen coat overalls and caps for this job, which makes the workroom look rather nice as well as being in keeping with the handling of foodstuffs. ('Madge Munro Talks to 2,000,000 People', *CWM*, Christmas 1932, 845)

Chocolate manufacture has been conceived in raced and gendered terms. A hierarchical progress narrative of the cocoa chain is constructed in which 'black and brown' workers (usually identified as men) farm the cocoa; white male workers in the west transform this into chocolate; white women render chocolate aesthetically pleasing through their feminine skills of decorating and packing; and white western consumers (particularly women) consume the finished product. The 'whiteness' of chocolate manufacture is re-emphasised materially and culturally in many ways. The addition of (white) milk in the factories of the 'metropolis' purifies the (black) cocoa, the gift of the colonies.[2] Meanwhile, discourses of food production employ assumptions about whiteness as representing hygiene and cleanliness. Thus female workers in the Rowntree factory wear white uniforms which make the workroom 'look rather nice', while Cadbury boasts of its 'vast factory as clean as a dairy. White-tiled walls . . . white-overalled workers'.[3] In such representations of the industry, non-white women, where they appear at all, are confined to the sphere of cocoa production.[4]

This chapter focuses on the experiences of women workers on the shopfloor of the Rowntree factory in York, drawing on a selection of oral histories conducted with retired workers. Although (white) women appear at strategic points in official company histories, they tend to be positioned as the grateful recipients of paternalist welfare, rather than as individual agents. The daily lives and attitudes of the ordinary women who had such a significant role in manufacturing confectionery in Britain have been largely ignored. Through the process of oral history, we can gain a better understanding of what working at Rowntree meant to individual women: of their relationship to the products, their colleagues and the company.

Although I draw on a number of interviews with white women, most of whom had been born in York, at the heart of this chapter will be the testimonies of three non-white women who migrated to the city. The first, Nellie, was born in Liverpool to Chinese parents, and moved to York during the Second World War. Carmen was recruited directly by Rowntree in Malta, arriving in York in the early 1960s. Finally, Julie travelled to York with her family in the early 1970s as a Ugandan Asian refugee and started work at Rowntree a year later.[5] Despite sources in the Rowntree archives confirming the long-term presence of people of diverse national and ethnic backgrounds on the shopfloor, in published histories the 'whiteness' of the chocolate workers is taken for granted, rendering the experiences of such non-white workers invisible. Popular perceptions of York as a city without any numerically significant non-white populations have compounded this problem. Yet it is the very absence of large migrant communities in York which makes it important to study the experiences of those women and men who did come to live and work in the city.[6]

Histories of women's labour, of diaspora and of race relations in Britain will be incomplete without studies that pay attention to the importance of local conditions. York and the Rowntree firm were situated within particular social, cultural and economic contexts. How did women living in this small relatively unindustrialised city, working at this 'local' factory with truly global connections, experience gender, race and class relations on the shopfloor? How did they conceptualise their own work in the chocolate industry? This chapter will by no means offer a representative study but it will prioritise women's own experiences and memories of work in the chocolate industry. Before moving on to these individual narratives, it is necessary to provide some broader historical context for the employment of women workers in confectionery production and for the employment of migrant workers at the York factory.

The human factor: Rowntree employment policies

'Rowntree lasses': the employment of women workers
Women were employed by Rowntree from the earliest days of the Tanner's Moat factory, founded in 1862. In her contribution to a

collection of reminiscences for the *CWM* in the early 1920s, Miss Lister, who joined the firm in May 1877, recalled between fifty and sixty 'girls' at the Tanner's Moat site in these early years. They performed the labour-intensive tasks of sorting, decorating and packing confectionery. Another pensioner, Mrs Beesley, started work at the factory aged twenty in November 1877. She described how girls of fourteen earned 3s 6p a week for sixty hours' work. More experienced women on piecework could earn around 14s to 15s but would have to pay for their own young helpers to 'knock out' the chocolate and fetch materials, leaving them with around 9s a week. Earnings would be less in summer, as production could be brought to a halt by the hot weather. By 1894 there were 416 women in the confectionery department and another fifty in the cake chocolate and cocoa department. Some of these early women workers amassed many years of service to the firm. Mrs Beesley became the first female Rowntree pensioner, retiring at the age of fifty-five in 1912.[7]

According to Mrs Beesley and the *CWM*, there had once been a parrot at the factory, 'which used to tell the lasses to get on with their work'.[8] Such fond memories of idiosyncratic, almost eccentric, approaches to management by the early Rowntree founders served to emphasise by contrast the increasingly formalised supervision of women workers. A Women's Employment Department, for example, had been created in 1896, under the direction of the first 'lady welfare supervisor', Miss Wood. The supervisors were charged with making all new appointments and overseeing the welfare of the girls both within the factory and at home. This was indicative of management's paternalist concern for the health, morality and general well-being of their growing female workforce, who were predominantly young, single women.[9]

From the early twentieth century, as the workforce continued to expand, still more systematic welfare measures were introduced. By 1904 there were 1,107 women employed in the confectionery department (compared to just 520 men), and 306 women in the cake chocolate department (with 299 men).[10] Rowntree set up a Domestic School in 1905, ostensibly to counter long-standing concerns that industrial employment of women threatened the very fabric of society by destroying family life – 'that it unfits the girls for the positions they have to take in the home'. Here female workers could learn to manage a household in specially designated cottages.[11] In 1943, this venture was renamed the Girls' Day Continuation School, allowing young workers to continue their general education for one day each week. Other welfare schemes included the provision of medical care, a library and 'music while you work'. There were also financial benefits, though as women had to leave the permanent staff if they married, pension and sick pay schemes were of limited value to many. Similar welfare measures had been taken at Cadbury, who also employed significant numbers of women workers.[12]

Despite a marriage bar being in operation at Rowntree, from 1912 married women could obtain temporary work as seasonal staff.[13] The efforts of women workers were crucial in meeting increased demand for confectionery at periods such as Easter and Christmas. Women would become still more vital in keeping production going during the First World War. The *CWM* celebrated their wartime roles with group photographs of all-female departments (accompanied by their male supervisors), captioned, 'Helping Us to Carry On'.[14] Yet full-time married women were still excluded from the status of 'permanent' employees (and would be for another fifty years). As the Rowntree business expanded from the mid-1930s, with several innovative new brands, employment opportunities for women increased (though their jobs were always vulnerable during periods of depression). Following the Second World War and the lifting of rationing, women workers were in still greater demand and management agonised over how to deal with a shortage of female staff in the 1950s and 1960s. In spite of recruitment problems, in 1959 women still made up over half the York factory workforce: there were 3,958 women (including temporary and permanent staff) compared to 3,707 men.[15]

Rowntree tried a number of measures to increase the proportion of female factory staff. A Board Minute from 1959 details the instiga-tion of an evening shift for married women in Cream Packing, with over 300 applications received for 200 appointments.[16] Several of the women I interviewed had worked this 'housewives' shift', which allowed them to complete housework and childcare duties during the day, and to hand children over to husbands as they left for work in the early evening. In addition, the firm broadened their search for women workers beyond the city, recruiting regionally and occasionally even internationally. In the 1960s, as will be discussed in more detail later, they sent a representative to Malta to recruit single girls. However, I have found no evidence of any such systematic recruitment of Commonwealth migrants from the Caribbean or from South East Asia.

The shortage of women workers gradually eroded some segregation of tasks by sex; men increasingly worked alongside women from 1960. Nevertheless, the ideological gendering of tasks remained. Women continued to be associated with the feminine abilities of creating pleas-ing luxury items, being able to handle delicate confectionery quickly and accurately, and working at speed on repetitive manual tasks such as packing. For the most part, these were seen as 'natural' skills, though pre-employment tests (manual and psychological) were designed to assign individual women to the most appropriate jobs.[17] Several of the women I interviewed had spent at least part of their time in the card box department, with box making privileged as a skilled 'trade'. Other tasks mentioned included sorting nuts; enrobing chocolates (covering assortment centres) by hand and by machine; piping designs onto chocolates; packing assortment boxes; hand-wrapping fruit pastilles; putting After Eight mints into boxes; and unwrapping waste chocolates. Work at the factory gradually became increasingly mechanised and fragmented. By the mid-1950s, instead of individually packing whole boxes of assorted chocolates at their own table, women would place one chocolate into a plastic tray as it moved past them on a conveyor belt. Even so, they could be called upon to pack by hand when machinery broke down, or for luxury products.[18]

Men controlled the processing of raw materials such as cocoa, as well as the dispersal of finished goods for retail around the country.[19] They were also employed as electricians, engineers, carpenters and builders. Although men did work on assembly lines (usually in different departments from women), male operatives were more likely to be moving around the factory, employed on 'indirect' tasks such as providing women with the necessary materials.[20] Lily, who worked

Figure 10 Undated photograph showing women hand-packing chocolate assortments using individual paper cups.

the afternoon shift in the late 1950s, remembered, 'women at the work, men . . . walking about doing other jobs'. Actual daily contact with male workers was limited. Even into the 1970s and 1980s, women remembered working primarily with other women. Julie stressed that 'there was only ladies where we worked . . . You don't work with men.' Although Nellie recalled men helping with piping, this was 'not for very long'. Working with men was a novelty rather than a daily occurrence: 'it was funny to have men working with you'. Male workers controlled the movement of confectionery into, around and out of the factory: the boundaries of the factory were thus effectively a male preserve.

The dearth of willing women factory workers did win them some benefits: full-time married women workers were finally allowed to join the permanent staff in 1962, granting them access to the pension scheme and sick pay, and the age at which they had to retire was raised from fifty-five to sixty in 1966.[21] However, such measures still did not benefit those women who formed the crucial seasonal labour force. Carmen spoke strongly about the injustice of this: 'We should have, by right, . . . we should get something paying – we are only part time, we come back every year, we should get some pension at least, if it's two pounds, one pound fair enough.' Assumptions about appropriate tasks and rewards for women chocolate workers were shifting, but in limited ways, in the 1950s and 1960s. Clearly, many women workers in York were either looking elsewhere for employment, or were choosing to work fewer hours at Rowntree, if indeed they were working at all. Whereas in 1952–53, the confectionery industry in York had recruited 41.1 per cent of secondary modern girl school leavers, by 1960–61 this figure had fallen to 18 per cent. Such changes were the result of complex factors, including the local availability of alternative employment, changing expectations as a result of longer periods in compulsory education, employment patterns of other family members, state provision of welfare and improved standards of living.[22]

Rowntree and migrant labour

As demonstrated in chapter four, Rowntree traded on their status as a local factory. Yet the firm and the city of York had never been detached from the global economics of imperialism. During the First World War, Indian men (many of them former sailors who had jumped ship) worked in various industries across Great Britain. Some had been enticed from their ships by offers of better wages at specific companies, others were recruited from the Labour Exchange.[23] A number of them found their way to York and to Rowntree. Male Indian workers at the factory were discriminated against as non-white men working amongst white women. In 1916, the Factory Manager, T. H. Appleton, stated that 'it would not do to employ [Hindu workmen] in any of the general rooms, or where there were girls'. Belgian refugees apparently caused no such anxiety.[24] In a situation where there were large numbers of single white women workers, an 'exotic' male sexuality was clearly seen as a threat. At this stage the firm was still able to exercise an individualised paternalistic surveillance of the welfare of its 'young ladies' and attempted to police – if only within the workplace – their relationships with male workers.[25]

The world wars were important historical moments in bringing migrants to York, as refugees fleeing persecution in Europe came to the city. Some of these women and men took jobs at the Rowntree factory. Polish girls attending English classes at the Continuation School featured in official company publicity of the late 1940s as young white workers happily assimilating into English culture.[26] Whilst the presence of white Europeans was openly celebrated, Rowntree kept quiet about their employment of non-white workers.[27] As Webster has observed, it was the European workers, who were officially aliens, who were accepted as potential Britons whilst black British subjects were constructed as 'other'.[28] Apart from Polish workers, migrant and non-white women are rarely found in the *CWM*, although their presence is suggested by the names listed in the sections announcing weddings and births. It is possible, for instance, to find Nellie's maiden name listed when she married in 1965. However, it is only through oral history that we can begin to gain a more detailed insight into the daily experiences of individual migrant women.[29]

Despite postwar government schemes to recruit more European labour, Rowntree experienced severe shortages of female employees in the 1950s and 1960s, as mentioned above.[30] The York Committee frequently discussed the topic, yet there is no reference in the minutes to the recruitment of non-white women or women from outside British borders. In particular, the 1964 scheme to recruit Maltese women is not mentioned. It is possible that such recruitment was dealt with by a separate department or was part of the Board of Directors' discussions rather than those of the Committee but it is strange that what must have been quite an expensive and time-consuming exercise gets no mention. The arrival of the girls does not even appear in the *CWM*, although the Maltese High Commissioner and his wife are featured when they come to monitor the girls' progress the following year.[31] Were these women perceived unproblematically as female Rowntree workers, part of a Commonwealth family perhaps? Or were management trying to diffuse any potential hostility about such recruitment by not drawing to it undue attention?

The Quaker heritage of the Rowntree firm, particularly in relation to the anti-slavery movement, set them up for criticism whenever they were seen to deviate from 'enlightened' employment policies. The scandal surrounding Rowntree involvement in São Tomé and Principe has already been discussed in some detail in chapter two. It is unsurprising, then, that Rowntree managers were keen to avoid any incident on the shopfloor which could lead to insinuations of racial discrimination. The York Committee minutes of 8 November 1966 illustrate just such a case, where negative press publicity had been given to 'the non-employment by the Company of an Anglo-Indian craftsman':

> The Chairman stated that this incident had highlighted the importance of referring such matters to him at an early stage, so that, if necessary, the Company Chairman could be consulted. Whilst the Chairman appreciated that Functional Heads must exercise their discretion in resolving problems, he emphasised that cases which appeared likely to develop into major policy issues should be submitted to him as quickly as possible.[32]

The worker's status as 'craftsman' no doubt enabled him to get greater coverage of his case. It is unlikely that a woman seeking seasonal employment would have evoked such interest in the press, or created such fear of her case developing into a 'major policy issue'.

The legacy of the Quakers' anti-slavery stance, and of the Rowntree investigations into poverty in Britain, was evident as late as the 1970s, when the York firm faced accusations of paying 'slave wages' in their South African subsidiary. A report in *The Guardian* 'named Wilson Rowntree as one of a number of British firms in South Africa paying African employees below the official subsistence level of from £10 to £11 a week for a family of five'.[33] This assertion was later withdrawn by the paper, but the spectre of race discrimination, particularly exploitation of black Africans, was never far from their door. The media has always been alert to opportunities to accuse Rowntree, and indeed Cadbury, of hypocrisy in labour relations.[34]

The *CWM* ends in 1970, just prior to the arrival of Ugandan Asians in York. Fortunately, other sources offer an insight into local policy and attitudes regarding employment, as well as the provision of accommodation and welfare services. A locally produced pamphlet entitled *Green for Come* referred to the national strategy of creating 'red' and 'green' zones: refugees were directed away from areas with existing Asian communities and towards so-called 'green' cities such as York, where they would be less of a 'strain' on local resources.[35] Although recording that this scheme was 'obviously a sensible one', the pamphlet hints at the racism which ultimately determined the zones: 'some of the areas listed . . . as 'red' were so listed more because of local protest than because of objectively measured pressure on their services – Leicester being the most obvious example'.[36] In York, too, there were protests that used fears about the 'pressure' on housing and jobs to try to prevent the settlement of what were very small numbers of refugees.[37] One angry letter to the *Yorkshire Evening Press* complained that the country was playing 'fairy Godmother' to 'ungrateful foreigners' and that the city was already suffering a housing shortage. Others advocated keeping numbers low so as not to cause tension in a city which currently had 'no racial discrimination whatsoever'.[38] Yet these racist views were strongly contested by letters and features urging Christian charity and invoking the figure of the 'Good Samaritan'.[39]

As an additional restriction to the relocation of refugees, it had been stated in a local authority ruling that homes in York would only be made available when the 'breadwinner' (usually but not always represented as male) had a job. Employment was seen as evidence that families were respectable, hard working and unlikely to make claims on local or national benefits.[40] The small number of refugees arriving in the city – around twenty-five families – made it possible for the local press to follow in detail their progress in finding work. This level of surveillance would have been impossible in the so-called 'immigrant cities', the 'red' areas. A front-page article in the *Yorkshire Evening Press* from 30 October 1972 reassured white readers, 'Three members of the first Ugandan Asian family to be found a permanent home in York have found jobs within a week . . . Mrudula Joshi, aged 24, a trained infant teacher, and her sister Illa, aged 20, have taken jobs as packers for Rowntree Mackintosh Ltd.' Mrs Archer, a York resettlement officer, is then quoted as saying, 'I think this shows that these people are prepared to work.'[41] The Rowntree firm thus had a part to play in the acceptance of refugees as workers, even as they were positioned as workers within a capitalist, racist and patriarchal system.

In the *Green for Come* report on York, it was noted that many Ugandan Asian refugees were working at Rowntree, and a number of possible reasons for this were put forward:

(a) that this is shift work, which frequently often has vacancies because of the inconvenience many people feel about doing the job
(b) it is relatively well-paid work with overtime readily available to anyone willing to work very hard
(c) the Asians themselves <u>want</u> to work and are therefore willing to take any job to get themselves established

(d) Rowntrees themselves as employers are very good to their employees.[42]

The tendency for migrant workers to take jobs considered unsuitable by the indigenous population is illustrated by points (a) and (c), although the reference to shift work suggests that this part of the report is referring to male workers. However, interviews conducted for the report confirmed that women saw Rowntree as a genuinely 'good' company to work for both in terms of welfare provision and job prospects:

'M' has nothing but praise for their working conditions and says how considerate Rowntrees are as employers. The girls' supervisor has visited them at home and seems to take a real interest in their welfare. She has suggested that 'I' goes on a day release scheme to learn shorthand and typing after which she could work in the offices.[43]

This type of surveillance of female employees was perhaps reassuring for some refugee families in the context of women entering paid work outside the home in an unfamiliar environment. It is also significant to note that Rowntree were offering a level of social mobility by encouraging girls to enter office work (as many young white women were doing at this time). This could have been attractive in that it offered the potential to move a little closer to the social status many families had enjoyed in Uganda.

Life before Rowntree: local, national and global transitions

Before turning to their experiences in the Rowntree factory, it is useful to sketch out very briefly the different backgrounds of the women who contributed to this project and the ways in which their individual biographies tie into local and national stories of women's labour, as well as into wider global movements of people and products. I begin with an analysis of how locally born white women came to be employed by the firm, considering both their individual motivations and the broader context of women's paid work in York. I then turn to the three women migrants, whose narratives reveal lives created and experienced within what Avtar Brah has termed the 'historical entanglements' of empire.[44] It is important to recognise the broader structural forces at work in histories of migration and I plot some of the trajectories which eventually brought each woman to the Rowntree factory. These are necessarily over-simplified and linear but they do give some sense of how the Rowntree factory has brought together in one place people, not just products, from across the empire.

'My gal's a Yorkshire gal': white women's lives in York
In 1932, a radio interview with a young Rowntree worker, Madge
Munro, suggested the regional affiliations of many women employees
through reference to their choice of songs whilst working: 'You know
the kind of song – "My gal's a Yorkshire gal" . . . with its kind words
to the "factory lass." The line which makes many visitors smile is
"Eh by goom she's a champion."'[45] This performance of gendered,
regional identities was not simply for the entertainment of visitors;
Yorkshire-ness was a regular motif of the *CWM* and had meaning for
the majority of workers.[46] All but one of the original thirteen women
interviewed for this project had been born and had lived most of their
lives in York. Only Alice came to the city as an adult, from a north-
east mining community. So how did white women from York come
to work for the Rowntree company?

At the time of the interviews in 2000, the women were aged
between sixty and eighty-eight years. Some had spent the majority of
their working lives at the factory, taking up jobs straight from leaving school at the age of fourteen and retiring at sixty (though usually
with at least one break in service). The oldest, Lillian (born in 1912),
started at Rowntree as a seasonal worker in 1936, aged twenty-four,
and retired in the early 1970s. She had previously worked at the Terry's
factory as a single girl. One woman, Brenda, left her Rowntree job after
just six months in 1939. Most of the women who took part in this
stage of my research started work in the 1940s and 1950s. They had
a variety of motivations for seeking work with the Rowntree company, which they did at various stages in their life cycle.

Upon leaving school at fourteen, unless they had full-time duties
within the home or in a family business, each woman had been expected
to take some form of paid work in order to contribute to the family
income. Mavis, who had gone straight to the firm from school, recalled,
'we had to tip up . . . you had to pay board and lodgings as it was called'.
As a major employer in the city, Rowntree recruited girls directly
from local schools and was often seen as both an obvious choice and
as a genuinely good firm to work for. Some women had family
already employed at the factory who encouraged them to apply. Sisters
Amy and Margaret grew up in company housing as their father was
a Rowntree fireman of some status. Margaret described her life as structured by the presence of the firm: 'Rowntrees has been the beginning
of my life, all my working life, practically, and the end'. Other
women, like Lily, initially rejected factory work despite such family
connections but turned to Rowntree as a source of convenient part-
time work later in life.

Young school-leavers worked full time, which was set from 1919 at forty-four hours a week.[47] Never-married women, widows and married women whose husbands had irregular or poorly paid jobs, would also often work full-time hours where possible. Lillian had to take up full-time seasonal employment when her husband was diagnosed as a diabetic in the 1930s: 'There was no National Health money and everything he had had to be paid for.' Alice's husband was also regularly out of work through illness and she took up part-time work at Rowntree in 1951. When she became a widow in the early 1960s, she went onto full-time shifts:

> as the women at work used to say, 'We work for greed but you work for need.' 'Cos they used to work when their husband had a good job ... everything was for pleasure and that and to better their lives and better their homes. But I had to work for necessity to keep the house going.

Alice sets up a clear division here between herself and other married women workers.

Single women workers may have expected to leave work upon getting married, and were officially encouraged to think in these terms by the company, but in practice this was not always the case. Increasingly it was the birth of children, rather than marriage itself, which affected working patterns.[48] Women described how they stopped work when they first had children but later returned, usually on part-time hours. Children themselves could be a motivation to work. Gladys, for example, applied to Rowntree when her daughter was accepted at a local grammar school: 'So I had to get all her stuff together ... and me only way was to start work meself, and me husband give an eye to t'children.' For the daughters of many of the women I spoke with, improvements in education brought changed expectations of the workplace. Ironically, Gladys's daughter also ended up at Rowntree for a period, as the secretarial work she had gained access to through secondary education did not pay the wages of her friends at the factory: 'she was palling on with girls who worked at the factory and all dressing up and that'. For later generations, then, Rowntree offered the possibility of conspicuous consumption through relatively high wages for women.

Lily went to Rowntree in the late 1950s at the age of forty-two as a married, part-time worker with a family. Working afternoons, she would put in around fifteen hours each week. In her own words, she was 'just earning a little bit to help ... normally ... to pay for holidays'. There is a danger, however, in underestimating the importance of some women's work by accepting without question their definition of it as just 'a little bit to help'. The emergence of a consumer culture had changed the nature of work so that, as Tilly and Scott put it, 'Greater expenses . . . replaced poverty as an incentive to work.'[49] By undermining the value of the money they earned, married women held in place the notion of the man's wage as the important one. Once the wages came in, they were often pooled by the woman and spent as she deemed fit, rather than saving one wage packet for 'luxuries'.[50] Women thus interpreted their working identities differently, according to their family situation. Where their husband had had a relatively well-paid, skilled job, they would play down their own contribution. However, if their husband's job had been either poorly paid or unstable, women took a pride in their own ability to contribute to their family's survival.[51]

'They call me Chinese Nell': Nellie's story

Nellie was born in Liverpool sometime before the Second World War – she chose not to reveal her exact birth date.[52] She had four brothers and four sisters, all born in England, and she was one of the youngest. Both her parents were Canton Chinese. Nellie cannot remember why or exactly when her parents arrived in Liverpool but it must have been the early part of the twentieth century, certainly by the 1930s. Liverpool is linked strongly for Nellie with the experience of Chinese culture, sustained through weekly visits to Chinatown in her youth. However, her early life was spent in Prescott Street where she told me there were no other Chinese people living at that time.[53] The traces of a Liverpudlian accent suggest Nellie's continuing affiliation with the city, despite living in York since the mid-1940s.[54]

Mainland China has never been directly subject to British imperial rule; nevertheless relations between the two countries have been structured by the economics of empire, particularly through the opium trade. As David Parker comments, 'The presence of Chinese people in Britain from the late eighteenth century onwards must be seen as part of a much larger story of imperial expansion and enforced global migration.'[55] Stereotypes of Chinese people, particularly men, as the 'yellow peril' – threatening white purity through drug abuse and sexual depravity – were formed in the context of British imperial hierarchies of race. There has been relatively little research on this long-term history of Chinese people in Britain, and even less on those living outside the key settlements of London and Liverpool. Yet York sources suggest the presence of at least one Chinese family very early in the twentieth century.[56] Moreover, the experiences of early women migrants such as Nellie's mother and of second-generation women like Nellie have been particularly under-researched. With the exception of Maria Lin Wong's important study of Chinese-Liverpudlians, the research that does exist on second-generation women mostly focuses on the children of post-Second World War migrants, particularly those working in the catering industry.[57]

Nellie came to York with her family during the Second World War, and worked in the family laundry business on Clarence Street. However, as the business suffered – partly due to automated 'launderettes' appearing in residential areas but also to the increasing ownership of washing machines and the loss of military contracts – Nellie sought work at Rowntree as a convenient local source of employment. Since much of the literature on first- and second-generation Chinese migrant women focuses on their labour in the family economy, Nellie's move into the sphere of waged labour in the Rowntree factory has meant that her experiences remain largely untheorised in the current scholarship.

'I've always wanted to come abroad': Carmen's story

Carmen was born in 1944, one of twelve children, and grew up in Birkirkara near Valletta in Malta. As a Maltese woman, she experienced life under the direct colonial rule of Britain. Although Malta was not 'conquered' or invaded by the British, colonialism was nonetheless a reality for the Maltese people.[58] The importance of the island as a 'fortress colony', guarding the entrance to Suez and thus to India from the Mediterranean, meant that absolute obedience from the local population was seen as particularly important. The impact of British rule was reflected in Carmen's memories of school, where she had to speak English: 'You have to. You have to. Because in class sometimes there'll be a big sign saying, "Please speak English." ' Having left school, like many other women, Carmen was employed as domestic labour for a British military family. With so much of the economy centred about the military, this was one of the few working opportunities: 'I enjoyed school very much but I had to leave because at that time there was not much anything to do and all that was is like more or less a chambermaid, like for the English people'.

Representations of the Maltese have tended to characterise them as hardworking and intelligent but stubborn about leaving the islands. They have been racialised as physically different from white English people, often as 'swarthy'. Where they have left Malta to come to Britain, they have been subject to more pejorative representations in the media. Geoff Dench reported in the 1970s on the negative images of Maltese men as being involved in criminal activity. The discourse of criminality has similarly been used in relation to Chinese people and to other migrant groups. Paul Gilroy illustrates how demands for immigration laws in the early twentieth century drew on such racist associations of migrants with crime.[59] The Maltese, however, have tended to be favoured in postwar immigration legislation, as demonstrated at a local level by Rowntree recruitment policy. They were actively encouraged to migrate to different parts of the empire, to populate areas such as Australia.[60] This suggests some important contrasts with perceptions of the Chinese and the impact of this on their experiences of migration, though both groups were subjected to discrimination.

Emigration from the Maltese islands was common between 1948 and 1966.[61] Young people, influenced partly by American culture and ideas, wanted greater freedom and sought it outside the strictly religious atmosphere of the islands. Carmen described her own departure from Malta in these terms: 'I've always wanted to come abroad, either England or Australia.' When she heard the advert for Rowntree workers on the radio, offering travel and accommodation, she headed for Valetta to apply. Carmen's emphasis on 'I' contrasts with Nellie's, 'we came to York', but particularly with Julie's collective narrative of migration. She presented her move very much as an individual choice and as something that would have happened eventually, even without the intervention of Rowntree. As a girl in Malta, Carmen felt the constrictions upon her time keenly as she was expected to help out with family childcare. The patriarchal ideology of Roman Catholicism (like that of many religions) also placed particular constraints upon women, even as they were empowered in gendered ways. Carmen longed to be able to go out and spend her leisure time freely. Waged work at Rowntree, though bringing its own constraints, allowed her the time and the resources to do this.

'And it was just a nightmare': Julie's story

Julie was born in 1940 in Zimbabwe, which had been a British colony since the 1890s. One of ten children, her family ran a clothing business. When she was eighteen she moved to Uganda, another British colony with a substantial Indian diaspora, to get married. She worked with her husband to run a small but successful clothing factory and enjoyed a comfortable lifestyle. In contrast to Nellie and Carmen, the moment of leaving 'home' is marked as a traumatic rupture in Julie's story. Julie began her oral history by telling me, 'We had our own business and we had quite a few people working for us. And it was just a nightmare and all of a sudden on the radio it came that all the Asians had to go.' The apparent prosperity of Asian communities in British Africa and their social distance from black Africans, created through the economics of British imperialism, were factors in allowing them to become scapegoats for black poverty in the post-independence

'Africanisation' era in Uganda. When Idi Amin – supported by the British initially – took over in 1971, the Asian population were deemed to have too much of the country's wealth and were subsequently violently expelled.[62]

The British treatment of East African Asians marks a shameful period in British politics. Julie and her family had British passports yet they entered Britain as refugees, constructed as racial others instead of as citizens, to be resettled as the authorities saw fit.[63] Her husband had to first secure a job at Rowntree before the family were able to leave the resettlement camp in Wales and move to York. On arriving in the city, they were settled in Rowntree-owned housing, paying four pounds rent a week. They would eventually buy this house and Julie was still living there at the time of the interview in 2002. By staying in York, Julie does not have a place in most histories of Asian migration. These focus on the 'centres' of British Asian settlement such as Bradford, Leicester and London, cities initially designated as 'red' zones but to which many refugees moved with the help of community connections.

Julie herself did not work for a year, whilst they were 'getting settled' in York. When she did begin to look for employment, Rowntree was not her first choice. Her social worker persuaded her to apply, rather than pursuing her dream of opening a nursery. Though she presents a largely positive picture of her time at the firm then, Rowntree and the local authorities had a significant level of control over Julie's early experiences of life in York. For Carmen and Julie, Rowntree's brand of industrial welfare – providing housing for instance – was situated within the context of immigration policy at the time. Defined respectively as a migrant worker and a refugee by the state, both women were dependent upon Rowntree to a certain extent even before they started work. The company thus benefited from the political climate around race and immigration in the 1960s and 1970s in finding solutions to a shortage of women workers.

'It was hard work': working lives

From a relatively small number of oral histories, we can already begin to see the complexity of Rowntree's female workforce. Women brought to the shopfloor very different life experiences and expectations of work. As Rowntree employees, however, they were expected to conform to set methods of working and to set patterns of behaviour designed to increase efficiency. I now turn to their daily lives at the factory to reach a better understanding of how women experienced their gendered roles in chocolate manufacture.

[193]

'It was a lovely presentation with hand-piping':
memories of chocolate production

Starting work at Rowntree could be a difficult time as women struggled to cope with the new, noisy environment and the tasks they had
to learn. Those who persevered developed not only the manual skills
required to keep up with (and even exceed) the set pace of work, but
also acquired knowledge about their tasks and the machines they
worked on. Many worked in various departments and so had a broad
sense of the scope of factory production, though they resented being
moved around too often, away from jobs they were used to and their
friendship group. Despite this investment in their work, women's
position in the factory (spatially and hierarchically) circumscribed
their view of chocolate manufacture. Their description of their work
tended to begin at the point at which men brought materials into the
room or, later, at the start of the conveyor belt.

Although, as discussed in chapter four, new starters were given
lectures on the origins of cocoa, and the *CWM* featured articles on
the subject, none of the women talked about this aspect of production unless specifically asked. Nellie told me the beans 'used to come
in big bags and like little – they look like coffee beans and they used
to come through this shoot and then that – I've never been to that
end'. Carmen did not recall any displays on how chocolate was made
and it was not until she worked in the Kit Kat department, many years
after she first started, that she remembered witnessing the process.
With the exception of women sorting through ingredients such as nuts,
women's work on the whole was tied much more closely to preparing the finished product. It is unsurprising, then, that they focused on
the appearance and quality of the confectionery. Whilst they used the
jargon of the factory in referring to 'enrobing' and 'cream packing', they
interchanged this with the language of marketing in referring to the
brand names of the items they were working on. As producers, and
as consumers, they were more familiar with the finished product than
with its components.

Women found pleasure in their work at Rowntree in a number of
different ways. Sometimes they liked a job simply because they were
able to do it or were 'used to it' (Lily). Alice told me how she loved
'cupping' – putting the Black Magic sweets into separate paper cups
– because she could 'just . . . do them very quick'. Though Carmen
found it difficult to get used to the speed of the work at first, she told
me, 'I loved the factory work, yeah. 'Cos it's . . . it's what I know, what
I've learned to do all them years you see.' These women took a
justifiable pride in their proficiency, though they played down their
skills as simply the product of endless repetition. The appearance of

the chocolates they were helping to create could also hold an intrinsic pleasure. The aesthetic quality of the confectionery allowed Lily to take creative pride in her work, despite its increasing mechanisation. She asserted that piping 'was quite artistic', implicitly working against the broader discourse of women as unskilled and stressing the quality of these mass-produced assortments. Although by that time women were only piping perhaps one line each onto endless rows of chocolates, it was still valued by Lily in contrast to what came later: 'It was a lovely presentation with hand-piping to what it is now with the machines . . . when I look at a box of chocolates I think to meself they're never as nice as when they were hand-piped.'

Box making was another area in which the creative abilities of the women had some outlet. Again, although the process was increasingly simplified and fragmented over the years, with 'flat-pack' or 'crash-lock' boxes becoming common,[64] women still derived a lot of satisfaction from seeing the completed product: 'it was quite exciting really to be able to make something from scratch and know that it was going to other departments and your work was being passed as A1' (Mavis). This pride in the product itself calls into question Glucksmann's assertion that women on assembly lines 'were actively excluded from work that contained any intrinsic meaning or that could ever be considered inherently satisfying'.[65]

Rowntree does, then, seem to have offered work that was indeed 'inherently satisfying' for some women. Not only did it produce a semi-luxury item, intended to be pleasing and of a high quality, it also drew on connections with the city of York, particularly in its advertising and packaging. Rowntree products fostered a pride in the city which was the birth-place of many of its workers. Showcases in the factory and photographs in the *CWM* displayed some of the more prized creations as a reminder of the company's significance and success: 'you couldn't beat what we did . . . they were superb . . . but they went to royalty' (Jean). The 'we' of Jean's narrative was very much the people of the York factory; none of the women gave any sense of having felt part of a larger enterprise. In reading the factory magazine, for example, women described turning to the births and marriages section to look for people they knew. There was little enthusiasm from Jean when the magazine began to include details on the 'country-wide' associated companies; she enjoyed it when it had been a 'proper magazine', 'when it was just ours, a York one, it was people you actually knew'.

Local loyalties and a genuine enjoyment of tasks did not produce entirely uncritical accounts of working at the Rowntree firm. The increasing fragmentation of tasks and demands for higher productivity created tensions in women's narratives. Alice complained, 'you used to have to put twenty-four boxes in an outer and it was horse-work . . . And sometimes they made the outers bigger and you put more in and your rates went up but you couldn't do the same amount.' The use of the term 'sweated labour' by different women suggests that this may have been an opinion voiced at the time. Despite this, few women in their final analysis will give anything but a positive account of their experiences. Alice, despite the criticisms above, frequently stated in her narrative, 'I couldn't say anything about Rowntrees, I've never ever said anything about Rowntrees.' However, she also emphasised her own agency: 'I thought it was a very good job – well I wouldn't have kept it twenty-four years would I? If I hadn't have thought it was a good job.'

The above-average wages Rowntree were renowned for in some way compensated for the high production targets: 'It was hard work at Rowntrees but you know you was getting paid . . . it was always, what do they call it? When you have to earn your money? Piecework' (Gladys). Use of the term 'earn', here, suggests that there are traces, if somewhat ambivalent, of a Victorian work ethic that saw hard work as intrinsically good.[66] Carmen and Julie each perceived of themselves as hard workers and stressed this in their narratives as interconnected with a sense of satisfaction and enjoyment in their time at the firm.[67] Carmen wished that she could have remained at the factory: 'I wish I was a lot younger, 'cos I would never part with Rowntrees, 'cos I loved that work, 'cos I'm not, like I say, I'm not frightened of hard work.' Julie also stressed the theme of hard work throughout her oral history: 'I've just worked very very hard in my life, you know . . . I've never taken a step back to say, "I'm not doing this." ' For Julie, paid work has been crucial to achieving a good standard of living in England. Working hard is a particularly important element of these migrant women's narratives in terms of 'composing' their lives in positive terms which emphasise their own agency and lack of dependence on either local charity or the welfare state.[68]

Working conditions: rules and regulations
Women's experiences of paid employment were structured by the imposition of company rules and regulations. These rules (created by the white male owners and managers of the firm), though supposedly applied equally to everyone of the same grade, could have different implications for different workers. This was not simply related to cultural difference but also to factors such as age, marital status and class. In this section, I consider some of the connections which existed between white and non-white women workers and how they related

to the company, but also how race and the experience of migration affected their experiences of working in the chocolate industry.[69]

Working time was highly regulated for all except the most senior employees, and was compartmentalised according to gender. Typically only men were permitted to work the better-paid 'shifts', with women limited to day working. The short evening shift, however, was gendered as feminine – the so-called 'housewives' shift' mentioned earlier in this chapter. Women 'blicked' in and out of the factory to record their precise working hours and faced loss of pay or disciplinary action if they were late.[70] Their relation to factory time could be nevertheless ambivalent; the routine of the factory being only one of the temporal domains in which they had to operate. Edna, for example, had her sick mother to look after and resisted threats of getting the sack for being persistently absent or late. Given such demands, the prestigious 'Blue Ribbon' award for perfect attendance in a year was an impossibility for many women.[71]

Once inside the factory walls, women's time was structured by a buzzer telling them when they could take a break and go to the canteen to eat. Nellie and Julie experienced the daily routine of the shopfloor in different ways. Nellie missed being able to get a cup of tea whenever she wanted, as she had been able to do in the family laundry business. Julie, on the other hand, did not always join her workmates at the regulated lunch break. When questioned, she would explain that she was fasting for Ramadan. In this way, Julie was resisting the control exercised by the firm over eating and drinking. Her experiences highlight the ethnocentric assumptions of the factory timetable and its roots in industrial, Christian Britain, which made its restrictions less obviously problematic for white York workers. Nevertheless, as explored below, these women did take back some control over their time through tactics such as extended toilet breaks.

Eating confectionery on the shopfloor was another means of resisting company directives about appropriate consumption within the workplace. Gladys vividly remembered an 'eye-opening' incident of an older woman defying factory rules on eating chocolates: 'her jaws was going and t'overlooker passed and she says, "Are you eating Mrs So and So?" But she was one of the old school, you know, been there years, and she says, "Yes, do you want one?" [laughs] She offered her this big tray . . . with t'sweets on. She said, "Yes, do you want one?" Well she didn't know where to put herself.' Other women were more discrete, putting a handful of sweets into their overall pocket to last them through a shift, or eating the small chocolates intended to make up the weight of selection boxes: 'And it was Dairy Box chocolate, which was lovely, lovely chocolate – milk chocolate, all milk chocolate

Dairy Box. And, it was so [much] easier [laughs] to put it in your mouth than put it back on the tray where you'd got it' (Lillian).[72] The imposed rules and logic of industrial food production clash against the allure of the commodity being produced and the pragmatic working methods of individual women. Ironically, the company itself was partly responsible for creating such pleasurable, irresistible versions of chocolate in its packaging and advertising (on display both within and outside the workplace).

The wearing of uniform could be a highly gendered, and gendering, activity. For many years it was only compulsory for female employees on the shopfloor. In 1947, a note followed the rule on uniform for women workers: 'A Clean Cap and Overall Properly Worn Make an Attractive Uniform. A Workmanlike Appearance Is the Best of Styles for the Workroom.'[73] There is an appeal to a perceived 'feminine' concern with 'attractiveness' and 'style' rather than an awareness of the practicalities of working with food, although the irony of the archetypal worker as male is striking. Five years later, uniform was compulsory for 'All factory employees and certain clerical and admin-istrative staff.'[74] Whilst this appears to be less discriminatory toward women, it is telling that clothing was now provided and renewed by the firm when necessary whereas previously the responsibility and expense of wearing a uniform had rested entirely with the women themselves.

Women's attitudes towards uniform wavered between acceptance of the rationale behind clothing rules in a food factory and small sub-versive acts which reasserted control over their own bodies. One of the only times Amy was reprimanded was for wearing her engagement ring; the other was for having nails that were deemed too long. Photographs from the *CWM* are highly suggestive of how women (par-ticularly young girls) would continue to follow the fashions of the day, as beehive hairstyles are scarcely covered by the regulation headgear intended to prevent any hair from contaminating the chocolate.[75] Nellie remembered that rules on uniform became stricter: 'Oh they're very strict in there . . . if you leave a bit of hair out she used to play pop with you – "Get that hat right down here." And not like when we first started, we used to have all the turbans up, we used to bleach it, starch it, make it all nice and up, used to dress up nice. Nowadays, no, everybody's same, everybody's same now.' The compulsory wearing of a uniform for women on the shopfloor was intended not only to regulate white femininity within the factory, it was also encoded with western ideologies of appropriate dress. The white overalls and 'turbans' (as they were popularly known) take on quite different con-notations when worn by British Asian women.[76] Still, the possibility of wearing personal clothes under the uniform could have been one factor in making the work more acceptable to Asian women and to their male relatives.

The relationship with authority, particularly female authority, was complicated. Amy remembered those in charge as strict but fair: 'they used to say, "Not you laughing again." 'Cos we always used to be sat laughing. But yet, that same person . . . when my uncle died . . . she saw how upset I was . . . she sent me home . . . She were very nice really.' Such individual kindnesses, whilst they could certainly be interpreted as resulting from the personality of the person in question, were interpreted by the women as indicative of Rowntree as a whole and thus reinforced loyalty to the firm. Where human contact was diminished, women felt resentment at being subjected to the will and gaze of their superiors. Thus, the practice of an overlooker sitting high on a chair in the centre of the room, watching over everything that went on, was critiqued by several women. Gladys remarked, 'She was bloomin' Queen o' Sheeba sat up there. She used to have her seat risen up so she could see everybody.'[77] Despite such feelings, women continued to stress to me their love of their job: 'you used to think, "God she's watching me." . . . So you used to talk with your head down and try and do as fast as you could – but it was all good fun' (Mavis). Again, there is ambiguity surrounding women's assertion of company loyalty as they navigate between positive and negative experiences of employment and a sense of duty to Rowntree as both former employees and York residents.

As an escape from the surveillance of supervisors and the relentless conveyor belt, the toilets provided a useful, female-only, relatively private space. In contrast to some factories, most women could take short toilet breaks between the regulated rest periods and many manipulated this to their advantage: 'sometimes it was just a break you know' (Lillian).[78] Although the phenomenon of being tied to the machines was experienced mainly by female operatives, they discussed this through the language of being treated like children rather than through any explicit awareness of gender oppression. This, in turn, allowed them to claim the power coterminous with the liminal state of childhood:

it was like being at school actually . . . you got crafty. You used to think, 'Yeah, I'm gonna tek me time here.' And, 'Ooh, I've got terrible stomach aches', and go to the toilet and it – you might say, 'Is it time of t'month?' – if it was a woman – 'Yeah.' And more times than not it wasn't. (Mavis)

Women were thus capable of reappropriating the means of their oppression to turn them to advantage. As 'girls' they could test the limits of authority, as women they could use the biology which consigned them to 'the weaker sex' to fight the demands of industry. Women's identity at work was thus unstable, allowing them to resist at some level the imposition of rules even as these tried to fix their identity as female employees.

Experience of the factory environment for women was as a gendered space where movement and behaviour was restricted. In the 1950s there were still separate canteens for men and women. Gendered rules on appropriate conduct in the workroom led to the separation of Maltese girls when they spent too much time talking amongst themselves. Carmen told me:

> Yeah they used to put us all together, but we used to make such a row, you know, if we heard a record or something, used to shout, 'Heya, Carmen, listen!' And the other one shout one another, and then they separate us, not to shout again – 'cos it used to be long belt, you know, when you're setting and packing and everything, we hear a nice record we used to shout, like reminders from home. And then they separate us . . . They put us back together – they were nice with us really, they were really good.

'Local' girls could also be separated for such disruptive behaviour.[79] Yet breaking up this ethnically distinct minority group of women, who were chatting in Maltese and sharing memories of Malta, had other implications, effectively isolating them so they would be less problematic for (white) supervisors.[80] Carmen expressed appreciation to the firm for allowing the Maltese girls to be reunited. In her later working life, Carmen felt picked on by one of the overlookers, always being selected for jobs she did not want to do. She attempted to become less visible by hiding behind her friends but to no avail. So rules worked in different ways, with different consequences, for migrant women.

Sallie Westwood has raised the question of whether women factory workers of different races were able to unite as women to fight inequality on the grounds of gender and of class position.[81] Certainly Julie remembers going out on strike with the other workers, although as is often the case in women's narratives of industrial relations at the factory, this is not presented as anything serious. Nellie also discusses her membership of the union and remembers the cry of 'all out' from her union representative:

> Oh yes, we all had to be in the union, you know, and – anything went wrong, say the machine went fast, . . . we used to say, "Call for the union woman." And she says, "All out." [laughs] And we all used to march to the lunchroom to have a little conversation, you know, to see what's what. Oh aye, they went by the union.

Carmen certainly believed that all the women workers should have been members: 'because at the end of the day, if . . . the money goes up . . . it's – everybody's gonna get it. They used to complain about some lasses, they never used to be in the union. But they should be because at the end of the day we get a rise, they would get it just the same.' Annie Phizacklea and Robert Miles have highlighted the complex class relations of migrant workers, identifying them as a class faction.[82] The notion of a 'faction' seems inappropriate in the York context, however, where migrant women came from such different backgrounds and arrived at very different moments under diverse conditions. These three women appear to have felt united with their white colleagues in working-class trade union politics, at least in the factory context.

'I loved the people there': interpersonal relationships on the shopfloor

A dominant theme in the narratives of all the women was the importance of interpersonal relationships. Their assessment of their working lives at Rowntree often rested ultimately on the quality of the friendships they made. As Gladys told me, 'I loved Rowntrees, well I loved the people there.' This section considers how women constructed friendships which would in many cases extend beyond the factory walls, and where they experienced conflict with fellow workers. Whilst some of my findings are echoed in other studies of women's factory work, I hope to demonstrate the importance of studying women's workplace cultures in a local, national and global context of production.[83] I will focus on the significance of discourses and understandings of femininity and race for everyday interactions between women workers.

'Different types of girls': negotiating femininity on the lines

As chocolate producers, women worked predominantly with other women. This could be a source of conflict. Those who went into the factory later in life, or from other jobs, were often shocked by the behaviour of their female colleagues: 'I didn't think I'd last a week there with the different types of girls which you had to cope with in a factory but, then, I was one of 'em at finish [laughs]' (Gladys). Many of the women I interviewed implicitly accepted the stereotype of the 'factory girl' even though they also emphasised the diversity of women they encountered and the basic goodness of their co-workers: 'Everybody used to think 'cos it was a factory you were rough. And you always get odd ones, don't you? But it wasn't like that at all – that was the very minority' (Jean).[84] Gladys identified with the other 'girls' after adjusting to factory life but still kept her distance from those who got 'boozed up'. Her definition of herself as 'just there for the money' was interesting as it enabled her to keep a level of distance from the disreputable behaviour of certain women yet also worked against the discourse of the Rowntree firm as providing more than just wages.[85]

Women could be separated both socially and physically in the factory environment. Part-time or seasonal married women workers were assigned to a separate conveyor, reinforcing divisions between them and the single girls. This was in keeping with middle-class fears about the 'bad influence' married women were having on 'innocent' single girls.[86] Women with more life experience could certainly make an impact on their co-workers. For Lillian, taking on seasonal employment as a newly married woman in the late 1930s, the experience was traumatic:

> I was very upset because I wasn't used to working with married women. They used to pull my leg because I was more or less innocent. . . . When I went home at night I used to cry and my husband said, 'For goodness sake, give your notice in, we'll manage.' And I said, 'No, it's only for a few weeks, I'll have to learn to stick up for meself.'

Separate conveyors did have practical implications as married women often did not have the pace of single girls and women (unless they had worked at the factory prior to marriage). Also, as workers on temporary contracts they were more likely to be moved around as required, whilst the conveyors for the single women could maintain a fairly stable, consistent workforce.

The spatial arrangement of the factory and of its workers, and the assignment of tasks, could both reaffirm and create differences, as well as connections, between women. These had (and continue to have) meaning not just within the factory but in a broader community context, as workplace friendships and antagonisms spilled out onto York streets: 'My first [overlooker] . . . she was a proper tartar . . . And I often see her now, and she's just a little old lady walking round same as meself' (Gladys). The comparatively small size of York, and the dominance of the Rowntree firm, has facilitated such interconnections between workplace and local communities.

'An unusual sight': detecting racial difference

Intertwined with perceptions of femininity and respectability, race and ethnicity could also define and divide women. Even those from different parts of Britain could be discriminated against. Amy's closest friend was a Scottish woman with whom no one else would work due to her strong accent.[87] As discussed, York did not witness any large-scale postwar immigration but in the context of national anxieties over race this only served to make any signs of racial difference particularly noticeable. Audrey remembered, 'there was a darkie girl . . . she was a half caste, a dark skinned girl – one or two used to come and live, work in the factories years ago – and it was an unusual sight because we never saw many dark people in the factory'. Audrey was friends with this girl and they would share a lift home but her skin colour was still something unusual to be remarked upon years later.

Racial difference was negotiated in the interviews according to current accepted standards of language and behaviour. It is therefore difficult to discern the form racism took in the factory at the time. Mavis was careful to contextualise any negative reactions to migrant workers:

> there was quite an influx of Pakistani workers that came in . . . And a lot of people used to say, 'Hum,' you know, 'there's a family of 'em coming and,' – which sounded a bit prejudicial but it wasn't like that – But that's how it seemed at the time, you know . . . And there was a lot of undercurrents as well because people were thinking they were coming in and taking our jobs off us and our own people.

This narrative of 'us' and 'our own people' places 'Pakistani' workers as 'other' – as not belonging to York, to Britain, or to Rowntree. Although a distinction is made between 'prejudice' and concerns about jobs, this highlights, even as it attempts to deny, the existence of racist feeling. However, the reference to 'undercurrents' is suggestive of an implicit racism never openly voiced. By using the term 'influx', Mavis suggests a feeling of being 'under seige', which, as Wendy Webster has demonstrated, was a narrative common to the postwar period at a national level.[88]

Gladys's narrative of workers of 'different nationalities', though less explicit in terms of race, still harboured internal contradictions typical of an attempt to reconcile a definite *sense* of difference with a desire not to appear prejudiced:

> only thing, you know, when they used to come smelling of garlic and that when it was on breakfast time – nobody wanted to work near 'em and that – the women you know? But really good workers for Rowntrees they was . . . they're made of something different to us . . . Tire you out watching them . . . They could earn twice as much as we could earn.

Gladys worked at Rowntree between 1950 and 1975, so it is possible that she was referring at least in part to the reaction to Ugandan Asian workers, though she chose not to be more specific. Reading between the lines, one can sense the tensions that existed on the shopfloor. 'They' were being watched and assessed; 'they' were essentially, biologically, 'different' even if this did make them better workers. Smell is identified as an important factor in determining difference. As Iris Marion Young points out, 'respectability' requires the elimination of bodily odours.[89]

Despite evidence of being made to feel different herself in various ways, Carmen hints at a reluctance to discuss difference, at least where it related simply to a different accent:

> you hear people – accents, but you daren't ask where they're from or anything, they're just – you think, 'oh they're – they came from somewhere' and everything and just let it be. And not many people used to talk like they are now ... in the olden days not many people used to start say a conversation where they come from or whatever, they more or less keep themselves to themselves.

This focus on accents suggests that the people Carmen refers to were perceived as racially white, at least until they spoke. Maltese people occupied an ambiguous position in relation to whiteness. Barry York has referred to this in the context of the 'White Australia' policy on immigration: 'the Maltese were racially "white" and British'; 'there was always recognition of the quiet diligence of the Mediterranean British subjects, but there was always reference to their racial status too'.[90] Skin colour is only mentioned once in Carmen's narrative and this is in relation to her nephew: 'he's ... not dark skinned like say Maltese are, but he's very – more on English side'. So, whilst Carmen distinguishes the physical characteristics of Maltese people from 'English' people, she does not refer in her narrative to any sense of physical difference. This could be because of her arrival in York as part of a distinct group of Maltese girls, with the mutual support network and group identity this provided.

Carmen also situates this silence over people's origins as typical of the 1960s, 'when I was single'. Nellie hinted that at one time people were unlikely to make open comments as they would 'now'. Certainly the arrival of the Ugandan Asian refugees in York prompted very open conversations about where people came from, and where they belonged. This suggests a different timescale to Iris Marion Young's dynamic projection of discussions of race in the US becoming less audible as racism effectively went 'underground'. Of course her frame of reference is that of an American professional class, rather than a British working class.[91] Changing attitudes in York should also be related to the particular historical context of the highly publicised arrival of the refugees (as opposed to immigration which was often constructed as a more long-term, insidious threat). Even so, Carmen's comment reveals a vital element of the ways in which difference was dealt with in York in the second half of the twentieth century. There is clearly a need here for more substantial research into the complexities of race as played out in a small northern city.

'They like our colour': celebrating difference
Nellie, Carmen and Julie each felt accepted by the white women of the factory, and present very positive narratives of their experiences. Still, there are signs in their narratives of an awareness of their visible difference from white colleagues, made more striking by being in such a minority. When asked about the presence of other workers from 'Europe or from China' at the factory, Nellie made an interesting response:

> No, I think I was about the only one, and me sister she worked in gum room. No, there weren't . . . really many, because Rowntrees are Quakers aren't they? And the – no, I don't think so, I think I was the only . . . Chinese girl working there, besides me sister.

Nellie did not clarify the significance of Rowntree being a Quaker family/firm, but she seemed to see the religion of the firm's founders as limiting the employment of Chinese people at the factory. When I rephrased the question to ask Nellie specifically about Polish and Ukrainian workers, she then told me that there were lots. As we have seen, racial difference on the shopfloor tended to be played down in official narratives unless it was 'safe' cultural difference amongst white Europeans. Nellie's narrative reflects this in some aspects. Yet she also suggests that the women on the shopfloor would deal with difference more openly.

From their appearance alone, it was assumed that neither Nellie nor Julie would be able to speak English. Julie related how when applying for the Rowntree job she surprised her interviewer by being able to communicate. Nellie jokingly regretted not taking fuller advantage of this situation to get further help as a new starter. She remembered how women on the shopfloor helped European workers who were struggling to speak and understand English: 'and the women were really good, because they tried to explain to them, you know? 'Cos when I first went there, they said to me, "CAN YOU UNDERSTAND ENGLISH?" I, I – I'm sorry I said yes, I wish I said no now.' Despite being born in Liverpool and still having traces of a Liverpool accent, Nellie told me that, 'well, they call me Chinese Nell, wouldn't they?' When she married, Nellie was still marked out as different by the continued, corrupted, use of her Chinese maiden name. Nellie relates this to the distinguishing of a German woman as 'German Margaret' even after she married an English man. Yet Nellie's nickname, however affectionate, is related to physical appearance rather than place of birth or nationality.[92]

Iris Marion Young provides a sophisticated analysis of such interactions as evidence of the ways in which racism now dwells 'in everyday habits and cultural meanings of which people are for the most part unaware'. For women and for non-white women in particular, 'Even if they successfully exhibit the norms of respectability, their physical presence continues to be marked, something others take note of.' In this way, Young asserts, non-white women may feel imprisoned in their bodies. However, her analysis focuses more on the experiences of people in a 'public', 'professional' context where reason as separate from the body is crucial. For Julie, shopfloor chatter involved a multitude of questions about her situation and culture: 'You were sitting so close to one another. And they wouldn't leave me. They telling me everything and, "How you come away?"' In the closeness of women's bodies on the line, it was her body which became the object of interest. Her skin colour and dress were the open subject of curiosity and comment. Questions could become very personal, for instance asking what she wore underneath her clothes. Such an obvious discussion of difference, which brings the 'private' into the 'public' realm of the shopfloor, shows these white working-class women ignoring the 'public etiquette' Young describes. Young rightly asserts that it is now generally seen as 'bad taste' to discuss difference so openly. Bridget Byrne also observes the middle-class tendency to 'see' but 'not see' difference. Such 'etiquette', however, may not apply in all circumstances for all women. The talk of women on the shopfloor, though taking place in a public environment, may well be of the kind Young associates with the semi-private 'locker room' or 'living room'. The assembly lines were effectively a female space where women felt able to discuss the private and personal.[93]

Julie was not simply the passive recipient of the questions and gaze of her co-workers and neighbours. She enjoyed the interest being shown and took pride in it, particularly as it related to her children: 'And you know everybody noticed them, "Hello, hello, hello."' Positioned as the exotic other, Julie focused on the ways in which this exotic difference was in one sense desired by her white colleagues. She remembered people's interest in her beautiful clothes and in family gatherings such as weddings: 'they like our colour'. The converse side of colonial desire, the fear and abjection of the 'other', is not recorded in her narrative. Certainly white workers seem to have understood her presence in the factory as a direct consequence of the situation in Uganda, commenting on how terrible it was. This allowed space for expressions of sympathy and interest rather than evoking worries over competition for jobs. Julie affirmed that questions were asked, 'In a nice way . . . They say, "Don't feel bad." ' This reveals the women's awareness that their 'curiosity' could be taken in the 'wrong' way, but also pre-empts any negative reaction by Julie, situating it as irrational.[94] Whether or not Julie experienced more overtly negative reactions, she is able to construct a story in which her difference is empowering – she is placed centre-stage. Yet she also situates herself within the shopfloor culture, stating, 'Time goes quick if you talk.' The monotony of the work itself meant that Julie recognised the import-ance of talking with her colleagues, even if it was about her personal life. Capitalism thus structured women's relationships to each other, even as they were resisting its demands.

Marital status, respectability, age and race were all identified by women as areas of difference and sometimes conflict between them. If the production process defined them as a 'homogenous group . . . united as a gender',[95] the diversity brought to light in these interviews brings a new dimension to the numerous official photographs of anonymous white women in the factory magazine, rendered almost identical by their pristine white uniforms. What emerged particularly strongly was a very individual subjectivity. Although at times women drew on broader local and national narratives relating to feminine respectability and racial difference, they tended to undercut these by reverting quickly to individual stories. Women believed that their expe-rience of work was personal and were often loath to speak for others: 'Well, they didn't all think the same way' (Lillian). Moreover, whilst 'difference' is always present in the narratives, it is not necessarily conceived as a problem. Difference also brought fun, pride and camaraderie. Nevertheless, in terms of perceived racial difference, the question remains as to whether the apparent post-imperial 'convivi-ality' of the shopfloor depended on the sense of security in numbers felt by white workers and the isolation of migrant women, at least to some extent, from large supportive cultural communities.[96]

'Like a family': acceptance and intimacy
Running alongside recognitions of difference in women's oral his-tories was a strong emphasis on genuine workplace friendships. Jean struggled to express to me the strength of the bonds between workers on the shopfloor: 'It just . . . bred camaraderie really, because . . . everybody was so good with everybody else. It was just helping every-body else to get what they needed to do – some working harder to help

others to catch up. It was just a real camaraderie thing . . . They were just good people I think. It just made people good people.' The physical position of women workers in many departments, particularly as the practice of assembly line production became more common, was conducive to the making of close friends, even as it enforced collective discipline. Women told me of their 'special' friends whom they sat next to for long periods: 'they were all good mates really but she was a special mate' (Amy).

For those who were not on the lines, perhaps as room examiners or checkweighers (positions of marginally increased status but little authority or higher pay), the isolation from the other women could prove hard to bear. Audrey, working the evening shift as a room examiner, felt left out: 'I wasn't so involved with all the tales they used to come out with.'[97] For many, the difficulties of leaving the community of the 'girls' for a more solitary job which involved the implementing of factory discipline were not worth the extra prestige: 'I didn't want to be bossing people about . . . I liked working with the girls as a group, not as one individual' (Amy). Even for those who felt excluded from the main work group, the activities of the other women (talking, singing, playing jokes) could be a source of strength in getting through the shift. Audrey, for example, liked to hum along with the songs of the women on the line. These informal, spontaneous aspects of workplace culture were more important for most women than trying to change conditions through formal mechanisms of resistance such as the Central Works Council and Trade Union.[98]

Westwood has usefully analysed the ways in which shopfloor culture in Britain draws upon western constructions and rituals of the family. However, she also cites the ways in which such rituals can nevertheless cross cultural boundaries to unite women on the shopfloor.[99] Some white women workers at Rowntree remembered being invited to the weddings of Asian friends and co-workers. Nellie also had fond memories of the shopfloor rituals surrounding marriage: 'if anybody got married, they all used to buy them presents, loads of presents, and then the girls getting married used to buy you a lunch'. These shared, gendered experiences united women workers in the factory. Such memories are used to bolster narratives of how 'good' the women were.

Rowntree was represented in company publicity as a 'family firm', in terms of being family run and adopting a paternalist system of welfare; yet women themselves were more likely to use tropes of the family to refer to relationships with fellow workers.[100] Although Alice undermined the notion of a workplace 'family', she also reaffirmed intimate connections amongst smaller social groups: 'you're not just all one big happy family – there was quite a few little families at Rowntrees'. The family metaphor, like 'camaraderie', is suggestive of the importance women attached to intimacy with other women. For the three 'non-white' women who had migrated to York, the language of family expressed a sense of acceptance. Julie described how work was 'like a family – it wasn't picky and choosy . . . they welcomed you . . . they were so loving'. Carmen also remembered work as 'like a family when you were working on a belt'. In her early days at the factory, when she was about nineteen years old, she remembered the older women she worked with as like mothers to her. Nellie also used the language of familial relations within the factory, calling one of her close (non-Chinese) friends, 'Aunty Amy'.

It was through Amy, that I first made contact with Nellie. In separate interviews they each told me the story of how they baffled a local bus driver on their way home from work. When the driver appeared confused by Nellie referring to her 'Aunty' Amy, Amy quipped, 'Me dad had a bike':

> when the bell went, you know, to go home, everybody run to the gates to get their buses, and I remember Amy and I getting on the bus and I said to her, 'Goodbye Aunty Amy!' And the bus driver looked, 'Are you –?' She said, 'Are you looking at –?' She said, 'Me dad had a bike.' [Laughs] Did she ever tell you that? Oh, she's funny. (Nellie)

The two women clearly took pleasure in their subversion of racialised expectations and family relationships, and in the playful treatment of miscegenation. Their humour relies on histories of British imperialism and imperial masculinities but it also subverts and ridicules them, partly through reference to the, by then, working-class transport of the bicycle. The bicycle also gives the joke a local resonance as the image of hundreds of workers on bikes travelling to and from the factory has gained an iconic status in the city.

The closeness of friendships and the good nature of women at the factory was emphasised by all three migrant women, echoing (but perhaps redefining in even stronger terms) the emphasis on 'camaraderie' and friendship expressed by many local 'white' workers. While within the Rowntree 'family' they may well have been controlled, their use of the family metaphor is inclusive and a positive representation of the attitudes of white women workers in the face of contemporary racism.[101] Though none of the women used the language of 'sisterhood', with its feminist resonances of supposed equality and unity, their use of familial tropes implied strong connections between women as mothers, daughters, aunts and nieces, even as differences were implicitly maintained through family hierarchies of age and status.[102]

'If I had to work, Rowntrees was the place for me': constructing company loyalty

We have seen how women conceptualised their relationship to their work and to their peers in largely positive terms. Within their narratives tensions have been resolved through reasserting their happy memories of work and the status of Rowntree as a 'good firm'. This final section focuses in more detail on how women expressed their relationship to the company itself. How did women construct narratives of company loyalty and how did they evaluate the Rowntree firm more broadly in terms of its local, national and international significance?

In the process of remembering their experience of working at Rowntree, women would take the time to evaluate their overall impressions of the firm and its legacy. Company loyalty was nearly always strong – particularly for those women who had been born in York – although, as discussed, this could be ambivalent. Certainly, nostalgia had its part to play; it was an important means of maintaining a sense of worth in retirement and of creating a safe haven in the past.[103] Women intertwined their nostalgia for the firm with that for a city, despite the factory being on the outskirts of York. Margaret, who lived near the factory, spoke of 'a lifetime of memories . . . at that side of town'. For Jean, Rowntree was 'a mainstay of the city' which 'held everything together'. Loyalty to Rowntree was closely interwoven with local loyalties and identities.[104] Such close connections between York and Rowntree led to a deep sense of loss in discussing the takeover by Swiss firm, Nestlé, in 1988. Jean placed this in both national and local frameworks: 'we wanted to keep it British . . . we didn't want it to go Swiss'; 'Rowntrees is York, or was York . . . sweets altogether are York . . . we didn't want to go foreign.'

Nellie, Carmen and Julie each employed the discourse of Rowntree as a 'good firm'. Significantly, these three women were all happy to be interviewed about their time at the firm and were still living in York. Women who did not enjoy working at the factory are more likely to have left for other jobs and thus not be motivated to volunteer for an oral history project researching the firm's history. Likewise, those women who were unhappy in York possibly moved away and thus would not have seen my adverts. It is interesting, nevertheless, to note the satisfaction with the company expressed by all three women. They were relatively uncritical of the firm as a whole, although they occasionally expressed moments of conflict with particular supervisors. Julie was grateful for the support of the firm when she was expecting her son: 'And they were very good at Rowntrees . . . when I was expecting.' However, there was not quite the same concern in their narratives to stress that Rowntree was a good firm as I had noted in those of women born in York. The firm itself was mentioned less frequently and this must be related to the other factors in their life histories which have been more dramatic in shaping their lives in York and their identities. They also perhaps did not have the same investment in (re)asserting Rowntree as representative of York, and as a focus for local as well as individual pride. It is interactions with people at the firm which are the focus of their enjoyment rather than an abstract version of the company itself. Nevertheless, Julie echoed the concerns of York-born women that Rowntree was no longer a local firm: 'But now the outsiders come. Outsiders come now.'

The acquisition of Rowntree in 1988 did not directly affect the majority of the women I spoke with, in the sense that most had already left the company. It is interesting, then, that the takeover was an uninitiated topic by everyone and was often placed significantly 'just after' they had left, regardless of chronological detail.[105] Comments ranged from the fact that it will 'all be different now', to more lengthy critiques of the economic cost of the takeover in terms of jobs. The preoccupation with referring to the present condition of the firm I sensed was due to two main factors. On one level it was a tactic of reiterating their sense of the limited worth of their own stories of the past. However, for many women it was indicative of their continuing interest in the company, suggesting that Rowntree was still an important aspect of their lives. Pride in Rowntree products was visible in material form: for example, in the Kit Kat mug in which I was served tea. Most women still used their 'waste card' to purchase cheap confectionery, although this was perhaps done by relatives and was most often used for the buying of gifts for others. A few women were also in receipt of a regular Christmas card and £10 voucher from the firm. This continuing link to the factory was highly valued as both a privilege and an entitlement. Company loyalty is thus enacted and sustained on a variety of levels, from the ideological, to the social, to the material.

Conclusion

The institution of Rowntree propounded a philosophy of human relations in industry and social advancement, which had an impact on both the factory environment and the city. Yet women workers in York were still exploited and oppressed in multiple ways. As part-time and seasonal employees, though crucial to meeting production targets, they did not have equal access to the range of benefits provided by the firm.

Though Rowntree offered relatively well-paid work, the feminine tasks of sorting, decorating and packing confectionery were not rated as highly as men's labour. On the whole, women were expected to be married, with husbands to support them, and this was used to justify their position within the factory.

Although all the women referred to Rowntree as a 'good' firm to work for, and stressed their happy times at the factory, they also constructed more ambivalent narratives. They often found the work demanding and criticised the move to an assembly line mode of production whereby their tasks became increasingly fragmented. Their comments suggest a real pride in the products they were producing, to the extent that they lamented the decrease in quality caused by mechanisation. These assessments were made through their consciousness of themselves as workers, indicating a real immersion in the production process. This did not extend, however, to any sustained engagement with the origins of the cocoa or other ingredients used. As men controlled what came into the factory, and were responsible for mixing the chocolate, women had little access to spaces where they could have seen the cocoa beans. Where they took a broader perspective of the industry, women tended to evaluate their work in relation to consumption.

In the face of hard work, and despite an acknowledgement of diversity, women constructed lasting friendships and supportive networks. The fact that many of the women had been born in York and lived there all their lives, combined with the comparatively small size of the city, facilitated the continuation of these friendships. The simple practice of saying 'hello' to people recognised within the factory has been carried over into the outside world, reinforcing the connection between Rowntree and its local context. Friends provide a nexus of support in the face of the harsh realities of women's lives but also encourage the retelling of narratives which attempt to make sense of these realities, often without challenging them. The role of the peer group in socialising women to the conditions of the factory was also important, highlighting the variety of roles women play in each other's lives.

The narratives of the three migrant women presented here give an important insight, highly personalised and individualised, into the experience of migration on a relatively small scale to a city and a factory perceived as having a homogenous 'white' population. All three women challenge expectations and assumed histories: Nellie, born in England before the arrival of Chinese migrants in the postwar period; Carmen, a single Maltese woman migrant; Julie, a Ugandan Asian born in Zimbabwe. Simply by being in York they do not have a place in most histories of migrants, which focus on the 'centres' of migration such as Bradford, London and Manchester. They have not been identified in official studies yet their personal histories demonstrate multiple, complicated migrations taking place within the context of empire. In coming to York and working at Rowntree, each woman entered into a new configuration of imperial relations: as non-white workers themselves, and as workers in an industry that relied on empire and colonialism. In the context of the demise of the British empire and postwar immigration from the Commonwealth, both Carmen and Julie were (re)situated in relation to the metropole; placed at the 'centre' rather than the 'peripheries', they symbolised the implosion of the British empire and yet they remained at the 'peripheries' of the metropole itself.

The work of Nellie, Carmen and Julie illustrates the ways in which the Rowntree firm is implicated in imperial and postcolonial histories, and in the wider story of race relations in Britain. The factory was an important site of (post)colonial encounters in the archetypal 'Old English' city. Though migrant women were employed by the firm on apparently equal terms to local women (with the attendant inequalities of class and gender), they still experienced individualised racial inequality on the shopfloor. Marked out as different they had to contend with a heightened visibility and with being the subject of the curiosity of other women. The three women did not, however, relate experiences of more explicit racism. There are important reasons for silencing such memories and historically shifting, generationally specific perceptions of what constitutes racism may be at work here. Nevertheless, it is significant that each of these women simply did not feel that they had been subjected to racial prejudice either within the factory or the city of York.

The absence of racist experiences is crucial to the positive life histories which these individual women composed at the time of being interviewed. Each woman was proud of the hard work she had put in, sometimes in the face of extreme difficulties, to achieve a better quality of life for herself and her family. There was also a sense of the respect earned from workmates and the local community. The women's narratives suggest the possibility of friendships amongst women workers which both transcended differences and kept 'difference' intact. We have a sense of their isolation and a heightened awareness of being 'different', but also of opportunities to 'belong' and to become 'local' (though this may have been partly dependent on their geographical separation from fellow migrants). Perhaps stories of racism would have detracted from the successes they are rightly proud of, giving too much prominence to the individuals and institutions who would have thwarted them in working to establish homes and communities in York.

All the women interviewed for this project had been both producers and consumers of Rowntree products. Consumption took place on the shopfloor as a pleasurable distraction from work and sometimes as an act of rebellion against supervisors. Away from the factory, women consumed chocolate bought with their waste card; these were not the high quality assortments they sent out to retailers but the products deemed unworthy of paying customers. Nevertheless, according to the women's narratives, these 'waste' chocolates were thoroughly enjoyed by family and friends. For industrial chocolate workers, then, consumption of chocolate was intricately connected to their labour. As we witnessed in chapter one, such labour was largely erased from official Rowntree marketing campaigns.

Notes

1 Quoted in Wagner, *Chocolate Conscience*, 94. Gwynne criticised the hypocrisy of Cadbury in buying slave-grown cocoa from São Tomé and Principe. 'Whiteness' thus served as a racial signifier but also suggested hands tellingly unblemished by the hard work of the plantations. The white chocolate makers were gendered as female in Gwynne's article.

2 Catherine Hall observed this trend in the Cadbury World exhibition. Catherine Hall, 'Turning a blind eye', 39. See also chapter one.

3 *CWM*, Christmas 1932, 845; Cadbury UK, 196/520/003552, 'Cadbury's Special Ads: From, May 1930 to, December 1932'. Hall notes of Cadbury that representations of 'the labour of an improved working class' at Bournville served to 'exorcise' the 'heat of the tropics' associated with raw cocoa. Hall, 'Turning a blind eye', 44. On the racist associations of whiteness and cleanliness, see McClintock, *Imperial Leather*; David Sibley, *Geographies of Exclusion: Society and Difference in the West* (London: Routledge, 1995), 22.

4 As discussed in the Introduction, I use the term 'non-white', despite its limitations, to highlight the ways in which certain women have been denied access to the privileged identity of 'whiteness'. The category of 'whiteness' itself is not static and it will be important during the course of this chapter to consider which women have been allowed to be defined and to define themselves as white – and how women chose to define their own racial identity.

5 I have anonymised the interviewees for the purpose of this book by using only first names.

6 As Laura Tabili points out, 'just because people didn't "see" or recall black Britons or overseas migrants does not mean they were not there'. She challenges the assumption that it has been 'excessive' numbers of migrants which has been the cause of conflict. Instead, she asks 'how many were too many' and suggests that the answer to this question has been historically contingent on domestic and imperial politics. Tabili, 'A homogenous society? Britain's internal "others", 1800–present', in Hall and Rose, (eds), *At Home with the Empire*, 56, 54. York as a 'white' city is sometimes compared unfavourably to 'vibrant', 'multicultural' Leeds but also functions as a counter to Bradford, with its 'problems' caused by large populations of non-white people living in distinct areas. In both cases, 'race' is defined in terms of the pleasures or problems it brings for white residents.

7 BI, Rowntree Company Archive, R/B4/THA/9, 'Reminiscences of R. & Co Pensioners by G. W. R. Wright', c.1921, 27, 8. In 1894 there were 177 men in the

confectionery department and 119 men in the cake chocolate department. The total York workforce was 861, rising to 2,945 over the next ten years. Workforce statistics are taken from *CWM*, February 1904, 148.

8 BI, Rowntree Company Archive, R/B4/THA/9, 'Reminiscences of R. & Co Pensioners by G. W. R. Wright', c.1921, 8. See also *CWM*, September 1912, 1355.

9 Fitzgerald, *Rowntree*, 225.

10 *CWM*, February 1904, 147.

11 BI, Rowntree Company Archive, R/DL/LD/5, 'Some Notes on Educational and Other Work', June 1913, 8.

12 By 1899, Cadbury had 1,885 women factory workers at its Bournville plant, more than twice the number of men. Chris Smith *et al.*, *Reshaping Work: The Cadbury Experience* (Cambridge: Cambridge University Press, 1990), 54. On the provision of music, see Emma Robertson *et al.*, 'Harmonious relations? Music at work in the Rowntree and Cadbury factories', *Business History*, 49: 2, (2007): 211–34.

13 Fitzgerald, *Rowntree*, 238.

14 *CWM*, October 1917, 1983.

15 BI, Rowntree Company Archive, R/DL/LE/4, 'Quarterly Staff Returns', figures for first quarter of 1959 (excluding overlookers).

16 BI, Rowntree Company Archive, R/BY/1/1, York Committee Minutes, July 1957– June 1960, No. 2095, 8 September 1959.

17 Manual tests included picking up and arranging wooden blocks. In psychological tests, women were classified according to types such as 'muddler' and 'careless'. BI, Rowntree Archive, R/DP/PC/23, 'Instructions for Overlookers etc.', Section XIII, 'Notes to Teachers Training Juniors', 1936, 25.

18 Smith *et al.* note the importance of women's skills in hand-packing as providing a shock absorber for packaging innovations, which would otherwise entail expensive changes to machinery. Smith *et al.*, *Reshaping Work*, 48.

19 Smith *et al.* describe the 'technological segregation' in confectionery production 'between male jobs in the "wet" end . . . (chocolate making, mixing, the manufacture of units for coating or enrobing and related activities) and women's activities in the "dry" end'. Smith *et al.*, *Reshaping Work*, 48.

20 On 'direct' and 'indirect' assembly line work, see Miriam Glucksmann, *Women Assemble: Women Workers and the New Industries in Inter-War Britain* (London: Routledge, 1990), 154–6.

21 BI, Rowntree Company Archive, R/BY/1/2, York Committee Minutes, June 1960– June 1962, No. 4234, 16 January 1962; and R/BY/1/4, York Committee Minutes, March 1965–December 1967, No. 7199, 22 November 1966.

22 The Employment Department concluded that for school leavers there had been 'a move away from "factory" work to work with greater social standing'. BI, Rowntree Company Archive, R/DL/LE/4, Quarterly Staff Returns, Appendix I, 'Employment of Secondary Modern Girl School Leavers in York, 1951–1961'.

23 Rozina Visram, *Asians in Britain* (London: Pluto Press, 2002), 196–8.

24 Appleton, Directors' Conferences, XXII, 20 November 1916, quoted in Fitzgerald, *Rowntree*, 247.

25 This is not to say that women were unable to resist such control. L. A. G. Strong asserts that women workers in the late nineteenth and early twentieth centuries sought 'revenge' for being strictly segregated from men: 'they used to link arms on the pavement outside, and force the men into the gutter'. L. A. G. Strong, *The Story of Rowntree* (York: unpublished, 1948), n.p.

26 See, for example, BI, Rowntree Company Archive, R/DL/S/6, Veronika Pietkiewicz and Zofja Bosacka, 'A Day at the Rowntree Cocoa Works', Girls' School Magazine, July 1949. The background of these girls is unclear. Poles were living in Britain not just as refugees, but as ex-British Army staff allowed to stay on after their contract ended. See Paul, *Whitewashing Britain*; Jerzy Zubrzycki, *Polish Immigrants in Britain: A Study of Adjustment* (The Hague: Martinus Nijhoff, 1956).

27 As women, these Polish workers may have been seen as relatively unthreatening. Shih found that employers in the USA were less concerned about the employment

of black women than of black men as they were seen to be more pliant and less confrontational. Johanna Shih, ' "... Yeah, I could hire this one, but I know it's gonna be a problem": how race, nativity and gender affect employers' perceptions of the manageability of job seekers', *Ethnic and Racial Studies*, 25: 1 (2002): 99–119. It may be that non-white, and even European male workers would also have been seen as more of a threat to local white male 'breadwinner' jobs and wages.

28 Webster, *Imagining Home*; Webster, 'Defining boundaries: European Volunteer Worker women in Britain and narratives of community', *Women's History Review*, 9: 2 (2000): 257–76. This was institutionalised in the 1960s and 1970s by legal measures such as the 1962 Commonwealth Immigration Act, which took away the automatic right of Commonwealth citizens to work and live in the UK.

29 Using last names to be a signifier of origins or of a minority ethnicity is problematic. As Magdalene Ang-Lygate observes, women usually lose their last name upon marriage and thus become invisible as ethnic minorities in the eyes of the state and even to each other. Conversely, white English women with typically 'English' maiden names may marry and take on a name marking them as 'different'. The act of naming has been highly politicised in the historical context of empire, in which 'English' names have been used to mark possessions of people, land and commodities. See Ang-Lygate, 'Women who move: experiences of diaspora', in Mary Maynard and June Purvis (eds), *New Frontiers in Women's Studies: Knowledge, Identity and Nationalism* (London: Taylor & Francis, 1996), 159.

30 The confectionery industry was not one of those identified as needing labour. Nevertheless, it did benefit from the labour of European workers as they became able to move around and away from the jobs to which they had originally been assigned. For a history of European Volunteer Workers, see Diana Kay and Robert Miles, *Refugees or Migrant Workers? European Volunteer Workers in Britain, 1946–1951* (London: Routledge, 1992).

31 *CWM*, Spring 1964, 5. The minutes of the Board of Directors are currently unavailable to researchers.

32 BI, Rowntree Company Archive, R/BY/1/4, York Committee Minutes, March 1965–December 1967, No. 7182.

33 *YEP*, 12 March 1973, 1.

34 As discussed in chapter three, this has continued with accusations over child slavery in West African cocoa farming from 2001.

35 See also Avtar Brah, *Cartographies of Diaspora: Contesting Identities* (London: Routledge, 1996), 34.

36 *Green for Come: A Report on the Rehousing and Settling of British Asians from Uganda in York and District between October 1972 and June 1973* (York: n.p., 1973), 3.

37 'At Whose Expense', letter from R. S. Slaughter. *YEP*, 12 October 1972, 3.

38 *YEP*, 9 September 1972, 4; *YEP*, 14 October 1972, 1.

39 See, for example, the speech by the Archbishop reported in the article, 'Asians: Abusive Letters to Dr. Coggan', *YEP*, 18 September 1972, 5. See also a letter from Mrs Hardy, *YEP*, 19 September 1972, 3.

40 According to the *Green for Come* report, 'Only a few areas (such as York) have required heads of household taking up houses to have pre-arranged jobs to go to.' *Green for Come*, 4. This meant that the heads of household had to travel to the city, sometimes repeatedly, which could be stressful, expensive and time-consuming. *Green for Come*, 20. The relationship between paid employment and the right to settle had been formalised in British immigration law through the work permit system, though such restrictions did not apply to holders of British passports until 1973. Jacqueline Bhabha and Sue Shutter, *Women's Movement: Women under Immigration, Nationality and Refugee Law* (Stoke-on-Trent: Trentham Books, 1994), 167.

41 *YEP*, 30 October 1972.

42 *Green for Come*, 20.

43 *Ibid.*, 20.

44 Brah, *Cartographies of Diaspora*, 1.
45 'Madge Munro Talks to 2,000,000 People', *CWM*, Christmas 1932, 845.
46 Nellie, Carmen and Julie used dialect words like 'lasses' in their narratives, suggesting their local affinities after having lived for so many years in the region.
47 BI, Rowntree Company Archive, R/DL/LS/1, Labour Research Report, 'History of Wage Arrangements' by Psychological Department, 30 April 1930, 2.
48 Deborah Simonton sees this as an important 'life-cycle change' in the period 1880–1980. Simonton, *A History of European Women's Work, 1700 to the Present* (London: Routledge, 1998), 191.
49 Louise A. Tilly and Joan W. Scott, *Women, Work and Family* (New York: Holt, Rinehart and Winston, 1978), 224.
50 Tilly and Scott feel that this in some way compensated for the sacrifices women made: 'as the family economy became a family consumer economy, the woman's position as financial manager of the household expanded'. *Ibid.*, 204.
51 Chinn stresses the power and economic independence of women of the urban poor but goes too far in suggesting that if these women lived in a patriarchal society they must therefore have 'chosen' to do so. Chinn, *They Worked All Their Lives*, 114.
52 Nellie did not wish to tell me her exact date of birth but she seems to have been fairly young during the war.
53 Maria Lin Wong suggests this was fairly typical for families engaged in the laundry business. Wong, *Chinese Liverpudlians: A History of the Chinese Community in Liverpool* (Birkenhead: Liver Press, 1989), 51.
54 In relating an anecdote of a 'Scouse' identity uniting black and white male Liverpudlians on holiday in Germany, Brah highlights that 'one may be positioned within more than one field of ethnicity depending on the criteria in play within a particular context'. Brah, *Cartographies of Diaspora*, 175. Nellie also has memories of being identified as from Liverpool through her accent.
55 David Parker, 'Chinese people in Britain: histories, futures and identities', in George Benton and Frank N. Pieke (eds), *The Chinese in Europe* (Basingstoke: Macmillan Press, 1998), 68.
56 See *YEP*, 22 July 1967, 5. One of the earliest Chinese residents in York had fled the Boxer Rebellion of 1900 (*YEP*, 12 August 1998, 5). In July 2008, an exhibition celebrating the lives of Chinese people in York opened at York Castle Museum. For an important recent article on the Chinese in Britain during the first half of the twentieth century, see John Seed, 'Limehouse blues: looking for Chinatown in the London Docks, 1900–1940', *History Workshop Journal*, 62 (2006), 58–85.
57 Wong, *Chinese Liverpudlians*; Sue Baxter and Geoff Raw, 'Fast food, fettered work: Chinese women in the ethnic catering industry', in Sallie Westwood and Parminder Bhachu (eds), *Enterprising Women: Ethnicity, Economy, and Gender Relations* (London: Routledge, 1988).
58 See Henry Frendo, 'Maltese colonial identity: Latin Mediterranean or British empire?' in Victor Mallia-Milanes (ed.), *The British Colonial Experience 1800–1964* (Msida, Malta: Mireva Publications, 1988), 190.
59 Geoff Dench, *Maltese in London: A Case-study in the Erosion of Ethnic Consciousness* (London: Routledge and Kegan Paul, 1975), 67–74; Suk-Tak Tam, 'Representations of "the Chinese" and "ethnicity" in British racial discourse', in Elizabeth Sinn (ed.), *The Last Half Century of Chinese Overseas* (Hong Kong: Hong Kong University Press, 1998), 82–3; Paul Gilroy, *'There Ain't No Black in the Union Jack': The Cultural Politics of Race and Nation* (London: Routledge, reprint edn, 1992), 72–113.
60 See Barry York, *Empire and Race: The Maltese in Australia 1881–1949* (Kensington, NSW: New South Wales University Press, 1990).
61 Carmel Cassar, 'Everyday life in Malta in the nineteenth and twentieth centuries', in Mallia-Milanes (ed.), *The British Colonial Experience*, 99.
62 Amin decreed that all Asians should leave, even those with Ugandan citizenship. Julie remembers the number expelled as 52,000, although official reports vary. Some

of the variations in statistics may be explained by the fact that some people had no passports and were effectively stateless. Not all those with British passports came to Britain, especially if it meant leaving behind one of their family who had no papers (people were expected to produce papers such as birth certificates of parents when applying for citizenship and passports, despite the fact that these had sometimes never been issued). For some idea of the chaos regarding passports and papers at the time, see Mahmood Mamdani, *From Citizen to Refugee: Ugandan Asians Come to Britain* (London: Frances Pinter, 1973).

63 Kathleen Paul discusses in detail the ways in which nationality and citizenship have been raced. Paul, *Whitewashing Britain*.

64 These were boxes assembled from a single flat piece of cardboard.

65 Glucksmann, *Women Assemble*, 220.

66 Elizabeth Roberts notes the increasingly complex relationship to the Victorian work ethic in the twentieth century. Certainly some women wanted more leisure time to themselves. Even so, hard work was still interlinked with respectability. Elizabeth Roberts, 'Working wives and their families', in Theo Barker and Michael Drake (eds), *Population and Society in Britain, 1850–1980* (London: Batsford Academic and Educational, 1982), 147.

67 Webster highlights the construction of migrant women as workers in contrast to the familial construction of native white women. Her research focuses on European Volunteer Workers but there are similarities with Carmen and Julie's oral histories. Webster, 'Defining boundaries'.

68 Penny Summerfield explores the layered meanings of 'composing' when applied to oral histories, suggesting the ways in which women actively 'compose' narratives whilst simultaneously striving to achieve personal 'composure' during the interview. Penny Summerfield, 'Dis/composing the subject: intersubjectivities in oral history', in Tess Cosslett, Celia Lury and Penny Summerfield (eds), *Feminism and Autobiography: Texts, Theories, Methods* (London: Routledge, 2000).

69 As suggested by Sallie Westwood and Parminder Bhachu, I want to go 'beyond an account of patriarchal relations and "women", positing instead the articulation between racism, class relations, cultural forms, and gender'. Westwood and Bhachu, 'Introduction', in Westwood and Bhachu (eds), *Enterprising Women*, 2.

70 This was the usual way of saying 'clocking in' as Rowntree used a machine made by Blick.

71 Miriam Glucksmann perceptively concludes that 'women's patterns of working time have always been more diverse than men's'. Glucksmann, *Cottons and Casuals: The Gendered Organisation of Labour in Time and Space* (Durham: Sociology Press, 2000), 125.

72 On the politics of eating within the workplace, see Eric Batstone, 'The hierarchy of maintenance and the maintenance of hierarchy: notes on food and industry', in Anne Murcott (ed.), *The Sociology of Food and Eating* (Aldershot, Hants: Gower Publishing Company, 1983).

73 BI, Rowntree Company Archive, R/DL/L/13, Works Rules, 6th Edition, 1947, rule 35.

74 BI, Rowntree Company Archive, R/DL/L/13, Works Rules, 7th Edition, 1953, rule 35.

75 *CWM*, Autumn 1964, 11. It is difficult to know whether to read this as a liberating act of choice or simply as the demands of fashion winning out against those of the workplace.

76 The racism inherent in apparently 'neutral', functional, uniform clothing has been repeatedly challenged. In 1974, Mr Rayat Singh and Mr Rehal Singh were suspended from employment on the Leeds buses for wearing their turbans to work. The men, supported by members of the Chapeltown community, fought the decision. See *Chapeltown News*, September 1974. Sikhs in Bradford had been allowed to wear turbans to work on the buses since 1966. See www.movinghere.org.uk/deliveryfiles/WYAS/WYL5046_5_1_01-8/0/1.pdf (accessed 4 January 2008).

77 The 'panoptic' arrangement of the workroom reduced workers on the shopfloor to 'scopophilic objects'. See Joel Sanders (ed.), *Stud: Architectures of Masculinity* (New York: Princeton Architectural Press, 1996), 22. It is interesting that Gladys

chose to draw on an exotic stereotype to critique her supervisor; 'tartar' was also used as a term of abuse for bosses (see later in this chapter). Thanks to Rachel Farebrother for highlighting this.

78 Peak Frean had stricter rules. See Glucksmann, *Women Assemble*, 106.

79 In the 1920s and 1930s, women packers were instructed to conduct themselves with decorum and to restrain from 'loud talking'. BI, Rowntree Company Archive, R/DP/PC/23, Cream Packing Department, 'General Instructions for Overlookers, Chargehands etc., c.1929–1938', 6.

80 Practices of breaking up and dispersing minorities, like the 'red' and 'green' resettlement policy already discussed, have bolstered popular impressions of York and Rowntree as 'white'.

81 Westwood suggests that 'black and white women share in the experience of exploitation under patriarchal capitalism, yet racism cuts through and across a potential unity'. However, she concedes that 'racism does not capture the hearts and minds of everyone and that individuals, though steeped in a racist culture, can often act in ways that belie this'. Sallie Westwood, *All Day Every Day: Factory and Family in the Making of Women's Lives* (London: Pluto Press, 1984), 234.

82 Robert Miles and Annie Phizacklea define the majority of 'New Commonwealth migrants' as working class in the sense that they 'offer their labour power for a wage'. However, this class identity has come to be understood 'through their experience of racism and discrimination'. They see this as creating a new division amongst the working class, which 'makes working-class unity both more difficult to achieve – but also even more necessary'. Miles and Phizacklea, *White Man's Country: Racism in British Politics* (London: Pluto Press, 1984), 161.

83 Andrew Phillips, for example, found a similar focus on workplace friendships in oral histories with women factory workers. Phillips, 'Women on the shop floor: the Colchester Rag 1918–1950', *Oral History*, 22 (Spring 1994), 62. See also Emma Robertson, 'It was just a real camaraderie thing: socialising, socialisation and shop floor culture at the Rowntree factory, York', in Krista Cowman and Louise Jackson (eds), *Women and Work Culture, Britain c. 1850–1950* (Aldershot: Ashgate, 2005), 107–20.

84 For an analysis of the 'factory girl' stereotype, see Chinn, *They Worked All Their Lives*, 91. L. A. G. Strong believes the 'Rowntree Girls' had a reputation as 'a rough crowd' in the past, which the women may have been working against. Strong, *The Story of Rowntree*, 19.

85 However, the firm did not wish to undermine the central concern of the workers to earn money: 'the earning of a good wage is the first consideration'. BI, Rowntree Company Archive, R/DP/PC/23, 'Instructions for Overlookers etc.', Section XIII, 'Notes to Teachers Training Juniors', 1936, 25.

86 Chinn, *They Worked All Their Lives*, 98. In contrast to my findings, Roberts claims, 'There is no evidence that women discussed sexual topics in the mill.' Roberts, 'Working wives and their families', 155.

87 As Laura Tabili points out, 'We cannot . . . assume all Britons uniformly perceived overseas migrants as more "other" or different from themselves than many native Britons.' Tabili, 'A homogenous society?' 55. As well as Scots, it is likely that there would have been second and third generation Irish workers in the factory, as York had had a significant number of Irish migrants during the nineteenth century. See Feinstein, 'Population', 121.

88 Webster, *Englishness and Empire*, 8 and chapter six.

89 Iris Marion Young, *Justice and the Politics of Difference* (Princeton: Princeton University Press, 1990), 137.

90 York, *Empire and Race*, 6. York separates 'quiet diligence' from 'racial status' yet the first description is also racialised in its attribution of immutable characteristics to Maltese people. York seems to accept the 'quiet diligence' of the Maltese as proven.

91 Young posits that, during the twentieth century, racism has receded from 'discursive consciousness' and that 'reactions of aversion' have become expressed through more

subconscious actions such as body language. Clearly Carmen feels that difference has come to be more openly discussed in York; though racism itself, in accordance with Young's theory, is denied. Young, *Justice*, 134.

92 Nevertheless, the persistence of ethnic and national identity through nicknames resists the denial of such identities by the state, which for many years dictated that a woman would take the nationality of her husband. It was only from 1948 that nationality was no longer automatically altered by marriage. See Bhabha and Shutter, *Women's Movement*, 26. These nicknames also challenge loss of identity for women within marriage through taking the husband's name.

93 Young, *Justice*, 124, 141, 132–3; Bridget Byrne, 'Learning whiteness – when is a mix not enough of a mix? A white middle-class mother talks about race, class and schools', in Ann Kaloski-Naylor et al. (eds), *White? Women* (York: Raw Nerve, 1999), 72. The bodily practices of 'aversion', which Young sees as accompanying the silencing of overtly racist language, would have been mitigated against by the demands of assembly line production in which women were working in such close physical proximity. However, Carmen does describe being put to work with other Maltese girls and there is evidence that Polish workers were also sitting together on the lines. BI, Rowntree Company Archive, R/DL/S/6, Veronika Pietkiewicz and Zofja Bosacka, 'A Day at the Rowntree Cocoa Works', Girls' School Magazine, July 1949.

94 Young questions the assumption that people 'do not have the right to complain of or condemn another person's behaviour if that person intends to be courteous and respectful'. She asserts that, 'If unconscious reactions, habits, and stereotypes reproduce ... oppression ... then they should be judged unjust, and therefore should be changed.' She does not believe that this should simply mean 'blaming' people but rather making them accept responsibility for their actions. Likewise I would feel uncomfortable berating the white women factory workers individually for their attitudes. This does not mean I cannot discuss their actions as racist and think about why this might be. Young, *Justice*, 150, 124.

95 Glucksmann, *Women Assemble*, 261.

96 Paul Gilroy's concept of 'conviviality' is useful in suggesting the everydayness and openness of some of the shopfloor relationships described in interviews. However, Gilroy's work is based on very different urban spaces and 'postcolonial cities'. In the York context, 'conviviality' springs from and takes place in a markedly different context. This further highlights the need to examine race in Britain at a local as well as a national, London-focused level. Gilroy, *After Empire: Melancholia or Convivial Culture?* (Abingdon: Routledge, 2004), xi.

97 Patricia Meyer Spacks is helpful in theorising Audrey's sense of exclusion: gossip can 'solidify a group's sense of itself by heightening consciousness of "outside" ... and "inside" (the temporarily secure territory of the talkers)'. Spacks, *Gossip* (New York: Alfred A. Knopf, 1985), 5.

98 Anna Pollert believes that working women's culture has been a matter of 'style' rather than substance, whilst Westwood locates the relative failure of working women's resistance to the demands of capitalism in the collusive nature of a 'culture of femininity' with 'patriarchy'. However, Westwood also recognises the 'oppositional, energetic and potentially very powerful' aspects of women's culture. Pollert, *Girls, Wives, Factory Lives* (Basingstoke: Macmillan Press, 1981), 151; Westwood, *All Day Every Day*, 22, 90.

99 Westwood, *All Day Every Day*, 230.

100 Jacquelyn Hall et al. have noted this negotiation with the family metaphor in other industry: 'they were not using this imagery to describe their dependence on a fatherly employer so much as they were exploring their relationships to one another'. Jacquelyn Dowd Hall et al., *Like a Family: The Making of a Southern Cotton Mill World* (Chapel Hill: University of North Carolina Press, 1987), xvii. Joan Sangster believes that the women she interviewed, who used the trope of the family to describe working at a paternalist factory, demonstrated 'the assimilation, at some level, of the familial metaphors employed by the company to promote its paternalism'. Joan Sangster, 'Telling our stories: feminist debates and the use of oral history', in Robert

B. Perks and Alistair Thomson (eds), *The Oral History Reader* (London: Routledge, 1998), 90. Rather than simply assimilating official tropes, women at Rowntree were complicating the usual associations of the paternalist 'family firm' and of the patriarchal family itself.

101 It may be that each woman was working against what they sensed would be my own expectations of racism, as well as the general construction of the working classes as racist by factions of the media and the government. This is also an example of the ways in which white women could indeed counter racism in their daily interactions.

102 The concept of 'sisterhood' and western feminist notions of the 'family' have been critiqued, particularly by black feminists, as eliding differences between women in terms of race and of class. See, for example, Hazel V. Carby, 'White woman listen! Black feminism and the boundaries of sisterhood', in Heidi Safia Mirza (ed.), *Black British Feminism: A Reader* (London: Routledge, 1997).

103 The negative associations of nostalgia as 'romantic sentimentality' are now being challenged. See, for example, Jo Tacchi, 'Nostalgia and radio sound', in Michael Bull and Les Back (eds), *The Auditory Culture Reader* (Oxford: Berg, 2003), 281–95.

104 Judith Modell and John Hinshaw have similarly linked the mill in Homestead, Pennsylvania to 'the cultural and psychological as well as the social and physical landscapes of the town'. Modell and Hinshaw, 'Male work and mill work', in Selma Leydesdorff *et al.* (eds), *Gender and Memory: International Yearbook of Oral History and Life Stories Vol. IV.* (Oxford: Oxford University Press, 1996), 133.

105 Portelli points out that the moving of events in time can have 'symbolic', 'psychological' and 'formal' significance. All three elements could be at work here. Portelli, *The Death of Luigi*, 26.

CONCLUSION

The retired Rowntree women interviewed for this project stressed the significant changes which had taken place both during and after their working lives – changes which had led to a very visible reduction in the size of the York workforce. Further technological, structural and economic changes in the confectionery sector in the first decade of the twentieth-first century, coupled with broader political and economic shifts in Europe and the wider world, have made the future of industrial chocolate manufacture in the city increasingly uncertain. The Terry's factory closed its doors in 2005, whilst the Nestlé Rowntree company has dramatically downsized and sold off much of the original factory site. Nevertheless, the association of York with chocolate appears to be far from over. New boutique-style shops have opened in the city, offering luxury 'handmade' products. 'Monk Bar Chocolatiers' trades explicitly on local connections through images of the ancient city gate near to where it is located. 'Hotel Chocolat', on the other hand, situated on the main shopping street, is a national chain proud to flaunt its 'Engaged Ethics' approach to chocolate production in St Lucia.

Such local developments are part of a broader national trend in the industry related to concerns over food quality and ethical consumption, as well as a belief in the health benefits of dark chocolate with a high cocoa content. Even the large industrial manufacturers have launched products containing over 50 per cent cocoa in order to appeal to a more 'discerning' consumer, though they have struggled to develop their fairtrade credentials. Ironically, chocolate has come full cycle with this return to a 'high quality', exclusive, expensive product made with beans grown on estates in the West Indies and South America. Yet contemporary consumers in Britain can at least take comfort in choosing packaging stamped with a 'fairtrade' (and ideally an 'organic') guarantee, even if the actual labour required for chocolate manufacture continues to remain just out of sight.

My purpose in this book has been to re-examine the history of chocolate at a local and a global level, linking together the legacies of early imperial exploitation and the continued global hegemony of western capitalists with the hard work of ordinary women in a British factory and on the cocoa farms of British West Africa. Chocolate in the west has always been invested with complex associations: from 'everyday' functionality, to romance and indulgence. Such cultural meanings have depended in part on its 'exotic' origins and on the conditions of its production – even where these have been rendered invisible. Indeed, the cocoa commodity chain has relied upon and perpetuated inequalities based on ideologies and structures of gender, race and class as formed within a context of British imperialism. The story of chocolate consumption and production therefore suggests new ways into an analysis of the British empire and its significance for women who have been positioned at different points along the chain.

The Rowntree firm provided a useful means of concentrating my analysis in the face of a huge global industry, and of grounding the study in a local context in which I was personally invested. However, many of the conclusions drawn could be applied to other western manufacturers, particularly the Quaker-founded firms of Cadbury and Fry. Although I have not engaged here with debates about the significance of the Quaker faith in business enterprises, the three firms certainly had a reputation for fair treatment of their workers, which drew on this religious heritage. The image of 'enlightened employer' was both more difficult to maintain and more problematic in relation to the production of key ingredients such as cocoa in British colonies. Rowntree, Cadbury and Fry did engage directly with colonial producers but in ways which often (re)produced inequalities. The colonial system undeniably worked to the advantage of British manufacturers and they were deeply implicated in maintaining imperial hierarchies.

The farming of cocoa in British West Africa, particularly Nigeria, has been generally understood to be the province of men. From listening to the oral histories of Nigerian women, it has become clear that this was not the case. The limitations of my study have been detailed in chapter three and I will not reiterate them here. Rather, I want to stress the need to look again at the involvement of Nigerian women at all stages of cocoa production. They described working hard under very difficult conditions to produce cocoa that is often undervalued. Although the situation is changing due to their own actions and the important role of cooperatives, there is clearly a long way to go before the profits of the chocolate industry will benefit these communities to the same extent to which they have benefited York.

Studying the Rowntree firm has underlined the diverse ways in which York has been connected to histories of imperialism, challenging configurations of the city as provincial backwater. 'Yorkshire' women and men have constructed regional identities sometimes in opposition to, but also in direct relation to, the rest of England, the British Isles and the empire. From Mr York's Plain York Chocolate, to Yorkshire Tea, to Kit Kat, the products of the empire have been a crucial (if disguised) aspect of these identities. Moreover, as Rowntree workers, women in York were part of a colonial industry, positioned within the gendered and raced hierarchies of the cocoa chain. Despite assertions of the absence of racial minorities in the factory and the city, the narratives of Nellie, Carmen and Julie are illustrative of the ways in which many white York women and men were actually in daily contact with non-white residents. Although I have found written evidence of racial tensions, the narratives of these individual women emphasise the acceptance and friendships they found in the factory and in the local community. They suggest the need to study histories of race in Britain at a local level and to find ways of conceptualising everyday experiences of difference outside the main urban centres.

Women were key workers in the chocolate industry in Britain, usually making up over half of the factory labour force. In chocolate marketing too, women featured heavily: as being in charge of family consumption, as independent consumers, and as the recipients of gifts in heterosexual courtship. These limited modes of feminine consumption tended to reinforce the prescribed roles of girlfriend, wife, housewife and mother. In the later twentieth century these gendered images were modernised to keep up with social change, but the emphasis on hegemonic models of femininity and masculinity continued. Intertwined with tropes of femininity, 'whiteness' has been used to sell a range of chocolate products. However, black characters were adopted in advertising for Rowntree's Cocoa in the immediate post-Second World War period. Little Coco and Honeybunch were cartoon versions of blackness. The colour of their skin connected them visually to the product, whilst their stereotyped racial characteristics made them 'genial', often comic spokespeople. At no point was there any recognition of the actual labour of women and men in British West Africa. The dominant vision was of the consumption of chocolate by a white British nation. Chocolate would create strong healthy citizens, capable of withstanding war and the collapse of empire. As a commodity to be sold across the world, it might also help to secure the continuation of British economic and cultural power.

There are clearly missing links from the cocoa chain as presented here. This has been partly due to limitations of time, resources and space, but is also the result of a deliberate decision to prioritise the lives of women at just two sites of production, and to explore broader connections between residents of York and the empire. Several areas have emerged as worthy of more detailed study. The two most important, in my mind, are the histories of women migrants in York and of Nigerian women cocoa farmers. This is not to undermine the validity of the women's narratives recorded in this book. Indeed, rather than simply extending the study, I wonder whether it might be possible to develop new methodologies which further explore the relationships between York and Nigeria, particularly between women. Perhaps the answer lies in more collaborative research methods: between academic institutions, between individual researchers, and between interviewers and interviewees.

I began this book, then, with the romance of the cocoa bean, food of the Gods, in which women tend to feature as either over-indulgent consumers or 'colourful' exotic workers performing the lighter side of cocoa farming. I want to end by emphasising the narratives told by women working in the industry. In these we can detect women's complex relationships to the former British empire and how such relations have been structured by the chocolate industry. Their oral histories expose the limitations of a strictly linear model of the cocoa chain, challenging us to look instead at the interconnections and interactions between people whose daily labours have been indispensable to the production and consumption of this symbolically charged commodity.

BIBLIOGRAPHY

Primary sources

Archival collections

Borthwick Institute of Historical Research (BI), University of York, York, UK:
  Parish Records
  Rowntree Company Archive
  Terry's Company Archive
Cadbury UK, Birmingham, UK:
  Cadbury Company Archive
Castle Museum, York:
  'Sweet Reason', Graduate Recruitment Booklet, c.1959
History of Advertising Trust (HAT), Norwich, UK:
  J. Walter Thompson Archive (JWT)
Nigerian National Archives (NNA), University of Ibadan, Nigeria:
  Government records and reports on the cocoa industry
University of Birmingham, Special Collections Department, Birmingham, UK:
  Cadbury Papers
York City Archives, York:
  'York Refugee Committee Book'

Published primary sources

Bareau, Paul. *Cocoa: A Crop with a Future*. Bournville: Cadbury Brothers, 1953.
Booth, General William. *In Darkest England and the Way Out*. London: International Headquarters of the Salvation Army, 1890.
British Broadcasting Corporation. *The Black and White Minstrel Show*. London: British Broadcasting Corporation, c.1962.
The Cocoa Chocolate and Confectionery Alliance. 'Report of the Cocoa Conference Held at Grosvenor House, London, W.1.' London, 1957.
Dahl, Roald. *Charlie and the Chocolate Factory*. London: George Allen & Unwin, 1967.
——. *Charlie and the Chocolate Factory*. London: Puffin Books, 1995.
'Enabling rural women'. Leaflet produced by Country Women Association of Nigeria (COWAN), n.d.
Gage, Thomas. *A New Survey of the West Indies*. London: George Routledge & Sons, 1928 [1648].
Green for Come: A Report on the Rehousing and Settling of British Asians from Uganda in York and District between October 1972 and June 1973. York: n.p., 1973.
Harris, Joanne. *Chocolat*. London: Black Swan, 2000.

Head, Brandon. *The Food of the Gods*. London: R. Brimley Johnson, 1903.

Historicus. *Cocoa: All About It*. London: Sampson Low, Marston and Company, 1896.

Knapp, A. W. *Cocoa and Chocolate: Their History from Plantation to Consumer*. London: Chapman and Hall, 1920.

Morrell, John Bowes. *The City of Our Dreams*. London: Fountain Press, 1940.

One Man's Vision: The Story of the Joseph Rowntree Village Trust. London: George Allen & Unwin, 1954.

Priestley, J. B. *English Journey*. London: William Heinemann, 1934.

Rowntree, Benjamin Seebohm. *Poverty: A Study of Town Life*. London: Macmillan, 1901.

——. *Poverty and Progress: A Second Social Survey of York*. London: Longmans, Green, 1941.

Steuart, Mary E. *Every Day Life on a Ceylon Cocoa Estate*. London: Henry J. Drane, 1905.

Stowe, Harriet Beecher. *Uncle Tom's Cabin or, Life among the Lowly*. London: Penguin Classics, 1986 [1852].

Urquhart, D. H. *Cocoa*. London, New York and Toronto: Longmans Green and Co., 1955.

Newspapers and magazines

Bournville Works Magazine (*BWM*)

Cocoa Express (Nigeria), June–July 2002

Cocoa Works Magazine (*CWM*)

Yorkshire Evening Press (*YEP*)

Secondary sources

Aalen, Frederick H. A. 'English origins', in Stephen V. Ward (ed.), *The Garden City: Past, Present and Future*. London: E. & F. N. Spon, 1992: 28–51.

Alcoff, Linda. 'The problem of speaking for others', *Cultural Critique*, 17 (1991): 5–32.

Allen, Theodore W. *The Invention of the White Race. Volume One: Racial Oppression and Social Control*. London: Verso, 1994.

Anderson, Benedict. *Imagined Communities: Reflections on the Origin and Spread of Nationalism*. London: Verso, revised edn, 1991.

Ang, Ien. 'On not speaking Chinese: postmodern ethnicity and the politics of diaspora', in Morag Shiach (ed.), *Feminism and Cultural Studies*. Oxford: Oxford University Press, 1999: 540–64.

Ang-Lygate, Magdalene. 'Women who move: experiences of diaspora', in Mary Maynard and June Purvis (eds), *New Frontiers in Women's Studies: Knowledge, Identity and Nationalism*. London: Taylor & Francis, 1996: 151–63.

Anon., 'The cocoa chain', *New Internationalist*, August 1998: 7–30.

Anzaldúa, Gloria. *Borderlands/La Frontera: The New Mestiza*. San Francisco: Aunt Lute, 2nd edn, 1999.

[227]

BIBLIOGRAPHY

Asare, Benjamin. 'Women in commercial agriculture: the cocoa economy of Southern Ghana', in James Valentine Udoh (ed.), *Women and Sustainable Development in Africa*. Westport: Praeger, 1995: 101–12.

Austin, Gareth. 'The emergence of capitalist relations in South Asante cocoa-farming, c.1916–33', *Journal of African History*, 28 (1987): 259–79.

——. 'Human pawning in Asante 1800–1950', in Toyin Falola and Paul E. Lovejoy (eds), *Pawnship in Africa: Debt Bondage in Historical Perspective*. Boulder: Westview Press, 1994: 119–59.

——. 'Mode of production or mode of cultivation: explaining the failure of European cocoa planters in competition with African farmers in colonial Ghana', in William Gervase Clarence-Smith (ed.), *Cocoa Pioneer Fronts since 1800: The Role of Smallholders, Planters and Merchants*. Basingstoke: Macmillan Press, 1996: 154–75.

Balibar, Etienne. 'Racism and nationalism', in Etienne Balibar and Immanuel Wallerstein (eds), *Race, Nation, Class: Ambiguous Identities*, translated by Chris Turner. London and New York: Verso, 1991: 37–67.

Barrientos, Stephanie and Diane Perrons. 'Gender and the global food chain: a comparative study of Chile and the U.K.', in Haleh Afshar and Stephanie Barrientos (eds), *Women, Globalisation and Fragmentation in the Developing World*. Basingstoke: Macmillan Press, 1999: 150–73.

Barrow, Christine. 'Small farm food production and gender in Barbados', in Janet H. Momsen (ed.), *Women and Change in the Caribbean: A Pan-Caribbean Perspective*. London: James Currey, 1993: 181–93.

Barthel, Diane. *Putting on Appearances: Gender and Advertising*. Philadelphia: Temple University Press, 1988.

——. 'Modernism and marketing: the chocolate box revisited', *Theory, Culture and Society*, 6 (1989): 429–38.

Bastian, Misty L. '"Vultures of the marketplace": southeastern Nigerian women and discourses of the *Ogu Umunwaanyi* (Women's War) of 1929', in Jean Allman, Susan Geiger and Nakanyike Musisi (eds), *Women in African Colonial Histories*. Bloomington: Indiana University Press, 2002: 260–81.

Batstone, Eric. 'The hierarchy of maintenance and the maintenance of hierarchy: notes on food and industry', in Anne Murcott (ed.), *The Sociology of Food and Eating*. Aldershot, Hants: Gower Publishing Company, 1983: 45–53.

Baxter, Sue and Geoff Raw. 'Fast food, fettered work: Chinese women in the ethnic catering industry', in Sallie Westwood and Parminder Bhachu (eds), *Enterprising Women: Ethnicity, Economy, and Gender Relations*. London: Routledge, 1988: 58–75.

BBC4, 'Black and White Minstrel Show – revisited'. Broadcast 6 June 2004.

Beddoe, Deirdre. *Back to Home and Duty: Women Between the Wars, 1918–1939*. London: Pandora, 1989.

Behar, Ruth. *Translated Woman: Crossing the Border with Esperanza's Story*. Boston: Beacon Press, 1993.

Benería, Lourdes and Gita Sen. 'Accumulation, reproduction and women's role in economic development: Boserup revisited', *Signs*, 7: 2 (1981): 279–98.

BIBLIOGRAPHY

Berry, Sara S. 'Christianity and the rise of cocoa-growing in Ibadan and Ondo', *Journal of the Historical Society of Nigeria*, 4: 3 (1968): 439–51.

——. 'The concept of innovation and the history of cocoa farming in western Nigeria', *Journal of African History*, 15: 1 (1974): 83–95.

——. *Cocoa, Custom and Socio-Economic Change in Rural Western Nigeria*. Oxford: Clarendon Press, 1975.

Bhabha, Jacqueline and Sue Shutter. *Women's Movement: Women Under Immigration, Nationality and Refugee Law*. Stoke-on-Trent: Trentham Books, 1994.

Blair, John. 'Blackface minstrels in cross-cultural perspective', *American Studies International*, 28: 2 (1990): 52–65.

Boserup, Ester. *Women's Role in Economic Development*. New York: St. Martin's Press, 1970.

Bourdieu, Pierre. *Distinction: A Social Critique of the Judgement of Taste*, translated by Richard Nice. London: Routledge, 1984.

Bradley, Ian Campbell. *Enlightened Entrepreneurs*. London: Weidenfeld and Nicolson, 1987.

Brah, Avtar. *Cartographies of Diaspora: Contesting Identities*. London: Routledge, 1996.

Breward, Christopher. 'Sartorial spectacle: clothing and masculine identities in the imperial city, 1860–1914', in Felix Driver and David Gilbert (eds), *Imperial Cities: Landscape, Display and Identity*. Manchester: Manchester University Press, 1999: 238–53.

Brewer, John and Frank Trentmann. 'Introduction: space, time and value in consuming cultures', in John Brewer and Frank Trentmann (eds), *Consuming Cultures, Global Perspectives: Historical Trajectories, Transnational Exchanges*. Oxford: Berg, 2006: 1–17.

Brierly, John S. 'A profile of Grenadian women small farmers', in Janet Henshall Momsen (ed.), *Women and Change in the Caribbean: A Pan-Caribbean Perspective*. London: James Currey, 1993: 194–204.

Burg, Judith. *A Guide to the Rowntree and Mackintosh Company Archives, 1862–1969*. York: University of York, 1997.

Burke, Timothy. *Lifebuoy Men, Lux Women: Commodification, Consumption, and Cleanliness in Modern Zimbabwe*. London: Leicester University Press, 1996: 216.

Burton, Antoinette. 'The white woman's burden: British feminists and the Indian woman, 1865–1915', *Women's Studies International Forum*, 13: 4 (1990): 295–308.

——. *Burdens of History*. Chapel Hill: University of North Carolina Press, 1994.

——. 'Who needs the nation? Interrogating "British" history', in Catherine Hall (ed.) *Cultures of Empire: A Reader*. Manchester: Manchester University Press, 2000: 137–53.

Byfield, Judith. 'Pawns and politics: the pawnship debate in western Nigeria', in Toyin Falola and Paul E. Lovejoy (eds), *Pawnship in Africa: Debt Bondage in Historical Perspective*. Boulder: Westview Press, 1994: 187–216.

[229]

Byrne, Bridget. 'Learning whiteness – when is a mix not enough of a mix? A white middle-class mother talks about race, class and schools', in Ann Kaloski-Naylor, Heloise Brown and Madi Gilkes (eds), *White? Women*. York: Raw Nerve, 1999: 63–77.

Callan, Hilary and Shirley Ardener (eds). *The Incorporated Wife*. London: Croon Helm, 1984.

Callaway, Helen. *Gender, Culture and Empire: European Women in Colonial Nigeria*. Basingstoke: Macmillan Press, 1987.

Carby, Hazel V. 'White woman listen! Black feminism and the boundaries of sisterhood', in Heidi Safia Mirza (ed.), *Black British Feminism: A Reader*. London: Routledge, 1997: 45–53.

——. 'Brown babies: the birth of Britain as a racialized state, 1942–1948', paper presented at American Research Seminar, Leeds University, UK. March 2007.

Cassar, Carmel. 'Everyday life in Malta in the nineteenth and twentieth centuries', in Victor Mallia-Milanes (ed.), *The British Colonial Experience, 1800–1964*. Msida, Malta: Mireva Publications, 1988: 91–126.

Caws, Mary Ann. 'Introduction: "the city on our mind"', in Mary Ann Caws (ed.), *City Images: Perspectives from Literature, Philosophy, and Film*. Reading: Gordon and Breach, 1991: 1–11.

Charles, Nickie and Marion Kerr. *Women, Food and Families*. Manchester: Manchester University Press, 1988.

Chinn, Carl. *They Worked All Their Lives: Women of the Urban Poor in England, 1880–1939*. Manchester: Manchester University Press, 1988.

Clampin, David. '"The war has turned our lives upside-down": the merit of commercial advertising in documenting the cultural history of the British Home Front in the Second World War', *Visual Resources*, 24: 2 (June 2008): 145–58.

Clarence-Smith, William Gervase. *Cocoa and Chocolate, 1765–1914*. London: Routledge, 2000.

—— and Francois Ruf. 'Cocoa pioneer fronts: the historical determinants', in W. G. Clarence-Smith (ed.), *Cocoa Pioneer Fronts since 1800: The Role of Smallholders, Planters and Merchants*. Basingstoke: Macmillan Press, 1996: 1–22.

—— and Steven Topik (eds). *The Global Coffee Economy in Africa, Asia, and Latin America, 1500–1989*. Cambridge: Cambridge University Press, 2003.

Clarke, Julian. 'Households and the political economy of small-scale cash crop production in south-western Nigeria', *Africa*, 51: 4 (1981): 807–23.

Coady, Chantal. *Chocolate: The Food of the Gods*. London: Pavilion Books, 1993.

Coe, Sophie D. and Michael D. Coe. *The True History of Chocolate*. London: Thames and Hudson, 1996.

Conekin, Becky E. *'The Autobiography of a Nation': The 1951 Festival of Britain*. Manchester: Manchester University Press, 2003.

Constantine, Stephen. '"Bringing the empire alive": the Empire Marketing Board and imperial propaganda, 1926–33', in John M. MacKenzie (ed.), *Imperialism and Popular Culture*. Manchester: Manchester University Press, 1986: 192–231.

Coombes, Annie E. *Reinventing Africa: Museums, Material Culture and the Popular Imagination*. New Haven: Yale University Press, 1994.

Cronin, Mike and Richard Holt. 'The imperial game in crisis: English cricket and decolonisation', in Stuart Ward (ed.), *British Culture and the End of Empire*. Manchester: Manchester University Press, 2001: 111–27.

Cross, Gary. 'Consumer history and the dilemmas of working-class history', *Labour History Review*, 62: 3 (1997): 261–74.

Cunningham, Valentine. ' "God and nature intended you for a missionary's wife": Mary Hill, Jane Eyre and other missionary women in the 1840s', in Fiona Bowie, Deborah Kirkwood and Shirley Ardener (eds), *Women and Missions: Past and Present. Anthropological and Historical Perceptions*. Oxford: Berg, 1993: 85–105.

Daley, Caroline. ' "He would know, but I just have a feeling": gender and oral history', *Women's History Review*, 7: 3 (1998): 343–59.

Davin, Anna. 'Imperialism and motherhood', in Frederick Cooper and Ann Laura Stoler (eds), *Tensions of Empire: Colonial Cultures in a Bourgeois World*. Berkeley: University of California Press, 1997: 87–151.

de Groot, Joanna. 'Metropolitan desires and colonial connections: reflections on consumption and empire', in Catherine Hall and Sonya O. Rose (eds), *At Home with the Empire: Metropolitan Culture and the Imperial World*. Cambridge: Cambridge University Press, 2006: 166–90.

Deloria, Philip J. *Playing Indian*. New Haven: Yale University Press, 1998.

de Mooij, Marieke. *Global Marketing and Advertising: Understanding Cultural Paradoxes*. London: Sage Publications, 1998.

Dench, Geoff. *Maltese in London: A Case-Study in the Erosion of Ethnic Consciousness*. London: Routledge and Kegan Paul, 1975.

Dixon-Mueller, Ruth. 'Women in agriculture: counting the labor force in developing countries', in Mary Margaret Fonow and Judith A. Cook (eds), *Beyond Methodology: Feminist Scholarship as Lived Research*. Bloomington: Indiana University Press, 1991: 226–47.

Dyer, Gillian. *Advertising as Communication*. London: Routledge, 1996.

Elsner, John and Roger Cardinal. ' "Unless you do these crazy things . . .": an interview with Robert Opie', in John Elsner and Roger Cardinal (eds), *The Cultures of Collecting*. London: Reaktion Books, 1994: 25–48.

Enloe, Cynthia. *Bananas, Beaches and Bases: Making Feminist Sense of International Politics*. London: Pandora, 1989.

Falola, Toyin. 'Pawnship in colonial southwestern Nigeria', in Toyin Falola and Paul E. Lovejoy (eds), *Pawnship in Africa: Debt Bondage in Historical Perspective*. Boulder: Westview Press, 1994: 245–66.

——. *Culture and Customs of Nigeria*. Westport: Greenwood Press, 2001.

Falola, Toyin and Paul E. Lovejoy (eds). *Pawnship in Africa: Debt Bondage in Historical Perspective*. Boulder: Westview Press, 1994.

Fara, Patricia. *Sex, Botany and Empire: The Story of Carl Linnaeus and Joseph Banks*. Cambridge: Icon Books, 2003.

Feinstein, Charles. 'Population, occupations and economic development, 1831–1981', in Charles Feinstein (ed.), *York 1831–1981: 150 Years of*

Scientific Endeavour and Social Change. York: The Ebor Press, 1981: 109–59.

Fitzgerald, Robert. *Rowntree and the Marketing Revolution, 1862–1969*. Cambridge: Cambridge University Press, 1995.

Frendo, Henry. 'Maltese colonial identity: Latin Mediterranean or British Empire?' in Victor Mallia-Milanes (ed.), *The British Colonial Experience 1800–1964*. Msida, Malta: Mireva Publications, 1988: 185–214.

Fryer, Peter. *Staying Power: The History of Black People in Britain*. London: Pluto Press, 1984.

Galletti, R., K. D. S. Baldwin and I. O. Dina. *Nigerian Cocoa Farmers: An Economic Survey of Yoruba Cocoa Farming Families*. Oxford: Oxford University Press, 1956.

Gates, Henry Louis, Jr (ed.). *'Race', Writing, and Difference*. Chicago: University of Chicago Press, 1986.

Gereffi, Gary and Miguel Korzeniewicz (eds). *Commodity Chains and Global Capitalism*. Westport: Greenwood Press, 1994.

Gilroy, Paul. *'There Ain't No Black in the Union Jack': The Cultural Politics of Race and Nation*. London: Routledge, reprint edn, 1992.

——. *After Empire: Melancholia or Convivial Culture?* Abingdon: Routledge, 2004.

Gluck, Sherna Berger and Daphne Patai (eds). *Women's Words: The Feminist Practice of Oral History*. London: Routledge, 1991.

Glucksmann, Miriam. *Women Assemble: Women Workers and the New Industries in Inter-War Britain*. London: Routledge, 1990.

——. *Cottons and Casuals: The Gendered Organisation of Labour in Time and Space*. Durham: Sociology Press, 2000.

Goodman, Philomena. *Women, Sexuality and War*. Basingstoke: Palgrave, 2002.

Gosden, Chris and Chantal Knowles. *Collecting Colonialism: Material Culture and Colonial Change*. Oxford: Berg, 2001.

Green, Jeffrey. *Black Edwardians: Black People in Britain 1901–1914*. London: Frank Cass, 1998.

Grier, Beverly. 'Pawns, porters, and petty traders: women in the transition to cash crop agriculture in colonial Ghana', in Toyin Falola and Paul E. Lovejoy (eds), *Pawnship in Africa: Debt Bondage in Historical Perspective*. Boulder: Westview Press, 1994: 161–86.

Guyer, Jane I. 'Food, cocoa, and the division of labour by sex in two West African societies', *Comparative Studies in Society and History*, 22 (1980): 355–73.

Hall, Catherine. 'Turning a blind eye: memories of empire', in Patricia Fara and Karalyn Patterson (eds), *Memory*. Cambridge: Cambridge University Press, 1998: 27–46.

——. 'Introduction: thinking the postcolonial, thinking the empire', in Catherine Hall (ed.), *Cultures of Empire: A Reader*. Manchester: Manchester University Press, 2000: 1–33.

——. *Civilising Subjects: Metropole and Colony in the English Imagination, 1830–1867*. Cambridge: Polity Press, 2002.

—— and Sonya O. Rose. 'Introduction: being at home with the empire', in Catherine Hall and Sonya O. Rose (eds), *At Home with the Empire: Metropolitan Culture and the Imperial World*. Cambridge: Cambridge University Press, 2006: 1–31.

Hall, Jacquelyn Dowd, James Leloudis, Robert Korstad, Mary Murphy, Lu Ann Jones and Christopher B. Daly. *Like A Family: The Making of a Southern Cotton Mill World*. Chapel Hill: University of North Carolina Press, 1987.

Hall, Stuart. 'Encoding/decoding', in Stuart Hall, Dorothy Hobson, Andrew Lowe and Paul Willis (eds), *Culture, Media, Language: Working Papers in Cultural Studies, 1972–1979*. London: Routledge, 1992, 128–38.

Hansen, Peter H. 'Coronation Everest: the empire and Commonwealth in the second Elizabethan age', in Stuart Ward (ed.), *British Culture and the End of Empire*. Manchester: Manchester University Press, 2001: 57–72.

Harry, Indra S. 'Women in agriculture in Trinidad: an overview', in Janet H. Momsen (ed.), *Women and Change in the Caribbean: A Pan-Caribbean Perspective*. London: James Currey, 1993: 205–18.

Hilden, Patricia Penn. *When Nickels Were Indians: An Urban, Mixed-Blood Story*. Washington: Smithsonian Institution Press, 1995.

Hill, Polly. *Migrant Cocoa Farmers of Southern Ghana*. London: Cambridge University Press, 1963.

Hopkins, A. G. 'Innovation in a colonial context: African origins of the Nigerian cocoa-farming industry, 1880–1920', in Clive Dewey and A. G. Hopkins (eds), *The Imperial Impact: Studies in the Economic History of Africa and India*. London: The Athlone Press, 1978: 83–96.

Hosein, Shaheeda. 'A space of their own: Indian women and land ownership in Trinidad 1870–1945', *Caribbean Review of Gender Studies*, 1 (April 2007): 1–17.

Howarth, Ken. *Oral History*. Stroud: Sutton Publishing, 1998.

Hutchinson, John and D. M. Palliser. *York: Bartholomew City Guides*. Edinburgh: John Bartholomew & Son, 1980.

Ignatiev, Noel. *How the Irish Became White*. London: Routledge, 1995.

James, Allison. 'The good, the bad and the delicious: the role of confectionery in British society', *Sociological Review*, 38: 4 (1990), 666–88.

Kay, Diana and Robert Miles. *Refugees or Migrant Workers? European Volunteer Workers in Britain, 1946–1951*. London: Routledge, 1992.

Kern-Foxworth, Marilyn. *Aunt Jemima, Uncle Ben, and Rastus: Blacks in Advertising, Yesterday, Today, and Tomorrow*. Westport: Greenwood Press, 1994.

King, Anthony D. *The Bungalow: The Production of a Global Culture*. London: Routledge and Kegan Paul, 1984.

King, Brenda. *Silk and Empire*. Manchester: Manchester University Press, 2005.

Koven, Seth. *Slumming: Sexual and Social Politics in Victorian London*. Princeton: Princeton University Press, 2004.

Loeb, Lori Anne. *Consuming Angels: Advertising and Victorian Women*. Oxford: Oxford University Press, 1994.

Lott, Eric. *Love and Theft: Blackface Minstrelsy and the American Working Class*. Oxford: Oxford University Press, 1995.

Macfadyen, Dugald. *Sir Ebenezer Howard and the Town Planning Movement*. Manchester: Manchester University Press, reprint edn, 1970.

MacKenzie, John M. *Propaganda and Empire: The Manipulation of Public Opinion, 1880–1960*. Manchester: Manchester University Press, 1984.

——. '"The Second City of the Empire": Glasgow – imperial municipality', in Felix Driver and David Gilbert (eds), *Imperial Cities: Landscape, Display and Identity*. Manchester: Manchester University Press, 1999: 215–37.

Maier, Karl. *This House Has Fallen: Nigeria in Crisis*. London: Penguin, 2000.

Mamdani, Mahmood. *From Citizen to Refugee: Ugandan Asians Come to Britain*. London: Frances Pinter, 1973.

Mangan, J. A. *The Games Ethic and Imperialism: Aspects of the Diffusion of an Ideal*. Middlesex: Viking, 1986.

Marcus, Julie. 'Racism, terror and the production of Australian auto/biographies', in Judith Okely and Helen Callaway (eds), *Anthropology and Autobiography*. London: Routledge, 1992: 100–15.

Mauss, Marcel. *The Gift: The Form and Reason for Exchange in Archaic Societies*, translated by W. D. Halls. London: Routledge Classics, 2002.

McClintock, Anne. *Imperial Leather: Race, Gender and Sexuality in the Colonial Contest*. London: Routledge, 1995.

Meredith, David. 'The Colonial Office, British business interests and the reform of cocoa marketing in West Africa, 1937–1945', *Journal of African History*, 29 (1988): 285–300.

Midgley, Clare. *Women Against Slavery: The British Campaigns, 1780–1870*. London: Routledge, 1992.

Mikell, Gwendolyn. *Cocoa and Chaos in Ghana*. New York: Paragon House, 1989.

Miles, John. 'Rural protest in the Gold Coast: the cocoa hold-ups, 1908–1938', in Clive Dewey and A. G. Hopkins (eds), *The Imperial Impact: Studies in the Economic History of Africa and India*. London: Athlone Press, 1978: 152–70.

Miles, Robert and Annie Phizacklea. *White Man's Country: Racism in British Politics*. London: Pluto Press, 1984.

Miller, Mervyn. *Raymond Unwin: Garden Cities and Town Planning*. Leicester: Leicester University Press, 1992.

Mills, James. *Cannabis Britannica*. Oxford: Oxford University Press, 2003.

Minister, Kristina. 'A feminist frame for the oral history interview', in Sherna Berger Gluck and Daphne Patai (eds), *Women's Words: The Feminist Practice of Oral History*. London: Routledge, 1991: 27–41.

Mintz, Sidney W. *Sweetness and Power: The Place of Sugar in Modern History*. London: Penguin, 1985.

Mitter, Swasti. *Common Fate, Common Bond: Women in the Global Economy*. London: Pluto Press, 1986.

Modell, Judith and John Hinshaw. 'Male work and mill work', in Selma Leydesdorff, Luisa Passerini and Paul Thompson (eds), *Gender and Memory:*

International Yearbook of Oral History and Life Stories Vol. IV. Oxford: Oxford University Press, 1996: 133–49.

Momsen, Janet Henshall. 'Gender roles in Caribbean agricultural labour', in Malcolm Cross and Gad Heuman (eds), *Labour in the Caribbean: From Emancipation to Independence.* Basingstoke: Macmillan, 1988: 141–58.

Morgan, Philip D. 'Encounters between British and "indigenous" peoples, c.1500–c.1800', in Martin Daunton and Rick Halpern (eds), *Empire and Others: British Encounters with Indigenous Peoples, 1600–1850.* Philadelphia: University of Pennsylvania Press, 1999: 42–78.

Morton, Marcia and Frederic Morton. *Chocolate: The Illustrated History.* New York: Crown Publishers, 1986.

Moxham, Roy. *Tea: Addiction, Exploitation and Empire.* London: Constable & Robinson, 2003.

Myers, Greg. *Words in Ads.* London: Edward Arnold, 1994.

Neave, David. 'The identity of the East Riding of Yorkshire', in Edward Royle (ed.), *Issues of Regional Identity: In Honour of John Marshall.* Manchester: Manchester University Press, 1998: 184–200.

Nuttgens, Patrick. *York: The Continuing City.* York: Maxiprint, 2nd edn, 1989.

Nye, David. *Image Worlds: Corporate Identities at General Electric.* Cambridge, Massachusetts: MIT Press, 1985.

O'Donohoe, Stephanie. 'Leaky boundaries: intertextuality and young adult experiences of advertising', in Mica Nava, Andrew Blake, Iain MacRury and Barry Richards (eds), *Buy This Book: Studies in Advertising and Consumption.* London: Routledge, 1997: 257–75.

Okali, Christine. *Cocoa and Kinship in Ghana: The Matrilineal Akan of Ghana.* London: Kegan Paul, 1983.

Olson, Karen and Linda Shopes. 'Crossing boundaries, building bridges: doing oral history among working-class women and men', in Sherna Berger Gluck and Daphne Patai (eds), *Women's Words: The Feminist Practice of Oral History.* London: Routledge, 1991: 189–204.

Ong, Aihwa. 'Colonialism and modernity: feminist re-presentations of women in non-western societies', *Inscriptions,* 3/4 (1988): 79–93.

Opie, Robert. *Rule Britannia: Trading on the British Image.* Harmondsworth: Penguin, 1985.

Othick, J. 'The cocoa and chocolate industry in the nineteenth century', in Derek Oddy and Derek Miller (eds), *The Making of the Modern British Diet.* London: Croon Helm, 1976: 77–90.

Parker, David. 'Chinese people in Britain: histories, futures and identities', in George Benton and Frank N. Pieke (eds), *The Chinese in Europe.* Basingstoke: Macmillan Press, 1998: 67–95.

Parker, Olive. *For the Family's Sake: A History of the Mothers' Union 1876–1976.* Folkestone: Bailey Brothers and Swinfen, 1975.

Patai, Daphne. 'U.S. academics and third world women: is ethical research possible?' in Sherna Berger Gluck and Daphne Patai (eds), *Women's Words: The Feminist Practice of Oral History.* London: Routledge, 1991: 137–53.

Paul, Kathleen. *Whitewashing Britain: Race and Citizenship in the Postwar Era*. Ithaca: Cornell University Press, 1997.

Phillips, Andrew, 'Women on the shop floor: the Colchester Rag 1918–1950', *Oral History*, 22 (Spring 1994): 56–65.

Phillips, Richard. *Sex, Politics and Empire: A Postcolonial Geography*. Manchester: Manchester University Press, 2006.

Phillips Lewis, Kathleen. 'Women in the Trinidadian cocoa industry, 1870–1945', *Journal of Caribbean History*, 34 (2000): 20–45.

Pickering, Michael. 'Mock blacks and racial mockery: the "nigger" minstrel and British imperialism', in J. S. Bratton, R. A. Cave, B. Gregory, H. J. Holder and M. Pickering (eds), *Acts of Supremacy: The British Empire and the Stage, 1790–1930*. Manchester: Manchester University Press, 1991: 179–236.

——. 'Race, gender and broadcast comedy: the case of the BBC's *Kentucky Minstrels*', *European Journal of Communication*, 9: 3 (1994): 311–33.

——. *Blackface Minstrelsy in Britain*. Aldershot: Ashgate, 2008.

Pieterse, Jan Nederveen. *White on Black: Images of Africa and Blacks in Western Popular Culture*. New Haven: Yale University Press, 1992.

Pollert, Anna. *Girls, Wives, Factory Lives*. Basingstoke: Macmillan Press, 1981.

Portelli, Alessandro. *The Death of Luigi Trastulli and Other Stories: Form and Meaning in Oral History*. Albany: State University of New York Press, 1991.

Porter, Bernard. *The Absent-Minded Imperialists: Empire, Society and Culture in Britain*. Oxford: Oxford University Press, 2004.

Potter, Simon J. 'Webs, networks, and systems: globalization and the mass media in the nineteenth- and twentieth-century British empire', *Journal of British Studies*, 46 (July 2007): 621–46.

Pratt, Mary Louise. *Imperial Eyes: Travel Writing and Transculturation*. London: Routledge, 1992.

Preston, Rebecca. 'The scenery of the torrid zone: imagined travels and the culture of exotics in nineteenth-century British gardens', in Felix Driver and David Gilbert (eds), *Imperial Cities: Landscape, Display and Identity*. Manchester: Manchester University Press, 1999: 194–211.

Purvis, June. 'From "women worthies" to poststructuralism? Debate and controversy in women's history in Britain', in June Purvis (ed.), *Women's History: Britain 1850–1945. An Introduction*. London: UCL Press, 1995: 1–22.

Radway, Janice A. *Reading the Romance: Women, Patriarchy, and Popular Literature*. London: Verso, 1987.

Ramamurthy, Anandi. *Imperial Persuaders: Images of Africa and Asia in British Advertising*. Manchester: Manchester University Press, 2003.

Ramusack, Barbara N. 'Cultural missionaries, maternal imperialists, feminist allies: British women activists in India, 1865–1945', *Women's Studies International Forum*, 13: 4 (1990): 309–21.

Reddock, Rhoda E. *Women, Labour and Politics in Trinidad and Tobago: A History*. London: Zed Books, 1994.

Richards, Jeffrey (ed.). *Imperialism and Juvenile Literature*. Manchester: Manchester University Press, 1989.

Riley, Denise. *'Am I That Name?' Feminism and the Category of Women in History*. Basingstoke: Macmillan, 1988.

Robbins, Bruce. 'Commodity Histories', *PMLA*, 120: 2 (March 2005): 454–63.

Roberts, Elizabeth. 'Working wives and their families', in Theo Barker and Michael Drake (eds), *Population and Society in Britain, 1850–1980*. London: Batsford Academic and Educational, 1982: 140–71.

Roberts, Mary Louise. 'The transnationalization of gender history', in *History and Theory*, 44 (October 2005): 456–68.

Roberts, Penelope A. 'Rural women's access to labor in West Africa', in Sharon B. Stichter and Jane L. Parpart (eds), *Patriarchy and Class: African Women in the Home and the Workforce*. Boulder: Westview Press, 1988: 97–114.

Robertson, Emma. '"On the whole, if I had to work, Rowntrees was the place for me": women's experiences of Rowntrees, 1936–1988', MA dissertation, University of York, 2000.

——. 'It was just a real camaraderie thing: socialising, socialisation and shop floor culture at the Rowntree factory, York', in Krista Cowman and Louise Jackson (eds), *Women and Work Culture, Britain c.1850–1950*. Aldershot: Ashgate, 2005: 107–20.

——. 'I get a real kick out of Big Ben: BBC versions of Britishness on the Empire and General Overseas Service, 1932–1948', *Historical Journal of Film, Radio and Television*, 28: 4 (October 2008): 459–73.

——, Marek Korczynski and Michael Pickering. 'Harmonious relations? Music at work in the Rowntree and Cadbury factories', *Business History*, 49: 2 (2007): 211–34.

Rose, Sonya O. 'Sex, citizenship, and the nation in World War II Britain', in Catherine Hall (ed.), *Cultures of Empire: A Reader*. Manchester: Manchester University Press, 2000: 246–77.

Rowlinson, Michael. 'The early application of scientific management by Cadbury', *Business History*, 30: 4 (1988): 377–95.

——. 'Quaker employers', *Historical Studies in Industrial Relations*, 6 (1998): 163–98.

Royle, Edward. 'Introduction: regions and identities', in Edward Royle (ed.), *Issues of Regional Identity: In Honour of John Marshall*. Manchester: Manchester University Press, 1998: 1–13.

Sanders, Joel (ed.). *Stud: Architectures of Masculinity*. New York: Princeton Architectural Press, 1996.

Sangster, Joan. 'Telling our stories: feminist debates and the use of oral history', in Robert B. Perks and Alistair Thomson (eds), *The Oral History Reader*. London: Routledge, 1998, 87–100.

Satre, Lowell J. *Chocolate on Trial: Slavery, Politics and the Ethics of Business*. Athens: Ohio University Press, 2005.

Seed, John. 'Limehouse blues: looking for Chinatown in the London Docks, 1900–1940', *History Workshop Journal*, 62 (2006), 58–85.

Senior, Olive. *Working Miracles: Women's Lives in the English-Speaking Caribbean*. London: James Currey, 1991.

Shepherd, Verene A. *Women in Caribbean History: The British Colonised Territories*. Oxford: James Currey, 1999.

Shih, Johanna. '"... Yeah, I could hire this one, but I know it's gonna be a problem": how race, nativity and gender affect employers' perceptions of the manageability of job seekers', *Ethnic and Racial Studies*, 25: 1 (2002): 99–119.

Sibley, David. *Geographies of Exclusion: Society and Difference in the West*. London: Routledge, 1995.

Simonton, Deborah. *A History of European Women's Work, 1700 to the Present*. London: Routledge, 1998.

Smith, Chris, John Child and Michael Rowlinson. *Reshaping Work: The Cadbury Experience*. Cambridge: Cambridge University Press, 1990.

Southall, Roger J. 'Cadbury on the Gold Coast, 1907–1938: the dilemma of the "model firm" in a colonial economy', PhD Dissertation, University of Birmingham, 1975.

Spacks, Patricia Meyer. *Gossip*. New York: Alfred A. Knopf, 1985.

Stewart, Gordon T. *Jute and Empire: The Calcutta Jute Wallahs and the Landscapes of Empire*. Manchester: Manchester University Press, 1998.

Strong, L. A. G. *The Story of Rowntree*. York: Unpublished, 1948.

Summerfield, Penny. 'Dis/composing the subject: intersubjectivities in oral history', in Tess Cosslett, Celia Lury and Penny Summerfield (eds), *Feminism and Autobiography: Texts, Theories, Methods*. London: Routledge, 2000: 91–106.

Tabili, Laura. 'A homogenous society? Britain's internal "others", 1800–present', in Catherine Hall and Sonya O. Rose (eds), *At Home with the Empire: Metropolitan Culture and the Imperial World*. Cambridge: Cambridge University Press, 2006: 53–76.

Tacchi, Jo. 'Nostalgia and radio sound', in Michael Bull and Les Back (eds), *The Auditory Culture Reader*. Oxford: Berg, 2003: 281–95.

Tam, Suk-Tak. 'Representations of "the Chinese" and "ethnicity" in British racial discourse', in Elizabeth Sinn (ed.), *The Last Half Century of Chinese Overseas*. Hong Kong: Hong Kong University Press, 1998: 81–90.

Terrio, Susan J. *Crafting the Culture and History of French Chocolate*. Berkeley: University of California Press, 2000.

Thomas, Nicholas. 'Colonial conversions: difference, hierarchy, and history in early twentieth-century evangelical propaganda', in Catherine Hall (ed.), *Cultures of Empire: A Reader*. Manchester: Manchester University Press, 2000: 298–328.

Thorne, Susan. 'Religion and empire at home', in Catherine Hall and Sonya O. Rose (eds), *At Home with the Empire: Metropolitan Culture and the Imperial World*. Cambridge: Cambridge University Press, 2006: 143–65.

Tilly, Louise A. and Joan W. Scott. *Women, Work and Family*. New York: Holt, Rinehart, and Winston, 1978.

Toll, Robert C. *Blacking Up: The Minstrel Show in Nineteenth-Century America*. New York: Oxford University Press, 1974.

Vellenga, Dorothy Dee. 'Matriliny, patriliny, and class formation among women cocoa farmers in two rural areas of Ghana', in Claire Robertson and Iris Berger (eds), *Women and Class in Africa*. New York: Africana Publishing Company, 1986: 62–77.

Vernon, Anne. *A Quaker Business Man*. London: George Allen & Unwin, 1958.

Visram, Rozina. *Asians in Britain*. London: Pluto Press, 2002.

Wagner, Gillian. *The Chocolate Conscience*. London: Chatto & Windus, 1987.

Walker, Ezekiel Ayodele. 'Structural change, the oil boom and the cocoa economy of southwestern Nigeria, 1973–1980s', *Journal of Modern African Studies*, 38: 1 (2000): 71–87.

Walker, Timothy. 'Slave labor and chocolate in Brazil: the culture of cacao plantations in Amazonia and Bahia (17th–19th centuries)', *Food and Foodways*, 15 (2007): 75–106.

Walvin, James. *Fruits of Empire: Exotic Produce and British Taste, 1660–1800*. Basingstoke: Macmillan Press, 1997.

Ward, Stephen V. (ed.) *The Garden City: Past, Present and Future*. London: E. & F. N. Spon, 1992.

Ward, Stuart. '"No nation could be broker": the satire boom and the demise of Britain's world role', in Stuart Ward (ed.), *British Culture and the End of Empire*. Manchester: Manchester University Press, 2001: 91–110.

—— (ed.). *British Culture and the End of Empire*. Manchester: Manchester University Press, 2001.

Warren, Allen. 'Citizens of the empire: Baden-Powell, Scouts and Guides, and an imperial ideal, 1900–40', in John M. MacKenzie (ed.) *Imperialism and Popular Culture*. Manchester: Manchester University Press, 1986: 232–56.

Webster, Wendy. *Imagining Home: Gender, 'Race' and National Identity, 1945–64*. London: UCL Press, 1998.

——. 'Defining boundaries: European Volunteer Worker women in Britain and narratives of community', *Women's History Review*, 9: 2 (2000): 257–76.

——. *Englishness and Empire, 1939–1965*. Oxford: Oxford University Press, 2005.

Weinberg, Bennett Alan and Bonnie K. Bealer, *The World of Caffeine*. London: Routledge, 2001.

West, John A. 'A brief history and botany of cacao', in Nelson Foster and Linda S. Cordell (eds), *Chilies to Chocolate: Food the Americas Gave the World*. Tucson: University of Arizona Press, 1992: 105–21.

Westwood, Sallie. *All Day Every Day: Factory and Family in the Making of Women's Lives*. London: Pluto Press, 1984.

—— and Parminder Bhachu. 'Introduction', in Sallie Westwood and Parminder Bhachu (eds), *Enterprising Women: Ethnicity, Economy, and Gender Relations*. London: Routledge, 1988: 1–19.

White, Deborah Gray. *Ar'n't I a Woman? Female Slaves in the Plantation South*. New York: W. W. Norton & Company, 1987.

Whitehead, Ann. 'Food symbolism, gender power and the family', in Barbara Harriss-White and Raymond Hoffenberg (eds), *Food: Multidisciplinary Perspectives*. Oxford: Blackwell, 1994: 116–29.

BIBLIOGRAPHY

Williams, Raymond. 'Advertising: the magic system', in Simon During (ed.), *The Cultural Studies Reader*. London: Routledge, 1993: 320–36.

Williamson, Judith A. *Decoding Advertisements: Ideology and Meaning in Advertising*. London: Marion Boyars, 1978.

Wilson, Van. *Number 26: The History of 26 St. Saviourgate, York*. n.p.: Voyager Publications, 1999.

Winship, Janice. 'Sexuality for sale', in Stuart Hall, Dorothy Hobson, Andrew Lowe and Paul Willis (eds), *Culture, Media, Language: Working Papers in Cultural Studies, 1972–1979*. London: Routledge, 1992: 217–23.

Wong, Maria Lin. *Chinese Liverpudlians: A History of the Chinese Community in Liverpool*. Birkenhead: Liver Press, 1989.

York, Barry. *Empire and Race: The Maltese in Australia 1881–1949*. Kensington, NSW: New South Wales University Press, 1990.

Young, Iris Marion. *Justice and the Politics of Difference*. Princeton: Princeton University Press, 1990.

Zubrzycki, Jerzy. *Polish Immigrants in Britain: A Study of Adjustment*. The Hague: Martinus Nijhoff, 1956.

Internet sources

Chapeltown News, September 1974, www.movinghere.org.uk/deliveryfiles/WYAS/WYL5046_5_1_01–8/0/1.pdf (accessed 4 January 2008).

'"Deal reached" in Nigeria oil protest', BBC News, 16 July 2002, http://news.bbc.co.uk/1/hi/world/africa/2129281.stm (accessed 7 July 2004).

International Institute of Tropical Agriculture, Sustainable Tree Crop Program, 'Child labor in the cocoa sector of West Africa: a synthesis of findings in Cameroon, Cote d'Ivoire, Ghana and Nigeria', August 2002, www.globalexchange.org/campaigns/fairtrade/cocoa/IITACocoaResearch.pdf (accessed 16 January 2008).

'Pact to end African "chocolate slavery"', BBC News, 2 May 2002, http://news.bbc.co.uk/2/hi/africa/1963617.stm (accessed 16 January 2008).

Pilgrim, David, 'The golliwog caricature', *Museum of Racist Memorabilia* (November 2000), www.ferris.edu/news/jimcrow/golliwog (accessed 19 June 2004).

INDEX

Page references for figures are in *italics*; those for notes are followed by n; for literary works, see under author's name

welfare 6, *9*, 119–22, 130n, 178–87
passim, 193, 196, 208
see also health; paternalism
West Africa 3, 7–12 *passim*, 16n,
36 — 40, 67–8, 70–86 *passim*,
90n, 98–101, 106–7, 110, 116,
121–2, 124, 142, 149, 153,
216n, 222–4
see also Africa; Ghana; Nigeria
West Indies 7, 10–11, 39, 47, 67,
70 — 4 *passim*, 81, 85–6, 92–3,
96 — 8, 124, 129, 142, 147–9,
159, 171n, 222
see also Caribbean; Jamaica;
Trinidad
'whiteness' 12, 15n, 16n, 28,
39–40, 59n, 81, *139*, 151,
164–5, 167, 178–9, 204,
214n, 224
see also 'blackness'; race
working class 1–2, 30, 56n, 130n
attitudes to empire 161–3, 169,
171n

consumers 2, 20, 23, 29, 31, 33
and race 130n, 167, 169, 201, 204,
206, 214n, 219n, 221n
see also class

York 5
connections to empire 7–9, 11,
16n, 85, 120–2, 124, 132–70
passim, 170n, 171n, 172n,
223–4
migration and race 7, 9, 12,
179, 183–6, 191–3, 201–5,
210–14, 214n, 217n, 219n,
220n
relationship with Rowntree firm
5–7, 39, 47, 50, 120–2, 195,
202, 210–12, 222
tourism 132, 140, 169, 172n
white women in 188–90, 212
York, Mr 39, 138–9, 172n, 223
Yorkshire 16n, 39, 59n, 132,
136–40, 152, 158, 170n,
188, 223

CPSIA information can be obtained at www.ICGtesting.com
Printed in the USA
BVOW06s1553120816

458443BV00013B/6/P